WORKING

WINDOWS

3RD EDITION

A Guide to the Repair and Restoration
of Wood Windows

TERRY MEANY

The Lyons Press
Guilford, Connecticut
An imprint of The Globe Pequot Press

The Lyons Press is an imprint of The Globe Pequot Press.

Images on pages 74, 75, and 78 copyright 3M. Used with permission. Images on page 127 courtesy of Ives. Used with permission. Image on page 129 courtesy of Rejuvenation. Used with permission. Image on page 143 courtesy of Vincent Whitney Company. Used with permission. Images on page 194 courtesy of M.A.G. Security. Used with permission. Images on page 198 courtesy of Ettore Products Company. Used with permission.

ISBN 978-1-59921-311-8

The Library of Congress has previously cataloged an earlier edition as follows:

Meany, Terry.
Working windows: a guide to the repair and restoration of wood windows /
Terence Meany.—Rev. and updated ed.
p. cm.
Includes index.
ISBN 1-59228-708-5 (trade paper)
1. Wooden windows—Maintenance and repair. I. Title.
TH2275.M43 2005
690'.1823—dc22
2005001312

Printed in the United States of America

10 9 8 7 6 5 4 3 2

TRADEMARKS

All terms mentioned in this book that are known to be or suspected of being trademark or service marks have been appropriately capitalized. These terms include, but are not limited to:

Abatron	Paint Peeler
Allied Window Co.	Peel-Away
Bahco	Pemko
Bondo	Pratt & Lambert
Bosch	Prazi
Chem Master	Purdy
DAP	Red Devil
Deft	Rustoleum
Duplex, Inc.	Sampson Rope
Dupont Tyvek	Sandvik
Eureka	Shark Corporation
Fein	Spackle
Festool	Speed Heater 1100
Glidden	Stanley
Intekplastics, Inc.	3M
Ives	Warner Tools
Jasco	Watco
Liquid Nails	Water Weld
M.A.G	WD-40
Makita	West System
Marvin	Whitco
Master Appliance	Wilson
McCloskey	Wonderbar
Milwaukee	Wooster
Minwax	Wright Products
Mordite Rope Caulk	Zinsser Company
North	

CONTENTS

CONTENTS

FOREWORD

After working in Seattle (lots of wind and rain) restoring residential structures as a general contractor and architectural historian since 1983, I can say that wood windows are renewable over an indefinite period of time with proper care and maintenance. In our increasingly "green" world, Terry Meany's book, *Working Windows: A Guide to the Repair and Restoration of Wood Windows*, provides a resource for people who want to keep, maintain and restore their traditional wood windows. I have recommended the first edition of his book over the years as the current, number one resource for information on window restoration and I look forward to continuing that recommendation with this latest edition.

The design of a traditional double hung wood window is a beautiful thing. The wood, glass and metal parts can be easily repaired or replaced. With proper weather stripping, they operate smoothly and draft free. When adding a traditional storm window, they can be more energy efficient than new units as the air space between the glass panes is often six to eight times that of new double-glazed unit.

The true "green" function of window repair is that instead of removing and replacing, we keep the old units out of the landfill and we don't set up a cycle for removing and replacing with new, vinyl, fiberglass or wood clad windows every 20 to 30 years as the new units fail or break beyond repair. A new window system has proprietary window parts made of plastic and metal that may or may not be available when they fail and need repair, so typically a new unit is installed rather than repairing the old. With double-insulated units, the seals often fail within 15 to 25 years, and the glazed unit needs to be replaced. Our landfills are burdened enough that we don't need to add a repairable green product to them. Over the years, I have often restored windows that were 60 to 100 years old, and original to the residence. After following the information in Terry's book, these windows are operating again, often better than when originally installed, and are ready to work for another 60 years.

Windows are one of the main recognizable and important features of older structures. As such, window restoration leads to a more faithful method of house restoration and preservation. *Working Windows* remains an important tool for professionals and homeowners engaged in the residential and commercial restoration of structures that contain traditional wood windows.

With all that said, Terry's book is a fun read as well. The information could have been presented as an authoritarian textbook puffed up inside its own covers. Instead the descriptions, wit and illustrations are easily accessible to anyone. Have fun with this book and pass on the information you gain, as we are all better off when we reuse instead of continuing with our throw-away, landfill world.

Rick Sever is a general contractor and architectural historian specializing in design, restoration and remodeling to the pre-1960 residence. He has worked in the Seattle area since 1983.

PREFACE

What does a window do?

A window provides a link with, and view of, the outside world. It's a source of light and ventilation as well as egress in case of emergencies. It can also be a source of frustration and expense in an older home if it is barely moving or inoperable.

I'm Mr. Window. I've repaired over 3,000 windows of all types in the Seattle area. That's right, over 3,000, enough to turn anyone into a fenestral drone (window drudge) whose vision of hell is an unending row of Victorian homes full of painted-shut windows which I must repair after signing a really bad contract with Satan (whose checks keep bouncing). I endured to share with you, the homeowner or curious carpenter, my practical knowledge of window repair. The information is both useful and realistic and can save you thousands of dollars in window replacement costs. If you live in hell, it can save you millions of dollars.

I am not a purist about old windows. There's something to be said for a new, high-quality vinyl window that never needs painting or glazing and remains problem free for years and years. Statements like these drive historic preservationists into a collective paroxysm, but these same people apparently have no problem with modern conveniences they favor such as dishwashers, furnaces, espresso makers, and the SUVs they drive to construction sites to protest the imminent destruction of historic outhouses. Still, there's much to be said about original wood windows from both a design and economic standpoint. If it's old-world charm you want, I'll show you how to keep a big part of it.

I'll explain repair techniques, describe tools and materials, and discuss the different types of windows found in older buildings and homes. I'll limit the text to approximately pre-1950 wood windows.

These fixes really work! I've repaired some horrible windows and they're still in service today. The procedures in this book will produce both historically correct and practical working results at an affordable price. Use them and you'll have operating, weather-tight, and attractive, albeit quaint, windows of your very own.

ACKNOWLEDGMENTS

After more edits and rewrites than I care to remember, I finished the original text of this book in 1997 and waved it good-bye, convinced I had turned out an intelligent and even witty tome on window repair. I sat back and waited for fat royalty checks to roll in along with a place on the *New York Times* bestseller list and a choice of movie deals. Looking at these shattered illusions some years later, I must have become more intelligent and upgraded my definition of wit. I decided a rewrite was in order (and then a third one as well)—and a second shot at Hollywood—with more detailed instructions and references. Although I've added a few illustrations, I want to express my gratitude to the original illustrators whose work greatly aided the text. I would once again like to thank Anita Lehmann, AIA, and Kathleen Rosales for their early help, Michael LaFond for the final drawings as well as Mike Littaker for reviewing the text. My thanks to Sandra Todd and Darlene Dubé at Todd/Dubé for setting the text and drawings, and to columnist Mark Hetts (Mr. Handyperson) for his thoughtful reviews and for introducing me to The Lyons Press.

I would also like to thank Rejuvenation of Portland, Oregon, the 3M Corporation, the Vincent Whitney Company, M.A.G. Engineering and Manufacturing Company, The Japan Woodworker, Ettore, and Ives Hardware for generously providing additional artwork for this edition.

INTRODUCTION

Most of my work has been in homes and buildings built between 1890 and the late 1940s. The wood windows of this period include the following types:

- Double-hung (most common)
- Casement
- Awning
- Hopper Vent
- Fixed
- Pivoting

Each window type has advantages and disadvantages in terms of maintenance and operation and will be described separately in the text. Original window systems can last for centuries with regular maintenance. Before you begin your repairs, ask yourself:

- Which windows do I need opened for safety and ventilation?

- What are my security considerations?

- If money is a concern, will I be in my home long enough to recoup my investment if I replace the windows?

- Will repaired windows give me the comfort and quiet of new insulated windows?

- My home's architecture isn't all that interesting so why not replace?

- If I do replace, what type of window should I purchase: aluminum, vinyl, or wood?

- Can Mr. Window show me, a strapped-to-my-desk, monitor-staring, keyboard-tapping, office-bound, reality-TV-show-addicted, can't-tell-a-hammer-from-a-spammer homeowner how to repair my own windows, proving to the world I can actually accomplish something besides move pixels around all day?

Home improvements often evolve around time, budget, and wishful thinking. Window considerations are no exception. Even if you feel like you're "all thumbs," with practice you'll be able to do any repair technique described in this book without resorting to exotic tools or materials.

For practice, start with a small window in a bedroom or closet and familiarize yourself with the work. Give yourself an afternoon to complete the job. I think you'll be pleased with the results.

The text starts with the simplest repairs—getting painted-shut windows opened—of double-hung windows, the most common style of windows in older homes, and progresses to complete disassemblies and repairs of rotted and weathered wood. I wouldn't advise jumping ahead to the tougher repairs without reading the earlier information first.

Please note: Any prices quoted are effective as of this printing.

CHAPTER 1

Double-Hung Windows

THE BASICS

Double-hung windows are the most common style of window in old American homes. An upper sash slides down and a lower sash slides up. They're a mystery to carpenters and homeowners, abused by painters, and often replaced instead of being understood and repaired. They are a model of simplicity and infinitely repairable regardless of how awful they appear. Once you've gotten them open and functioning again, you'll wonder why you didn't fix them sooner.

The most basic repair is simply getting a window open after it's been painted shut. From there, you can deal with rope replacement, installing new glass, wood repair, and painting. Before strapping on the tool belt and conquering your fenestration anxieties, you'll need some details about window construction and obstruction. You'll also need some tools and materials depending on how much work you intend on doing. These will be noted in the text, but please see the Tool and Materials Appendix on pages 207–214 for further enlightenment.

THE DETAILS

Double-hung windows have an upper and a lower sash (the movable sections that hold the glass) that slide up and down and look like this:

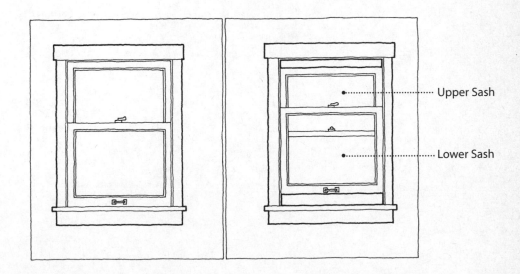

Upper Sash

Lower Sash

Naming Names: What to call all those parts (instead of, "Oh, you know, that little wheel thingy that the rope goes through").

· A sash is the section that moves and holds the glass. It has two horizontal members called rails and two vertical members called stiles.

· The jamb is the larger window frame in which the sashes slide.

· Window weights counterbalance the sashes so they remain open.

· The pulleys facilitate the movement of the weights.

· When present, the pocket covers provide access to the weights.

· Parting beads separate the upper and lower sashes so they can slide past each other.

· The interior stop and the blind stop hold the sashes in place.

· Casings are the vertical wood trim which set the window in place and help stabilize it. On brick and stucco buildings, the exterior trim is usually brick molding.

· The sill is the sloped, horizontal, exterior base of the window.

· The stool is the horizontal trim at the bottom of the window; it butts up against the lower sash.

· An apron is the horizontal trim under the stool.

· Hook lifts and sash lifts assist in opening and closing a sash.

What? You don't have pulleys or pocket covers? Don't worry, I'll cover those, too.

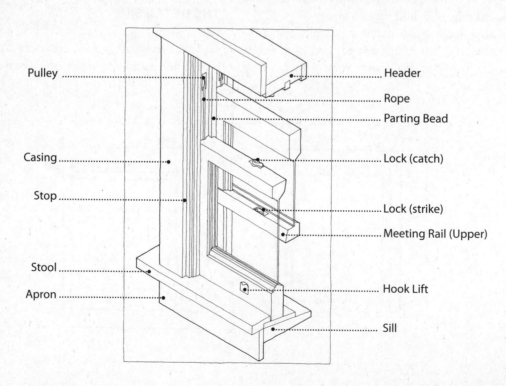

Pulley .... Header

Rope

Parting Bead

Casing .... Lock (catch)

Stop .... Lock (strike)

Meeting Rail (Upper)

Stool .... Hook Lift

Apron ....

Sill

The two sashes join at the meeting rail.

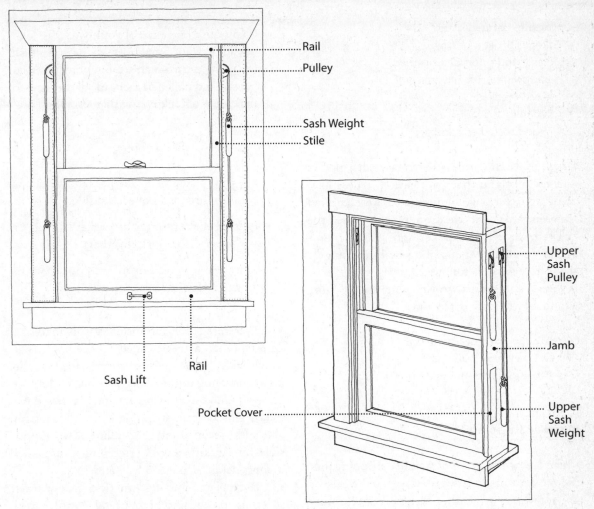

Rail
Pulley

Sash Weight
Stile

Sash Lift

Rail

Pocket Cover

Upper
Sash
Pulley

Jamb

Upper
Sash
Weight

NOTE: In a single-hung window, only the lower sash moves. I've only run across one of these and it was a replacement window, not the original; they're almost unheard of in old homes. In newer homes, single-hung vinyl windows are typical. The problem with a single-hung window is you cannot paint the meeting rail, the horizontal section you see full of gloppy paint drips whenever you open a lower sash. If you can't lower the upper sash, paint will drip unless you tape off the rail with masking tape (and the rail would have to have been taped off every time it was previously painted, which is the impossible dream).

Triple-hung windows, a feature of some Greek Revival houses, operate on the same principle as double-hung windows with the addition of a third operating sash.

TYPICAL PROBLEMS

· Sashes painted shut
· Ropes broken or frayed
· Paint and putty deteriorated
· Hardware broken or missing
· Glass cracked
· Not weather tight
· Wood rotted or damaged

Once upon a time, in a land far away, all windows opened (all right, that's not entirely true, I have come across a few windows that were painted shut since new, but these are rarities). Then the painters came and stale air and stifling rooms and the weeping and wailing and gnashing of serial homeowners followed for years and years. Before attempting to open your double-hung windows, you must determine:

· Are they weather-stripped?
· Do they have pulleys?
· What kind of pulleys do they have?

Weather Stripping

There are several types of weather stripping, but the most common types used with old windows are interlocking weather stripping and spring bronze. Interlocking is a hindrance to work around, especially if a window is painted shut. The diagrams below show a typical section of this material. To determine if your windows are weather-stripped:

· Find a window that works and open the lower sash to see if any metal weather stripping is nailed to the jamb. Usually if one window is weather-stripped, they all are.

· If you can't open any of your windows, look outside at the lower corners of the upper sash for a one- or two-inch section of metal sticking out and nailed to each side of the jamb to indicate interlocking weather stripping.

Interlocking weather stripping:

· Fits into a channel (called a dado) which is cut into three sides of each sash.

· Is fitted at the meeting rail (where the upper and lower sashes lock together).

· Must line up precisely in order for the window to slide and lock properly.

There are some variations of this material. One type has a piece nailed to the sash itself which slides into a second piece nailed to the jamb. Installing interlocking material in double-hung windows is quite an art and is rarely done today. This weather stripping is usually salvageable and I recommend reinstalling it when possible. Interlocking weather stripping is discussed in more detail on pages 52–59 and 149.

To replace missing interlocking weather stripping, contact Accurate Metal Weather-strip Company (800-536-6043 or www.accurateweatherstrip.com).

NOTE: Sometimes, the weather stripping does not extend down at the corners of the upper sash. Look carefully for the ends of the weather stripping.

Spring bronze consists of thin, flat, continuous sections of brass. The sashes press against it forming a seal. It's much easier to work around than interlocking, but it normally isn't salvageable once it's removed and should be replaced (see pages 144–149).

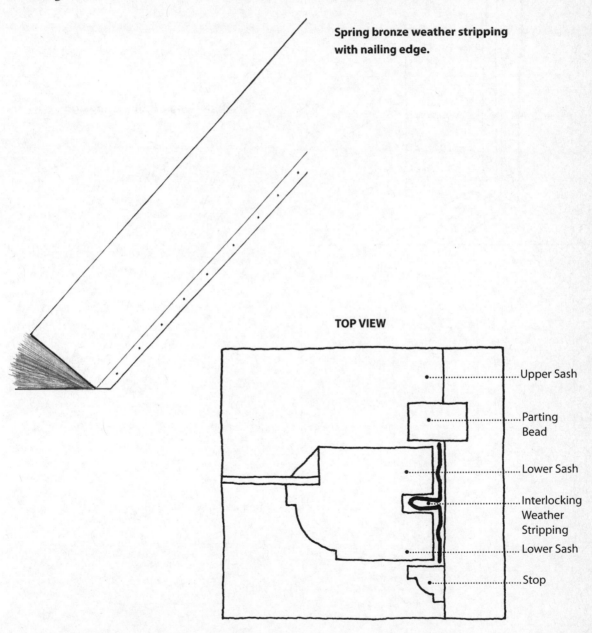

Spring bronze weather stripping with nailing edge.

TOP VIEW

Upper Sash

Parting Bead

Lower Sash

Interlocking Weather Stripping

Lower Sash

Stop

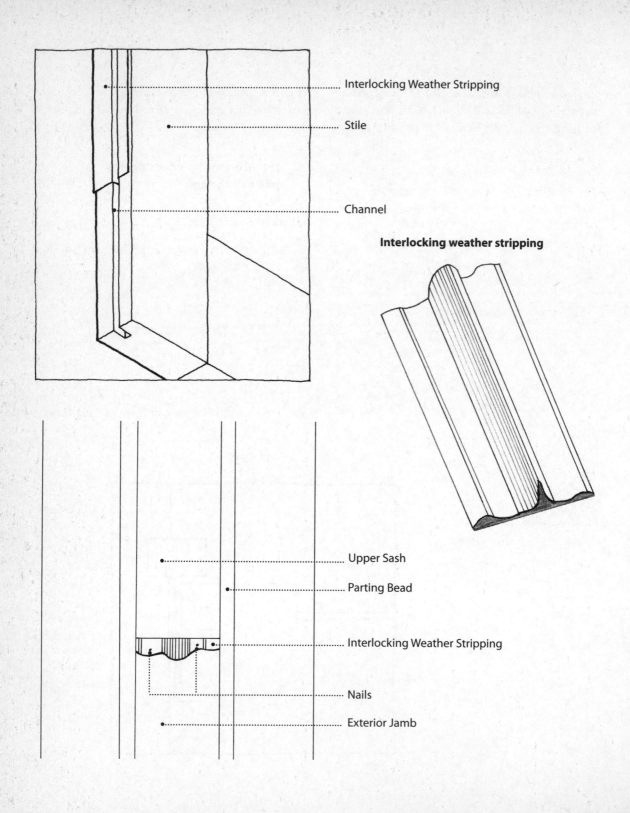

Interlocking Weather Stripping

Stile

Channel

Interlocking weather stripping

Upper Sash

Parting Bead

Interlocking Weather Stripping

Nails

Exterior Jamb

Pulleys

Next, determine if you have pulleys, which is simple enough to do. For pre-1950s windows, you will either have the fixed (wheel) type or a duplex pulley. Most are the fixed type. Duplex pulleys or spring sash balances were introduced in the 1940s; an example of each is shown below.

A duplex pulley is a metal box, installed in the jamb, containing spring-wound cables. A large window will have two duplex pulleys. One end of a cable is attached to the lower corner or corners of each sash. Old cables are prone to snapping if they are not removed carefully.

What was the point of duplex pulleys when the fixed type was so simple and worked so well? Cost, of course. Duplex pulleys eliminated weights, ropes, and the fixed pulleys. The window could

be assembled in the factory or on-site. We tend to view past home construction as the height of slow and steady craftsmanship and attention to details, but whenever a time and money-saving innovation could be introduced, homebuilders grabbed it, which is no different than construction today.

If you do not have duplex pulleys and do not have fixed pulleys and you do not have sash pins (yes, yet another piece of hardware shown below), then STOP! The builder never intended this window to open but did intend for it to be fixed shut. Usually, you'll find this in a group of 3–4 or more double-hung windows where only the end windows or every other window opens. Those smart builders probably saved, oh, maybe a dollar a window installing them without pulleys and weights.

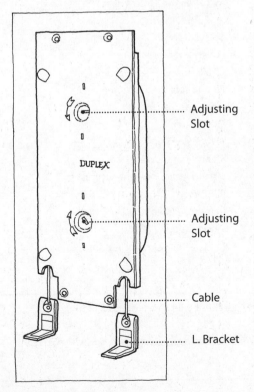

Adjusting Slot

DUPLEX

Adjusting Slot

Cable

L. Bracket

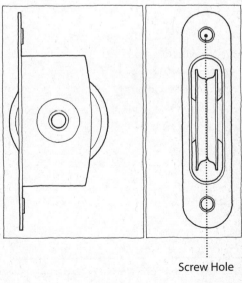

Screw Hole

We'll never see these prices again...

The following prices were supplied in 1937 by the Detroit Steel Products Company, a former manufacturer of steel casement windows trying to make its case for homebuilders to install their metal windows rather than wood double-hung windows in new homes.

Cost of a typical, single frame, double-hung window (13 sq. ft. including interior casings)

Frame and sashes (uninstalled):	$6.20
Other materials*:	4.00
Installation labor**:	6.15
Total cost:	**$16.35**

* All or some of the following:

- Weights
- Sash rope
- Sash lift and window lock
- Interior trim
- Parting beads
- Glass and putty
- Weather stripping
- Full screen

**Includes the following:

- Set, plumb, and brace frame
- Fit and hang sash
- Caulk frame
- Fit and attach inside trim, apron, and stool
- Glaze sash
- Attach hardware
- Fit and hang screen
- Fit and attach weather stripping
- Paint sash (2 coats)
- Paint trim (3 coats)
- Paint screen (2 coats)
- Refit sash after completion

(The cost of the company's installed steel Fenestra Casement window came to $14.97.)

Source: Home Owners' Catalog: A Guide to the Selection of Building Materials, Equipment, and Furnishings (1937), published by the F.W. Dodge Corporation

Fixed double-hung windows may still need repairs. If so, follow the repair instructions for double-hung windows. Just because they're fixed doesn't mean they have to stay that way. To turn a fixed double-hung or casement window into an operable window, see pages 138–142.

 There are replacement pulleys that use a self-winding steel tape instead of ropes and weights. I would stick with the original system when possible. It's simple, can always be repaired, and replacement duplicate pulleys are available if needed.

Sash Pins

What are sash pins? They are spring-loaded pins, also called sash spring bolts, installed into the sides of a sash in lieu of ropes and weights. When the pins are pulled inward, the sash can be raised. Released, the ends of the pins insert and lock into holes drilled into the jamb every six inches or so. This prevents the sash from dropping. Sash pins do the job, although the movement of the sash will be choppy. Replacement pins are still manufactured. Windows with sash pins are also called guillotine windows for reasons that are readily apparent if you've ever opened one.

Sash pins might be stuck due to paint buildup. To loosen them, you have to twist and pull them loose with a vise-grips or pliers. If a pin is damaged and needs to be replaced, you must remove the sash and gently tap the end of the pin near the glass with a hammer. The pins are held in by friction (the metal casing pushes against the drilled hole the pin sits in). As it's forced out of the hole, you'll be able to grab the other end with pliers and twist it out completely. Replace both pins in each sash you remove. Sash pins are not a common hardware item. Some older, been-in-town forever types of hardware stores might have them in stock so call around (see Resources); many hardware stores won't have the faintest idea what you're talking about. One advantage of windows with sash pins is they're much more difficult for some ne'er-do-well prowler to pry open, if that's any consolation.

Q Geez, Mr. Window, I've got sash pins and they're kind of a pain. The windows don't open real smoothly and when I go to close the big ones, all I can say is watch out below, they do drop like guillotines. What's the deal, are these some kind of weird French Revolution retro windows or something?

A *We can't blame this one on the French and calling them freedom windows won't make them any better. Sash pins were used because they were cheap. Builders have always had budgets to work with and sash pins represent a lower budget. Sometimes, though, you'll find a mix of windows in the same house, some with pulleys and some (basement and closet windows, for instance) with sash pins.*

Stuck with sash pins? After freeing an upper sash, nail a small block of wood under the bottom rail of the sash, outside on each side of the jamb. The blocks should be located so the meeting rail of the sash can move down low enough to be painted when the lower sash is all the way open. The blocks will stop the sash from falling down to the sill should you lose your hold on the pins when closing it from its lowest open position.

Sash Pin

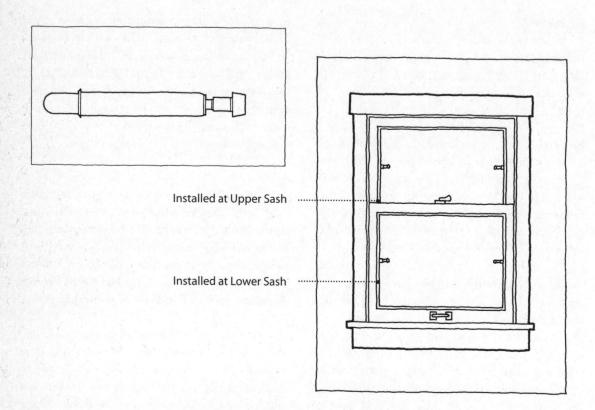

Installed at Upper Sash

Installed at Lower Sash

An alternative to sash pins on the lower sash are ventilating bolts, which are sliding, spring-loaded bolts that attach to the stiles. The bolts lock into small strike plates, set at different heights, which are installed on the window stops. Ventilating bolts are more expensive than sash pins.

Ventilating Bolt

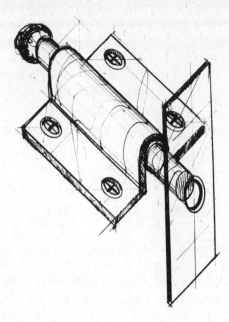

PROBLEMS AND PROBLEM SOLVING

Opening the Window

Let's say all you want to do is get the lower sash open. You don't have any weather stripping. You can have either type of pulley; it doesn't matter at this point.

BEWARE: Sometimes the bottom rails are quite loose and can drop off when opening the sash (don't worry, they can be repaired). Telltale signs are gaps in the corners and a generally funky looking sash. The glass may also be loose. Hold onto these as best you can while opening the sash. If the glass is badly cracked, be absolutely sure to tape the cracks with duct tape or masking tape, preferably on both sides! This prevents the glass from falling out while removing the sash.

WARNING! The sash may be nailed or screwed shut. This is more likely if the window is in an area vulnerable to break-ins (basement windows, for instance) or if your home was formerly owned by rabid survivalists. The nails are inevitably on the interior side. To deal with these pesky fasteners, see "Windows Nailed Shut" on page 21.

To open the lower sash, you have to break the paint seal on three sides, and usually at the meeting rail, as well as any caulk sealing the sash shut. You can do this by using:

· A wide, sharp, chisel-type putty knife and hammer
· A heat gun
· Chemical paint remover
· A window zipper

The putty knife and hammer are the least messy, although these will not remove the paint, only break the seal, which is normally all that's necessary. The heat gun and paint remover will remove much of the excess paint, but will require a lot of cleanup and repainting. A window zipper is a small hand tool with a serrated triangular or heart-shaped head that cuts through dried paint. I've never liked any of the models because they're not as easy to control as a putty knife (all right, they're not as easy for Mr. Window to control). Window zippers are inexpensive and available at most paint and hardware stores if you want to give one a try.

Window Zipper

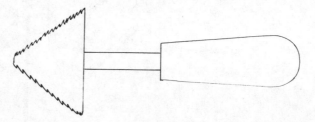

The diagram below shows where to break the paint. This is an interior view. For this job, you really should break the paint seal on the outside as well so you can pry the sash upward. There are no guarantees just breaking the paint on the inside will be sufficient for opening the window. Working on the outside normally means working off ladders. Please see "Ladder Safety" on page 15 before you go crawling around like Spider Man/Woman/Other.

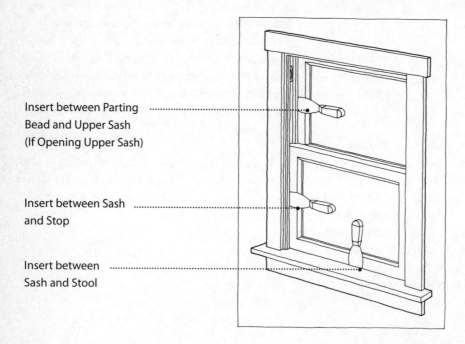

Insert between Parting
Bead and Upper Sash
(If Opening Upper Sash)

Insert between Sash
and Stop

Insert between
Sash and Stool

If you are using a putty knife to open the sash:

· Be sure the lock is open before you start (I know, that sounds obvious, but you can forget and then go outside and try and force the sash up, all the while going nuts wondering why it isn't budging because you forgot to flip the lock).

· Run the pointed corner end of the blade against the paint seal all around between the sash and the stops and stool. You don't have to dig very hard, just enough to cut into the paint. This cut helps prevent the paint from chipping when you begin pounding on the putty knife with a hammer. Old oil paint is brittle and can break off in large chips, which means more filling and painting after the sash is opened.

· After cutting into the paint, place the blade of the putty knife against the seal and tap the putty knife with a hammer, breaking the paint on the inside. If accessible, repeat these steps on the outside of the sash.

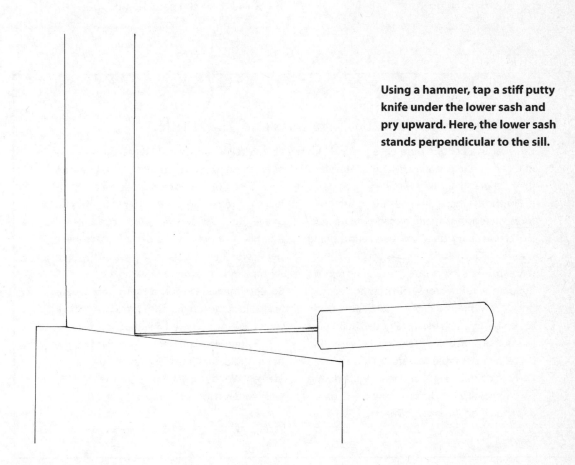

Using a hammer, tap a stiff putty knife under the lower sash and pry upward. Here, the lower sash stands perpendicular to the sill.

· Spray some silicone or WD-40 on the jamb so the sash will slide more easily (liquid soap will do, too, if you object to chemicals).

· Next, insert the knife outside under the bottom rail of the sash, between it and the sill, and pry up. You might have to insert a flat pry bar (see pry bar comment below) under the putty knife blade to provide more force if the sash is really stuck. Don't use a screwdriver, it will gouge the wood (I've found a zillion screwdriver marks in sashes over the years and had to fill and repair plenty of them)!

· If you cannot get to the outside, you might be able to pull up on the sash lifts and open it from the inside, but if it starts feeling like a labor of Hercules, let it go. You'll have to remove the stops (see below).

Another way to break the paint seal is to use a heat gun or chemical paint remover (see pages 80–85). Both methods are messy because they loosen and remove the paint surrounding the paint seal. If it's your intent to strip paint off the window, by all means use heat or chemicals to loosen up the sash. Otherwise, stick with hand tools and leave the paint intact.

The Wonderful World of Pry Bars and Nail Pullers

Crowbar is a generic term covering all kinds of tools used to pry apart, up, and out—walls, floors, framing lumber, windows—you name it. For those whose business it is to use these tools, there are distinctions made when speaking of wrecking bars, pry bars, and ripping bars. For your window work, you'll need the flatter pry bars to pry open sashes and remove molding, window stops, and parting beads.

A few brands and specific tools come to mind. An 8" SharkGrip Pry Bar/Nail Puller (www.sharkcorp.com) features a very thin flat end, a desirable feature because it's less likely to damage walls and woodwork during your removal work. It runs around $12 on up depending on the vendor. The Red Devil 8 $^3/_8$"

Scrape 'N Pry Bar (www.reddevil.com) also has a very thin flat end and currently costs between $6 and $7. Both tools can also serve as scrapers when removing paint with paint remover. Stanley Tools (www.stanleytools.com) makes a terrific 7"-long Wonder Bar II Pry Bar that's perfect for tight spaces; I use mine all the time for trim and molding removal. It runs around $6. Both the Red Devil and Stanley brands are available at most hardware stores while Shark tools have more limited distribution.

Sometimes, you need more heft to force open a reluctant sash. Try one of the larger Stanley Wonder Bars, such as the 55-525, which offers a lot of leverage.

WARNING! Don't push up on the upper rail of the lower sash to try to force the sash open. Pushing hard enough can loosen the rail and even break it at the corners or loosen the glass. Mr. Window is not speaking theoretically here and feels fortunate there were no witnesses (a regular and repeating feeling during his career) when he popped a few rails loose. The meeting rail is fairly narrow, more a function of aesthetics than practicality, and is particularly tenuous on large, wide sashes. Pull up on the sash lifts instead. On the upper sash, which never has sash lifts (I think it should and advocate installing them), push down only at the corners of the lower rail and then only after it's been adequately loosened. In either case, don't push at the center of either meeting rail as this puts the most stress on them.

Ladder Safety

Here's a cheery statistic: Hundreds of thousands of ladder accidents happen every year in the United States, several thousand resulting in deaths. Extension ladders offer plenty of opportunities for injuries since they allow you to fall from a higher distance. Mr. Window, who has never been too fond of heights and ladders, will admit he hasn't always followed the rules and guidelines he's about to list. His living to tell about it is no justification for you not being smarter about ladder use.

For all you ladder newbies, there are four types of ladders, three of which you might find yourself using:

- Fixed (a single length, non-adjustable ladder)
- Step (folding ladder with flat steps instead of rungs)
- Extension (a two-piece ladder, with rungs, that can extend in length)
- Articulated (a multi-adjustable ladder that can be used as an extension or stepladder as well as a platform)

When using an extension ladder:

- Buy or rent an appropriately rated ladder for the job and the weight the ladder will be supporting. In descending order, the ratings are Type IA (duty rating of 300 lbs, extra-heavy duty), Type I (250 lbs, heavy duty), Type II (225 lbs, medium use), and Type III (200 lbs, light-duty use). Be sure the ladder is long enough for the job (its working length will be three feet less than its stated or dimensional length).

- Check that your ladder is in safe working condition. Wood ladders should have tight joints and fasteners and the wood rungs intact. Aluminum ladders should not have cracks or broken welds. With any type of extension ladder, the ropes, hooks, and locks should be in good working order. Stay off of shaky, wobbly ladders! Clean any grease or dirt from the rungs before using.

- Angle the ladder close to 75 degrees from the ground. This is roughly the same as having the base of the ladder set out from the wall the same distance as one-fourth of the ladder's height to its top support point. If the ladder hits the house at 20 feet from the ground, the base should be five feet from the wall. In other words, one foot out for every four feet up.

- Be sure the base or legs of the ladder are resting firmly on the ground. If the ground is too uneven, place some 2x6 boards or larger under the leg needing support. No bricks or buckets, they can slip and then so can you. The ladder should be standing straight and even.

- Stay away from overhead electrical wires. If you must set up near them, use a fiberglass ladder instead of an aluminum one or use a dry wood ladder. Avoid this scenario in wet weather, however.

- To set up the ladder, lay it down perpendicular to wall with the foot of the ladder against the wall. Lift the top of the ladder over your head and walk under the ladder, raising it as you go, rung by rung. Once the ladder is vertical and against the house, lift it slightly and pull the base out. Reverse these steps to take the ladder down. The heavier duty rating, the heavier the ladder so be sure you have the strength to set up the ladder. Once the ladder is vertical, adjust the height to the area where you will be working.

- Pound a stake, pipe, or large wedge into the ground and against each leg of the ladder to prevent it from slipping. On driveways, tie one end of a rope to the lowest rung and the other end to a secure point of attachment.

- For extension ladders up to 36 feet long, there should be three feet of overlap between the two sections, meaning you can't just keep sliding the movable section of the ladder until the two sections are almost coming apart; leave three feet of the movable section overlapping the bottom section.

- Be sure the ladder locking mechanisms (the fly locks that lock into the rungs) are fully engaged.

- If you're feeling a bit too insecure, tie off the top of the ladder with rope or baling wire (attach a screw-in eye to the windowsill and fill the hole in later when you remove it).

- Climb the ladder carefully, keeping yourself centered with the rungs.

- Instead of carrying heavy tools with you, put them in a bucket and pull them up with a rope. A ladder hook, which slips over a rung and is available at paint stores, will give you something to hang the bucket on (or you can just tie it with small piece of rope or wire).

- Stay off the top three rungs of the ladder.

- Don't overreach! Everyone does this and it's a bad idea. Overreaching means you move your body's trunk beyond the side rails instead of staying centered. It's tempting. You figure, what's the big deal, I'm right here, why go down and move the ladder if I don't have to? Trust me, go down and move the ladder. Also, don't try and move the ladder while standing on it. I've watched painters do this, bouncing the ladder up and down and sliding it over because getting down and moving it for that last foot of siding they're trying to paint is just a nuisance, but these are guys who smell paint fumes all day so that explains that.

- Only one person on the ladder at one time!

- If you must place a ladder in front of an entry door, be sure the door is locked and you've put a sign on the inside warning that you're working on a ladder outside the door. Otherwise, the door opens, someone walks out, and it's surprise time for you.

- Store wood ladders in a dry area, off the floor. Aluminum and fiberglass ladders should also be stored in a dry area to preserve the ropes and avoid corrosion. Lubricate the locking mechanisms from time to time. Tighten all fasteners on wood ladders. Never paint a wood ladder (the paint can hide deterioration and damage), but treat with wood preservative.

When using stepladders:

- Be sure the ladder is tall enough for the job at hand and has a duty rating that will match the workload.

- Lock the spreaders, the metal devices that hold the ladder open, completely before standing on the ladder.

- Place the ladder securely on the ground so it doesn't lean.

- Stay off the top step (you know, the one that says, "THIS IS NOT A STEP").

- Check that the ladder is tight and not wobbling.

- Store the ladder in a clean, dry place, applying the same maintenance standards as those for wooden extension ladders.

Articulated ladders are the multiple personalities of the ladder world. The models and features vary by manufacturer, but some of these ladders can be broken down into smaller individual ladders, extension ladders, and fixed ladders. They even turn into scaffolding and ladders for staircases (the legs adjust to the different heights of the steps). If you've ever watched the infomercial for Little Giant Ladder Systems (this isn't an endorsement, just a comment), you'll know what these strange mutants can do. You'll also probably never be able to manipulate the ladders as fast as the product demonstrator on TV who handles the

Little Giant with the same ease as a carnival clown sculpting balloons into zoo animals. The main thing to watch for when you use an articulated ladder is that all the hinges are completely locked and in good working order. The same safety, storage, and maintenance rules apply to an articulated ladder as apply to an aluminum extension ladder.

Removing the Stops

If the sash will barely budge or you cannot access the outside and get a putty knife between the bottom rail and the sill, then you will have to remove the stops. The easiest way to do this is shown on page 19.

NOTE: If your window has duplex pulleys, see pages 23, 50–51.

Here are the steps:

· You will need a hammer, a block of wood, stiff putty knife, small pry bar, and a pair of wire cutters or pliers.

· If you haven't already done so, run the edge of a putty knife between the sash and the stop to cut into the paint seal.

· Next, run the knife along the intersection of the stop and the casing as it faces you. This can be hard to find if it's glopped with layers of paint and filled with caulk. Gently run the knife down this seam. If you use both hands, there's less chance of the knife slipping and scratching the casing.

· Place a block of wood against the upper sash (you can also use the handle of the putty knife); this provides leverage for the claw hammer and prevents the claw end from chewing up the stop.

· Place the head of the hammer on the block of wood and the end of the claw against the back side of the stop where it's nailed into the jamb.

· Pull on the hammer and the back of the stop will come loose. You only need to get it out a half an inch or so, but further is OK, too.

· The stop should now be slightly loose just above the top of the lower sash. Insert a small crowbar or stiff putty knife under the stop near the casing and slowly bend it out a little at a time so it doesn't crack or split.

· Work your way up and down the stop, gradually pulling it out further. There will be at least four to six nails holding it in unless it's been removed in the past and reinstalled with fewer nails.

· Pull the nails out from the backside of the stop—don't nail them through the front, they can split the wood at the surface—using a wire cutters or pliers. Grab them tightly with the tool and turn the handles of the pliers or wire cutters in a circle, bending the nails. This will pull them out.

Some restorers suggest starting at the bottom of the stop and working your way up, but I disagree. Often there is so much paint buildup at the stool that it prevents the end of the stop from easily sliding out. I recommend loosening as much of the stop as you can, an inch or so at a time starting in the middle, and then repeating, moving the stop out further. As it bows out, the stop gives you more leeway at the bottom by taking some of the pressure off the ends of the stop. When a stop is especially tight, you can insert a

wire cutter or hacksaw blade against the exposed nails and cut through them, which will greatly relax the stop and make it easier to remove. It really depends on how much paint you're dealing with. The more layers at the stool, the tighter the stop. Keep in mind that each stop is cut for a particular window. If you're working on more than one opening, mark the stops so you'll know where to reinstall them in case they get mixed up with stops from other windows.

Removing the stops to free up the sashes is especially useful when you're working on windows on the second floor or higher and aren't interested in climbing ladders to break the paint seal outside.

Removal of Stop

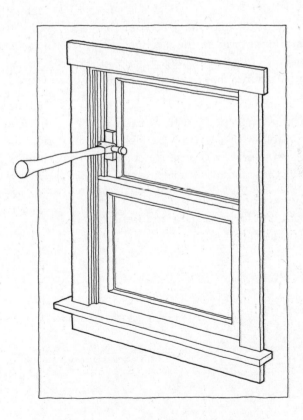

IF YOU HAVE SASH PINS: Loosen the pins and pull them out as far as they will come. Wedge a sliver of wood between the pin and its casing so the pins will not lock into the jamb again. This way, you can loosen the sash and pull it forward and out. If you have four hands (one for each pin and one each for the hammer and putty knife) and presumably two bodies, you can ignore this advice. My perspective is written for someone bravely and courageously doing the work alone, keeping America number one in window restoration. It is simply coincidental that Mr. Window matches this description.

With both stops removed:

· Carefully insert the putty knife between the upper and lower sash at the meeting rail. The sashes lock together at a slight angle, so don't try to hammer the putty knife straight down.

· Tap the knife moderately with a hammer and it will follow the angle of the meeting rail. The two sashes will separate, as you work along the length of the meeting rail.

· Pull the lower sash towards you and work it slowly back and forth several times until it breaks free and can be raised.

· Don't pull one end out at too much of an angle before freeing the entire length of the sash! You can stress and bend the glass and it can crack. Watch if either the glass or bottom rail is loose as you raise the sash and secure them as you go.

· The meeting rail might be full of caulk or Spackle requiring you to be more aggressive when tapping the putty knife. Aggression can be a good thing, but don't haul off like you're chopping wood for the winter. Patience really is a virtue when it comes to window restoration.

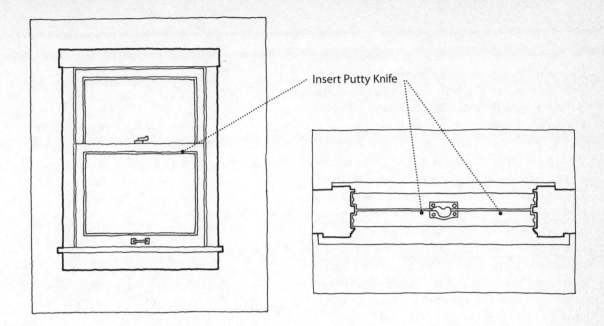

Insert Putty Knife

After moving the sash back and forth a few times, it should be ready to open upwards. Spray the pulleys with plenty of WD-40 or spray silicone and be careful with the old ropes! They're often covered with a lot of paint, making them stiff and prone to break if moved too abruptly. If the ropes are painted tight to the jamb, carefully loosen them by forcing a flexible putty knife between the ropes and the jamb and prying the ropes off the jamb. Slowly work the sash up and down until the paint on the ropes breaks and the ropes move through the pulleys. Even if there isn't much paint buildup, old cotton ropes are tenuous, but still serviceable. Mr. Window does recommend you replace them if time and skills permit since replacement is always a good idea.

How long will an old rope last? There's no way of saying; it could go years without breaking or it could break the same day you free up the window. I would say if basic ventilation is your immediate goal or you're living in a rental unit and working on the windows because your landlord thinks it builds character (your character), worry about rope replacement later unless you've got the interest and easy access to the window weights. You can also install sash controls in lieu of ropes (see pages 39–42).

The edges of the stops and the sash will probably be caked with paint. Scrape off the excess paint from the stops before reinstalling (please see section on lead-based paint first, pages 72–73) with a scraper or coarse sandpaper. For complete stripping, see pages 79–90, Chapter 4.

Windows Nailed Shut

Most nailed-shut windows are not in residences. Occasionally I would run across them in commercial buildings and school buildings. I never figured out the latter category unless too many kids were bailing out on test days.

If your windows are stained and varnished, and thus unpainted and easier to open, and you still can't budge the sash, even with the stops removed, look for nails. Slide a stiff blade putty knife between the vertical stiles and the jamb and check for an obstruction. Hit something? Pry the two apart slightly. Find a nail? Force the end of the putty knife (use an old one as this isn't exactly tool-friendly activity) against the nail and hammer down on it until the nail either breaks or bends loose from the jamb. When the sash is removed, pull the bent nail out of the jamb and the sash with pliers or wire cutters. If it's a screw, try to find the head and unscrew it. Otherwise, cut the shaft of the screw with a hacksaw blade (just the blade, removed from the saw).

When an upper sash is nailed shut, the nails are most often either under or nailed through its lower two corners on the exterior section of the jamb. Smart and thoughtful people in the past who wanted to nail an upper sash shut would nail a block of wood under the sash to keep it closed so present people like you could easily find it and remove it. Unfortunately, many smart or thoughtful people were trumped by people in a hurry who slammed nails into upper sashes so you're stuck pulling these nails out.

Usually, I find the nail heads at upper sashes sticking out enough to make them noticeable and they can then be pulled with a vise-grips or small crowbar. When the nails have been set and the heads aren't easy to pull with a tool:

- Take an old screwdriver and dig away a small amount of wood from around the head of the nail.

- Grab the nail head with a pliers (not needle-nose, you'll need something stronger, like

slip-joint pliers or vise-grips) and turn it back and forth in half circles.

- When the nail has loosened, pull it out. The hole in the sash can be patched with filler (see pages 107–110).

Nails inserted on the inside of an upper sash can be cut or bent at the jamb after removing the parting beads (see page 34).

Reinstalling the Stops

When reinstalling the stops:

- Clean any accumulated paint and caulk gunk off the ends and edges of the stops.

- Allow enough room between the stops and the sash so the sash will slide easily. I usually line up the stops, partially hammer one nail close to the center, and then raise and lower the sash and check for adjustment before nailing the rest of the stop. A good way of spacing is to insert a stiff putty knife between the sash and the stop and use this as a guide. Remember, you will be at least touching up the paint, if not completely repainting or varnishing, and the putty knife allows for the space between the stop and the sash getting brushed with either coating.

- If the sash is tight or sticking, check the position of the stops and spray the jamb and the area where the sash runs against the stops with lubricant. Spray liberally, but wipe off any lubricant from areas you expect to paint.

- When a stop seems too long for its opening because of all the paint buildup on it and the casings, you can take a hacksaw and trim 1/32" off the bottom to ease the reinstallation.

· Once you're satisfied with the movement of the sash, finish nailing the stops, checking one more time before you set the nails. You only need three to five nails depending on its length so don't go overboard here. Use a nail set—an inexpensive tool used to drive finish nails into wood so their heads are under the surface—to set the nails. Fill the nail holes with Spackle, wood filler, or painter's putty and, if painted, caulk the seam where the stop meets the casing with latex caulk.

Q I followed your advice, Mr. Window, and everything was going really nice and I set all the nails and then found out this stupid sash was sticking on one side. It's too tight against the stop and no matter how many times I think about being here now and chanting my patience chant, all I want to do is yank this stop off and stomp on it. My inner child isn't happy about this one bit.

A *Nor is your outer adult, I bet. Depending on the spacing of your nails, you might be able to raise the sash until it jams up against the stop and then hammer in a finish nail with just a few taps (you don't want it going into the jamb) into the stop. Next, insert a wide, stiff putty knife between the sash and the stop and force the stop away from the sash by bending the putty knife away from the sash. Now slam the nail in and remove your putty knife. The stop should no longer be impeding the sash. This method will not work if the other nails in the stop are too close to the sticking point in which case you'll have to remove the stop and reinstall.*

WARNING! If you have duplex pulleys:

· Slowly move the sash back and forth and gently lift it up and out.

· The cables are attached to the sash via small corner irons (also called corner brackets or angle irons). These can be corroded as can the cables, which have a nasty habit of snapping if handled too roughly.

· Rub the cable with some medium or fine steel wool to remove any corrosion and then apply a small amount of oil or bicycle grease. Spray some lubricant inside the pulley mechanism as well.

Installing a new duplex pulley (see pages 50–52) requires disassembling both sashes and the parting beads. These pulleys are a specialty item available through wholesale hardware suppliers or call Duplex, Inc., (909) 397-9003, in Pomona, California. Always call the supplier first before trudging down only to find out your local hardware store has never heard of duplex pulleys.

Replacing the Ropes

You can rope the lower sash alone or rope both the upper and lower sashes, using either sash rope or sash chain to attach the sash to the weights. Sash chain is costlier—up to ten times more expensive—than rope and is used with very heavy sashes, industrial windows, or in expensive homes and apartments with standard-size windows. Some restorers insist on installing chain when repairing double-hung windows, but this is overkill given the good quality of sash rope available today. Heavy sash chain will, under most circumstances, last forever—something to consider when weighing its cost.

Although pure cotton sash rope is still sold, a blend of cotton and synthetic material is a better choice since it is stronger and more durable than cotton. Sash rope is sold by number (#7, #8, etc.) which indicates its diameter. Number eight rope with a $1/4''$ diameter is more than sufficient for most uses, certainly for residential use. If it isn't available at a local hardware store, try a rope supplier (listed in the Yellow Pages, or see Resources).

One hundred percent solid braid polyester rope is also a good choice, but lacks the traditional feel and appearance of cotton offered by the cotton/poly mix. The appearance issue is really very minor and it's questionable that most people would even notice. Additionally, tradition has its price as the outer cotton section of the cotton/poly mix rope will gradually deteriorate (and it will show). The cotton/poly mix is easier to work with, though, and some polyester rope, depending on the braid, can unravel at the ends, requiring you to take a flame to the ends to fuse them together. Nylon rope will stretch, a bad idea when attaching to window weights, so avoid it.

NOTE: There is an alternative to replacing the ropes: You can install sash controls (see p. 39), which are quick, simple, and cheap, but not as reliable as new ropes (sometimes the controls drop out) nor will you end up with as smoothly an operating window. For a fast fix, though, there's a lot to be said for sash controls.

Lower Sash Rope Replacement and Pocket Covers

With the lower sash removed, look for a pocket cover. Pocket covers are found in one of two locations:

· Exterior or outside pocket covers are more often found in pre-1900 (give or take) houses. These covers are cut into the exterior portion of the jamb where the upper sash slides down, about 6" from the sill. This cover is difficult to see under the usual couple hundred layers of paint, but look closely for its outline.

· Interior or inside pocket covers are cut into the section of the jamb where the lower sash slides, a few inches above the sill.

· Each pocket cover comes with—surprise—its own peculiarities, but they're better than having no pocket covers and offer easy rope and weight access.

Exterior/Outside Pocket Covers

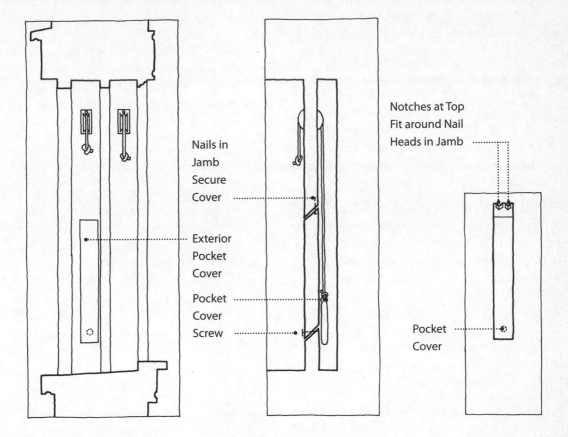

Nails in Jamb Secure Cover

Exterior Pocket Cover

Pocket Cover Screw

Notches at Top Fit around Nail Heads in Jamb

Pocket Cover

A small screw secures the bottom of the exterior cover to the jamb; both the top and bottom are cut at a 45-degree angle. The top end has two notches cut into it that wedge against two nails in the jamb as shown in the diagram. To remove the cover:

· Break the paint on its two vertical sides with a putty knife or score with the edge of a sharp blade.

· Use an old screwdriver and a hammer and chip away the paint and filler in the slotted head of the screw and then remove the screw (if it doesn't come out, just loosen it).

· Slowly pry the cover out starting near the bottom by inserting a narrow, thin putty knife at the bottom edge of the pocket cover, tapping it with a hammer (remember to follow the 45-degree angle here), and slowly force the cover out while pulling it down.

· Alternatively, you can wedge a stiff putty knife between the parting bead and the cover and another knife between both the exterior blind stop and the parting bead and the cover and gradually force it out of the jamb.

· Keep in mind a finish nail from the outside casing occasionally finds itself nailed through an exterior pocket cover. It doesn't happen often—carpenters knew better back then—but it can happen. As the pocket cover separates from the jamb, you can cut any nails with a hacksaw blade detached from its saw.

Once the cover is a little loose from either method, you can then pull it out completely. Combining both methods is often best. Keep in mind if it hasn't been removed in years it will resist, even if resistance is futile.

With the cover removed, you should see one or both (if the rope is broken for the lower sash) of the window weights at the bottom of the pocket. Either way, you could have a problem because:

· The weight from the upper sash can block easy access to the weight from the lower sash (while the upper sash is closed or in the up position, its weight will be at the bottom of the pocket or close to it).

· If both the ropes are broken, the weights can be tightly wedged together.

· When both sashes are the same size, you can always attach the rope for the lower sash to either weight, whichever is more accessible. When sashes are different sizes, you'll have to use the correct weight.

Dividers

Although it's rare in the exterior pocket cover era, your home or building might have wood or metal dividers separating the weights. These dividers:

· Are about as wide as the pocket itself, attach to the top of the weight pocket, and loosely hang down the length of the pocket to separate the weights.

· Limit access to the lower sash weight if the upper sash weight is at the bottom of the pocket.

· Are more often found in public or commercial buildings with large windows.

To work around these dividers:

- With small weights, the dividers are flexible enough to be bent or bowed towards the outside of the window, giving you access to the lower sash weight.

- With large weights, you can try to force the upper sash weight toward the pulley, pull it out of the pocket, cut it from its rope and remove it, or loosen and open the upper sash and pull the weight up completely.

- You can snap off the lower twelve inches or so of a wood divider or take metal snips to a metal divider, but even this doesn't always provide enough access to a large lower sash weight.

With dividers, you're often better off re-roping both sashes. As I mentioned earlier, these dividers are rare but someone reading this book will run into them and Mr. Window believes this lone reader should get the benefit of his startling amount of knowledge about dividers.

If the weights are jammed against each other, try forcing a large screwdriver or crowbar between the weights and shift them around until you can attach the rope. Spraying them with a lot of lubricant can help. Let loose with the WD-40 and don't worry about ozone depletion as WD-40 is cheerfully chlorofluorocarbon-free. If the weights are too wedged to move in any direction, you'll have to take the casing off (see pages 43–46) and access them from the front.

Interior/Inside Pocket Covers

An inside pocket cover is on the inside portion of the jamb where the lower sash slides. This pocket cover is:

- More visible and can be seen after raising the lower sash.

- Normally fastened with two screws, one at the top and one at the bottom.

- Sometimes held in with one bottom screw or even a small nail at each end.

- The outer lip of the cover is under the parting bead, which will have to be pried out slightly in order to remove the cover.

NOTE: On a few occasions, I have run across pocket covers that were not completely cut out during manufacturing and weren't even held in by any kind of fastener. They're kind of weird. You have to slowly pry them and snap them out of the jamb and possibly insert a hacksaw blade and cut away at one side. When reinstalling, use small wire nails or weather-stripping nails to secure.

To remove an inside pocket cover:

- Start at the bottom of the parting bead and, using a stiff putty knife, break the paint seal on the outside face.

- Scrape away, or chisel away, any accumulated paint on the windowsill in front of the parting bead. If the paint isn't cleared away, the parting bead sticks here and has a wonderful tendency to split a few inches up while you're removing it.

- Hammer the putty knife into the jamb where the bead is inserted and slowly bend the bead out from the bottom.

- Next, insert a small pry bar under the now loosened bead and continue loosening it. Go slow; it can still snap on you. You'll have to stop short of the upper sash, otherwise the bead will break.

- After the parting bead has been loosened and pulled out a ways, put a small block of wood between the end of the bead and the jamb to keep it away from the pocket cover.

- Unscrew the cover and pry it out at the bottom, gradually pulling it down and out. If there are no screws, just pry the cover off.

While the sash is removed, it is an opportune time to strip off or sand the paint and repaint, replace any broken glass or putty, install weather stripping, or even clean the glass. Please see Chapter 4 for the details of this work.

Inside Pocket Cover

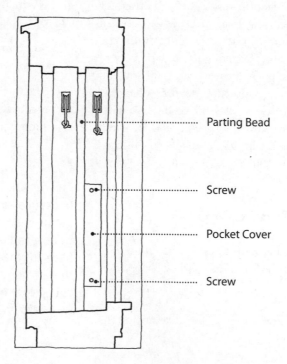

Parting Bead

Screw

Pocket Cover

Screw

Installing the New Rope

Is the old rope still intact? Cut the knotted end coming out of the pulley, let the weight drop to the bottom of the pocket, and pull the rope into the pocket from the top of the weight. Now what? Let's assume the cover is removed and you have plenty of room (hey, it happens) inside the pocket. How do you get the new rope down the pocket? Well, you could try feeding it through and down the pulley by itself and, hope springing eternal, believe that the end will drop right to the bottom and your eagerly awaiting hand. Or you could do what Mr. Window does:

- Get a small piece of chain (plumber's chain, sash chain, etc.) at a hardware store, attach a wire twist (such as those that come with plastic trash bags) to one end and then wrap the other end of the twist around the end of the rope.

NOTE: Buy a couple feet or so of chain and cut off some 6-inch pieces. It's good to have extra around because sometimes the chain comes loose from the rope and ends up at the bottom of the pocket where it can be hard to retrieve.

- Feed the chain down through the pulley and then gradually feed the rope through. Keep your hand inside the pocket to catch the chain if it detaches from the rope and drops off.

- Seconds later, the rope will reach your eagerly awaiting hand, unless it gets hung up on something and then you have to pull it out and feed it through again. You particularly don't want it to get wrapped around the rope for the other sash.

- Cut the old rope away from the weight and pass the end of the new rope through the weight's knot hole.

- Tie an overhand knot (for all you non-knot types, it's the first knot you form when tying your shoes; if you only wear loafers, you're out of luck) at the end of the rope and then take that knotted end and tie an overhand knot tight to the weight with the rest of the rope. The first knot prevents the rope's second knot from coming undone. There are plenty of other Boy Scout/Girl Scout/Army/Navy/Marine/Coast Guard knots to choose from, just use one that won't slip after the window is reassembled.

- With the weight at the bottom of the pocket, cut the rope about four inches out from the pulley and knot the end. Tug on the weight a few times to be sure the knot is tight.

- Move the weight up and down to check that it moves freely with the pulley. If it did get wrapped around the other existing rope, detach the weight, pull the rope out of the pulley, feed it down to the weight, and reattach.

How long should the rope be?

- With the lower sash in place and tilted out towards you and with the weight at the bottom of the pocket, pull on the rope until the weight is at the top of the pocket, up at the pulley.

- Let the weight drop down slightly (so it's not jammed into the pulley), hold the rope against the side of the sash at its knot hole, and then cut it about 4–5″ beyond the hole.

- Tie an overhand knot at the end of the rope and force it into the hole.

- If the hole is large, you can loop the rope around twice when tying your overhand knot so you'll have a larger knot to fill the hole (this is a double overhand knot).

- If the hole is small or not holding the rope securely, hammer a small nail (a shingle nail is good) through the knot and into the sash. Nail it at a downward angle to be sure it doesn't go through and strike the edge of the glass and crack it (personal experience writing here). Even if the knot is fitting tautly inside the knot hole, it's a good idea to nail it in anyway. It's a small added precaution that takes very little time to do.

Sometimes it's difficult to push the chain through the pulley wheel and you have to remove the pulley, but this is rare. In these cases, you can unscrew and remove the pulley and then feed the rope through it. By removing the pulley, you normally won't have to attach a chain to the rope, just knot the end of it and push it down into the pocket. For more pulley information, including removal (there are a couple of steps) and types of pulleys, see pages 128–129.

Q Hey, Mr. Window, I notice you use the words "sometimes," "often," "mostly," "should," "could," and all kinds of other qualifiers that strike me as being some kind of mamby-pamby, new age, passive, afraid-to-take-a-stand writing, the kind of writing I'd expect from someone who, say, eats quiche. What's going on? You one of those quiche eaters?

A *Mr. Window not only eats quiche, he bakes them, too, but to answer your question: It would be great if all windows and window situations were the same, like servings of Coca-Cola, but they're not. Some windows didn't work well when they were installed. Some were painted shut from the beginning and have never opened. Others have tight weight pockets. It's not unlike solving problems with Windows on your computer. When was the last time any of those problems could be described in a straightforward, I-eat-steak-for-breakfast-and-drive-a-half-ton pickup way? Or the solutions? I describe the situations as clearly as I can while allowing for all the variations I've run across over the years. At least when you're finished, these windows won't crash.*

Don't have a piece of chain? Try a piece of string with a bolt or small weight attached to it. As long as it fits through the pulley and it's weighted it should work. Don't have any string? That's desperation, but if the old rope is still intact:

- Pull the knotted end until the weight is up near the pulley.
- At the pulley, wrap the rope around a piece of scrap wood or cardboard to prevent the weight from dropping.
- Cut the knot.
- Butt the new rope up to the old and tape the two ends together.
- Unwrap the rope from the cardboard.
- Slowly lower the weight.
- Pull the old rope down the pocket with the new rope trailing it.

NOTE: Well, there is one type of pulley into which you can feed the rope directly without attaching it to a chain (in fact, you can't get a chain through these pulleys). Hooded pulleys were designed in the 1940s to prevent the rope from getting jammed at the side of the wheel. Be sure the end of the rope has been cut clean; you can cut the end at a slight angle, which helps in pushing it through the pulley. Rubbing some liquid soap on it will also help. If it gets stuck, twist the rope and keep pushing. You may have to remove the pulley and grab the end of the rope with tweezers or needle-nose pliers as it comes around the wheel.

Q **Hold on, Mr. Window, I pulled off the pocket cover between two of my windows and all I could see were two big weights with a little wheel pulley thingy wired to the** top of each one. Other than possibly being a suspected FBI listening device, as are many other items in my house, what's the deal? I don't get it.

A *These are not FBI listening devices, although you might take a second look at your doorbell chimes. Two side-by-side double-hung windows normally will share one pocket for their respective weights. If the pocket is too narrow to hold four weights (one for each upper sash and one for each lower sash), a single weight will be used, commensurately heavy enough to counterbalance two sashes. In order for this trick to work, a small pulley is attached with baling wire to the hole at the top of the weight and a single rope is passed through it and attached to both sashes.*

Hooded Pulley

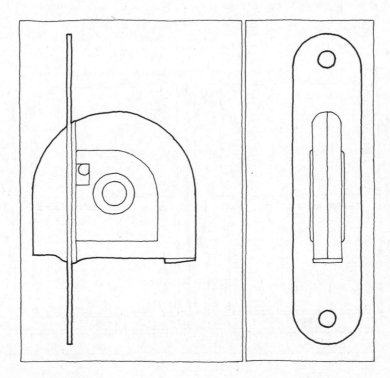

Q **Terrific. And just how do I rope these, Mr. Window? I'd have to be a magician or genius or nano-robot or something.**

A *Or you'd have to be Mr. Window. There are a couple things you can do, depending on whether the old rope is intact. With an intact rope, you don't even need the top of the weight accessible with the pocket cover removed, although it's easier. Here are the steps:*

- Undo the knot at one of the pulleys and cut the end of the old rope clean and straight.

- Butt this end up against the end of the new rope, also cut straight.

- Tape the two ends together using electrical tape (I use this because it's smooth and can be pulled tight). Be sure the taped connection is taut so it doesn't come apart when passing through the pulley on top of the weight.

- Slowly pull the other end of the old rope through its pulley on the other side.

- Feed the new rope through the first sash pulley and through the small pulley on top of the weight, while pulling the other end of the rope until it comes out the second sash pulley.

Side-by-side sashes sharing weight, center pocket.

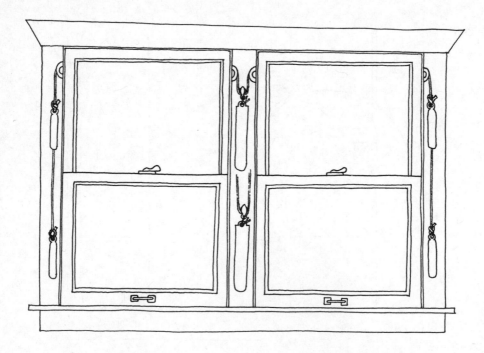

- Remove the tape and knot that end of the new rope, allowing about four inches to hang out of the pulley.

- Pull the other end of the rope a little snug, allow a couple of inches out from the pulley, cut the rope, and knot it.

As an alternative, if you can reach the top of the weight, you can:

- Cut one knotted end of the old rope at the pulley.

- Pull the rope down into the pocket while it's still running through the pulley at the top of the weight, but don't pull it out of this pulley.

- Feed the new rope through the sash pulley and into the pocket.

- Tape the new and old rope ends together before pulling the new rope up through the weight's pulley and through the other sash pulley.

I offer this alternative because sometimes it's easier to tape the old and new rope ends together inside the pocket if the old rope's knots are tight against the pulleys in the jamb.

NOTE: If the top of the shared weight is too tall to reach with the pocket cover off and the old rope is missing or broken or has been pulled through the pulley at the top of the weight, you'll have to remove the casing in order to install the new rope.

When the old rope is broken or missing, but you can get to the top of the window weight:

- Feed a new rope down one side through a sash pulley.

- Push the end of this rope through the pulley at the top of the weight.

- Feed a second piece of rope, even scrap rope, through the other sash pulley and into the pocket.

- Tape the two rope ends together in order to pull the new rope up and through the second pulley.

After the new rope ends have been cut and knotted:

- Attach the rope to one sash and lower that sash to the closed position.

- Pull the other end of the rope until the weight has reached the pulleys, but don't jam the weight against them.

- Cut this end of the rope about four inches past the knot hole of the second sash, knot the end, and insert it into the knot hole.

- Test the sash for movement.

- Raise both sashes to the full open position to check the rope length.

You don't find side-by-side windows sharing weights all that often; they started to show up in the 1920s. If the mullion—the vertical member between side-by-side sashes/windows—looks too narrow to have a pocket that can accommodate four sash weights, you can figure on dealing with these larger, shared weights.

NOTE: While the lower sash is out, paint over the paint drips on the meeting rail on both sashes. It's best to scrape and sand the old paint first, as it will be thick and chunky, but keep in mind it's probably lead-based paint so you'll have to take appropriate precautions (see pages 72–78).

Removing Both Sashes and Replacing the Parting Beads

Not satisfied to leave well enough alone, you've decided to pull out the upper sash and have it operable as well. This offers an opportunity for minor destruction, which can be gratifying. Keep a trash bag nearby to toss the rope and parting bead scraps.

Why bother with the upper sash?

- Improved ventilation for one thing. Opening an upper sash instead of a lower can be a safety issue if you have young children or pets in your home, but still want ventilation.

- In an office, an open lower sash is an invitation for papers to blow around, but not so with an open upper sash.

- The meeting rails can be painted and you won't have to look at paint drips from your future painting jobs.

- It's just kind of cool to pull the upper sash down.

Most people don't even know an upper sash can open! Repair these sashes and the following could happen:

- Awed strangers will knock on your door asking you how you got your windows to work.

- TV talk shows will solicit you as a guest host.

- Publishers will request your autobiography.

- Marriage proposals from independently wealthy and extremely open-minded potential mates will come in by the dozen.

To find out if any of the preceding could happen, here's how you remove and rope an upper sash:

- With the lower sash removed, it will be necessary to remove the parting beads before removing the upper sash. The parting bead is seated in a groove or dado in the jamb about ⅜″ deep.

- Take a stiff putty knife and break the paint seal all along the parting bead, inside and out, anywhere it meets the jamb.

- If, by some chance, the winds of homeowners' fate have provided you with upper sashes that open, then simply lower the sash down to the sill and, starting at the top, pry the parting bead out from the top down. Use a pry bar on the backside of the upper section of the parting bead, the side that faces the outside, near the pulley. Any dents or dings you make in the window jamb won't be seen if you pry from this side. Hammer the pry bar in at a slight angle where the parting bead meets the jamb in order to force it out.

- After you've loosened the upper half of the parting bead, the rest should come out with just a little coaxing and pry bar action on the other side of the parting bead, the side that faces inward. Try as best you can to remove it in one piece and lift it up and away from the windowsill.

- The parting bead can be reused if it comes out in one piece, but as this is a common item at many lumberyards, it can be replaced (note sizes and other considerations on page 42), too. Current sizes do not always measure up to the old dimensions, however, and can be undersized enough to render a loose fit.

- If the sash already opens, you only have to remove one parting bead to remove the sash. It's a good idea to remove both, however, and either replace them or scrape or sand off the worst of the built-up paint.

If the upper sash and parting beads are cemented in with paint—a very likely and common situation—and the upper sash won't budge:

- Break the paint at the edges of each parting bead first.

- With a stiff putty knife or the straight end of a small pry bar and a hammer, chip and pry away at one parting bead, putting the end of the blade against the parting bead but slightly away from where it fits in the jamb. The parting bead will split and you'll remove it in pieces.

- The bottom section of the parting bead near the sill will probably come out in one piece and then snap off at the bottom of the upper sash.

- Be aggressive with the upper section, but not so much as to mar the jamb excessively.

- Remove the second parting bead. You only have to remove the vertical pieces, not the horizontal parting bead at the header.

NOTE: As you remove the parting beads and break the upper sash loose, it might fall suddenly if its ropes are broken, so be prepared to catch it. As a precaution, especially with a large sash, pound a 16d nail into each side of the jamb, a few inches under the bottom rail of the sash, to catch it if it begins to move. Sashes with layer after layer of paint aren't fast movers as a rule and they normally stay put until you pull them loose.

After removing both parting beads, it would be ideal if you could break the entire paint seal between the outside of the sash and the blind stop, especially if it's been caulked. This is easy enough using a ladder on first-floor windows, less so on second-story, and forget it on the third floor unless you like climbing thirty-six-foot ladders. Mr. Window has done this and isn't especially fond of it. A fair amount of the paint seal can be broken from inside your house if you don't mind leaning out and challenging a few worker safety rules. Here are some techniques you can use at your own risk (Mr. Window must add such caveats to avoid becoming Mr. Lawsuit Defendant):

- Start with placing the putty knife between the lower corners of the sash and the blind stops. Hammer it in and pull inward. This will initially break the seal and can be sufficient for loosening the sash. Grab the lower sash corners and move the now loose sash back and forth a few times, gently pulling downward. If it breaks loose at the top, you're in good shape.

- Still stuck? Sit on the sill, straddling it with one leg out the window, and draw the corner of a stiff putty knife blade against the paint seal. You can also sit on the sill and lean out, but put your feet against a toolbox or something heavy to brace yourself.

- Instead of a putty knife, consider using a dovetail or other fine-tooth saw and carefully saw through the seal. This might sound a bit extreme, but not if the sash has been thickly caulked shut.

- If you have a tall window whose top can't easily be reached, you can attach a wide stiff putty knife to the end of a three or four-foot-long board, such as a 2x2, reach out and insert the blade at the paint seal, and carefully tap it with a hammer to break the seal. To attach, screw and tape the putty knife tightly to the wood. Working several stories up over a lively pedestrian area? Drill a hole in the other end of the board, tie a cord through it, and loop the rest of the cord around your wrist so you don't drop your fun new tool on or near someone below. Mr. Window is writing from personal and mostly forgotten experience here.

After the paint seal has been broken, and you're back inside with both feet on the floor, grab the bottom corners and slowly work the sash back and forth, pulling it down at the same time. Remove the sash and install the ropes. Unlike the lower sash, the upper sash ropes have to be cut to a more exacting length.

Here is the easiest way to figure out the right rope length:

Break the exterior paint seal all around the upper sash.

Stiff putty knife screwed to 2"x 2" lumber.

Insert a putty knife up and down the length of the parting bead, including between the upper sash and the bead, and pry it out.

Upper sash

Side view, lower sash removed

- After installing and tying the upper ropes to their weights, allow 4″ or so of extra length out of the pulley.

- Cut the rope, knot it, and pull the weight up to the top of the pulley.

- Wrap the rope around an old piece of rope or scrap of cardboard at the pulley so the weight stays up. This way, the weights are not in each others' way at the bottom of the pocket when you're measuring the remaining ropes for the lower sashes. This is especially helpful if you have two windows side by side with four weights in a shared pocket and several of the old ropes have snapped.

- Install the lower ropes and pull the weights up and out of the way as well, wrapping the ropes around a scrap piece of rope or cardboard.

- When all the ropes have been installed, place the upper sash on the stool and pull one upper weight up tight to the pulley.

- Cut the rope about 2–3″ from the knot hole, knot the end, and secure the knot in the sash knot hole. Repeat for the other rope.

- Slide the sash all the way up and be sure it closes tightly and without its weights hitting the lower sash weights; these should already be up and out of the way. If it does drop open, check inside the pocket and see if the weights have hit the bottom. If they have hit the bottom, then shorten the ropes.

The lengths for the upper ropes have to be accurate or the weights will hit the bottom of the pocket before the sash is closed all the way. What happens if the weights haven't hit bottom, but the sash still doesn't close? It means the weights are too light. You can do one of the following:

- Add some weight
- Weather-strip the sash (this often tightens it up sufficiently)
- Add a sash control to one or both sides

How do you add weight? Just about anything that the rope can fit through will do: large washers, old gears, etc. Put the rope through the added-on weights first and then tie it onto the sash weight. Or, if you're adding something that won't accommodate the rope (it can't pass through the added weight), you can add to the bottom of the weight by wrapping baling wire to the sash weight and the additional weight, connecting one to the other. I wrap the wire around the weights, cinch it tightly with pliers, and then wrap it all with several layers (OK, a lot of layers) of electrical tape or duct tape. It may not look very elegant, but it works. One time, with nothing else available, I taped a small rock to a weight. It did the job and was, like, very organic.

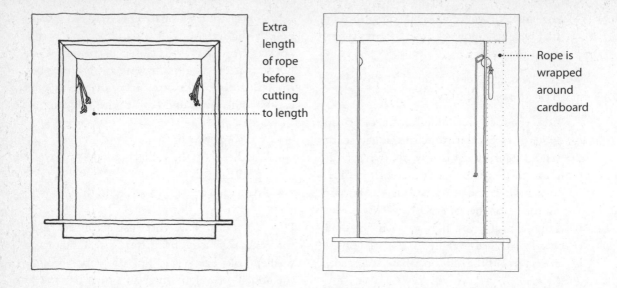

Extra length of rope before cutting to length

Rope is wrapped around cardboard

Scrap metal salvage yards and architectural salvage specialty shops sometimes have old window weights. You can also buy new window weights, but this is an expensive way to go. Kilian Hardware (www.kilianhardware.com, 215-247-0945), for instance, sells new sash weights for $3 a pound with a price break at 100- and 500-pound orders (I can't imagine the shipping costs).

Contractors often throw old weights away when remodeling if they're tearing into the walls and replacing the windows. Grab some of these if you need heavier weights. You can take weights that are too big for your purposes and break them with a framing hammer or small sledge hammer to get something closer to what you need (I've also broken one weight against another); cast iron window weights break pretty effortlessly. Breaking weights with hammers isn't an exact science so grab several extra weights when they're available. You can also contact a company that installs new windows and inquire if you can procure some weights from one of their jobs after any old windows are removed.

Q You know, Mr. Window, you sure want these ropes awfully long coming out of the pulley. I mean, I leave a few inches out like you say and knot them and then when I go to install them in the sash, I have a lot of rope to cut off, sometimes half a foot. If the three to four million people I suspect will buy this extraordinary repair book do the same thing, that's a bunch of extra rope, like maybe enough to go to the moon and back. Why so much waste?

A Well, every six inches of rope tossed out by four million people actually equals 378.787878... miles of rope, which could go from Wendover, Utah, to Las Vegas, Nevada, with enough left over for you to leave a trail of it to help you find your way back from the free outdoor show at Treasure Island to your room at the Jackpot Motel. I suggest the extra length because sometimes a rope slips while you're tying knots in the end coming out of the pulley. The extra length usually prevents the entire rope from going into the pocket and your having to re-rope all over again. When a heavy weight drops, even after you've tied the knot, the rope can still slip down into the pocket, knot and all, if there isn't any excess coming out of the pulley. Knot holes on sashes are cut in different locations, some lower than others, requiring longer rope. As you get more comfortable installing ropes, by all means cut them closer to the required length and save yourself some rope. I've just found having the extra length available saved me some grief.

Sash Controls

What is a sash control? It's a piece of spring metal, sold in pairs, installed between the sash and the jamb, and used in place of broken ropes. They slip in and are held in by friction, small prongs that imbed into the jamb, and/or by small nails. There are at least two styles made, the most common being Wright Products V21 Window Sash Control (www.wright-products.com/products/misc_hardware/MWdwHardware) and at least one type should be available in a decent-sized hardware store. The movement of the sash won't be as smooth as with ropes, but sash controls do provide a quick fix. They can also be used to supplement ropes when the sash is either too heavy or too light for the existing weights. A sash can be too heavy, for example, when the glass has been

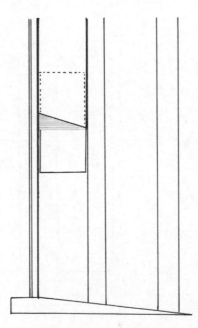

Lower sash in open position because of sash control mechanism.

changed and a heavier piece added, such as security glass or translucent glass in a bathroom (for privacy). You may only need one control or even half of one (cut lengthwise). Given the low cost (a few dollars) and ease of installation, it's very easy to experiment with sash controls until you get the right combination for your windows.

A sash control will compress spring bronze weather stripping thereby decreasing its effectiveness. A sash control cut in half lengthwise can be installed if you have interlocking weather stripping.

Q Hey, wait a minute Mr. Window, why are you telling me now that all I have to do is install a sash control, which is cheap and quick and doesn't require tearing the window apart? What's with all this re-roping stuff?

A *Hmm, it would make a much shorter book, wouldn't it? Besides, I did reference sash controls earlier, if you had been paying attention, so there. Sash controls are great as a quick fix or to take care of the mismatch between sash and weights when one is too heavy or too light. Sash controls can fall out when a sash is opened beyond where the control was installed (for this reason, they are sometimes secured at their centers with a small nail) and the movement of the sash is stiff, which makes them hard for some people to open, especially upper sashes. Sash ropes or chains are a better choice than sash controls when you have the time to work on your windows.*

Once the upper sash is secured and happy, install the old parting bead or replace with a new one cut to length.

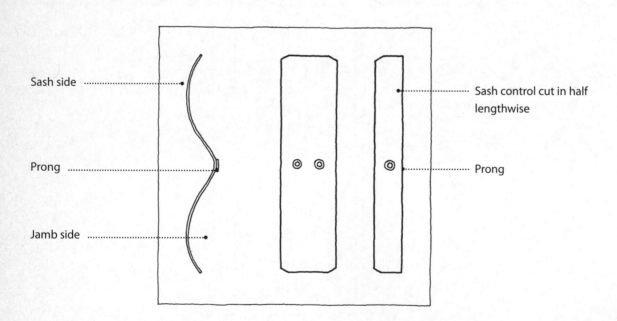

Sash side

Prong

Jamb side

Sash control cut in half lengthwise

Prong

To install the parting bead:

- Lower the sash to the sill or as close as it will go.

- Poke the end of the parting bead in between the corner of the sash (at the bottom rail which is always notched to accommodate the parting bead as is the upper rail of the lower sash) and the jamb. Note that the end of the parting bead, which sits on the sill, is cut at a slight angle to accommodate the slope of the sill.

- Work the parting bead in all the way to the top of the jamb, placing a six-inch or so

block of wood (a piece of 2x4 works very nicely) against it and tapping the block with a hammer to secure it. Tapping can turn to pounding if it's a tight fit, but that's fine; you don't want the parting bead popping out. A loose parting bead can be secured with two or three small brads or finish nails. A parting bead that both resists your pounding and begins to splinter where it enters the dado in the jamb is a parting bead that's too big. Stop your pounding, remove the parting bead, and plane or sand down the two edges going into the dado for a smooth fit.

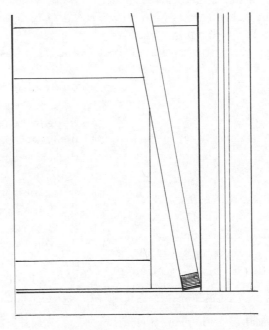

Upper sash lowered to sill; parting bead installed at an angle until inserted into jamb. The parting bead is cut at an angle to match the sill.

- The simplest way to plane down a parting bead is with a Stanley 21-399 Surform Pocket Plane, available at hardware and lumber stores everywhere. It's a great tool and takes very little skill to use. I don't mean this disparagingly, but a regular carpenter's plane takes practice and more practice to use well; the Surform takes about 60 seconds, which is assuredly Mr. Window's speed. The Surform costs around $7 or so, a decent bargain.

- Run the upper sash up and down. Pound the parting bead in further at any point the sash binds with it. You want the parting bead to be uniform its entire length.

- If you trimmed the inner edge or the section of the parting bead that fits inside the dado down a fair amount, check that it sits at a 90-degree angle to the jamb. In other words, you don't want it to go in crooked as it sits in the dado. A crooked parting bead can be straightened out by pulling on it with your hands, pushing on it with the palms of your hands, or whacking it with a block of wood and hammer.

Parting Bead Dimensions

Parting beads come in several different sizes. The most common, and usually available, is ¾" x ½". Other sizes include ¾" x ⅜" and ⅞" x ⅜". Unless you want to have these nonstandard sizes milled, you'll have to work around what's available.

You can fake the ⅜" figure by planing or sanding down one side of a ¾" x ½" parting bead. The ⅞" x ⅜" is a little tougher. You can take ¾" x ½" material, slightly plane down the

½" dimension, stuff it into the jamb until it stops and still allows the sashes to slide, secure it with small wire nails or finish nails, and call it good. Done right, it will fill out the extra needed ⅛". Of course, Mr. Window would never consider doing anything like this since it isn't historically pure and proper.

Not all ¾" by ½" parting beads are the same size. They will vary with different suppliers and can be undersized to some degree. Another sign of sliding standards and increased cost of raw materials, I suppose. It's best if you can find a lumberyard that carries material truer to the stated dimensions (take a section of your parting bead with you for comparison).

What if your lumberyard sells parting beads that are narrow enough to fit in the dado but not as wide as the originals? This can be a problem because the sash can actually slip past the parting beads if they're not wide enough and move in and out, which isn't exactly a desirable result. This happened to me in one house in San Francisco and there was no time to run out a custom-size parting bead. There was plenty of time, however, to install a half-dozen drywall screws inside the dado in the jamb every eight inches or so, tightening them just enough that when I inserted the undersized parting beads against the heads of the screws, the parting beads stuck out just as far as the originals did. I nailed the parting beads to secure them and they worked perfectly. Of course, the house painters came along and painted half the windows shut, but that's another story.

You can solve this problem with drywall screws in the dado as I did or by inserting strips of closed-cell weather stripping instead (press one parting bead hard against it to be sure it will stick out as far as you need it to). This is one of those situations that calls for some minor creativity to solve the problem at hand instead of stopping the job. Window restoration and repair call for a certain amount of adaptability if you want to get the job done at a reasonable cost, in a reasonable amount of time, and with good results. A historical purist would insist on running the exact size parting beads or stops out of recycled old growth lumber, soaking them in linseed oil, and brushing four coats of high-gloss oil finish on them. This is fine if your house is a museum and you're on the museum's restoration staff with nothing else to do except make reproduction window parts. Otherwise, artistic interpretation is just fine.

After both parting beads are in, slide the upper sash up and down a few times for good measure, checking for binding and smooth movement. Next, install the lower sash and the stops.

Again, while the sashes are out, you have an opportune time to strip and repaint them or install weather stripping (see pages 143–152). The exterior trim, sill, and jambs can also be worked on from inside the room without using an extension ladder outside. See Chapter 4 for further discussion.

No Pocket Covers

Q **So, Mr. Window, what do I do if I haven't got any pocket covers? Am I forever condemned to a life of inferior windows, which in turn will affect my ability to find a job, go on dates, and become a Jeopardy contestant?**

A *I can't help you with jobs or dates, but one hint for Jeopardy tryout: John Adams was the first vice president as well as being the second president, bone up on your Shakespeare, and know your potent potables. Now, back to windows. Presumably, manufacturers eliminated pocket covers because of the cost. Maybe the builder saved a big $1 a window, but made future rope replacement very difficult. So much for old-world craftsmanship. You can still access the weights, you'll just have to spend more time doing so.*

You have three choices for accessing the weights:

- Remove the interior casings
- Remove the exterior casings or brick molding
- Drill an access hole in the jamb

There are three common styles of interior casings:

- Vertical casings that butt up against an upper horizontal casing (Victorian styles often butt up against bull's-eye molding)

- Vertical casings that are miter cut at a 45-degree angle against the upper casing and often have an additional piece of trim (a backband) around the outer edge

- Vertical casings butted to a horizontal casing with a backband around the edge.

As a broad guideline, windows with mitered casings (usually the 1920s and later) are less likely to have pocket covers, although this isn't absolute. I don't know why this is; I'm just going by what I've run into over the years. It could be some strange past cult of collusive architects, carpenters, and window designers in the Northwest who came up with this just to annoy people eighty years later. In addition, these casings are also a bit more difficult to remove.

The easiest way to remove either type, after the stops are taken off, is to:

- Run the edge of a stiff putty knife where the plaster meets the vertical casings to break the paint seal.

- Insert the putty knife between the casing and the jamb and slowly pry out against the casing at the midway point.

- After working your way up and down the casing, and having moved it out ½″ or so, insert a hacksaw blade between the casing and jamb and cut the nails (there will be four to five of them). You can also snip the nails with a wire cutter if there's enough room to accommodate it.

- Stuff the straight end of a long pry bar in under the casing and pry against the other edge of it which sits against the plaster.

- To pull the other side of the casing from the plaster, place a small block of wood or stiff putty knife under the bend in the crowbar as you pry against the wood. If you put the crowbar directly on the plaster, you'll probably dent the wall.

- Gradually pull the casing out. Again, cut the nails as they become exposed.

Common casing styles

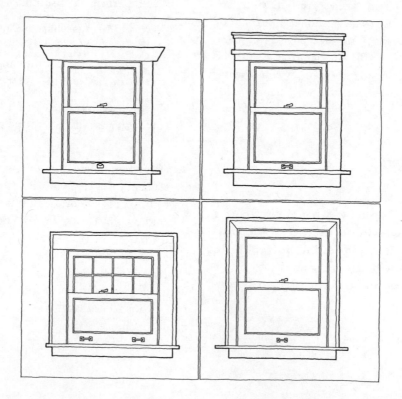

WARNING! When removing these casings, a piece of lath can also start coming out, which will pull the plaster along with it. If the lath starts to loosen, force it back in and keep pushing against it with a putty knife or pry bar while continuing to remove the casing.

If the casing is mitered, there will also be one or two nails holding the mitered corner together, usually nailed from the top casing into the vertical casings. Sometimes, with either style of casing, there will be one or two nails pounded through the stool up into the casing. It seems clear the guys who built these houses never intended you to disassemble anything, broken rope or not. Either that or they were paid by the nail. (Please see Chapter 5 for more information on casings).

With the casing removed, you should find that a hole has been cut into the lath and plaster near the top of the window. This was cut when the window was originally installed so the carpenters could drop the weights into the pockets. If the old ropes are intact but need replacement, these holes—which you can expand with a hacksaw blade or keyhole saw—are quite helpful because you can pull the weight up and remove it, feed a new rope through the pulley and easily attach it to the weight (you'll have to hold the old weight by poking a screwdriver shaft or awl through the knot hole at the top unless you can grab the weight with your fingers). When the weights are stuck at the bottom of the pocket and the ropes broken, you will have to cut away the lath and plaster at the top of the weight and drop your rope down.

To find the top of the weight when the old rope is broken:

- Chop out a small bit of plaster a foot or so from the bottom of the pocket and push a narrow putty knife through between the lath.

- If you hit the weight, saw off the lath from that point upward until you have exposed the top of the weight.

- If you cannot feel the weight, then cut down from that point.

NOTE: You can use a reciprocating saw (this is like a heavy-duty electric carving knife) to cut through the lath, but you risk jerking some lath loose and cracking the plaster beyond the material you want to remove. I use either a hacksaw blade or a small keyhole saw, both of which are much less disruptive.

After removing butted casings without the backband, you may find the whole pocket is exposed and that the plaster and lath were not run all the way to the jamb. This is often the case if the house was built roughly prior to 1920. Houses built in the 1920s and thereafter usually had the plaster and lath installed right up to the jamb based on what I've seen.

There are always variations. You may have wood walls covered with wallpaper and no plaster at all. You may have had a replacement window installed without pocket covers and with plywood covering the pocket under the casing. I have tried to describe the most common situations. My observations have been extensive, but by no means all-inclusive.

Exterior Casings and Brick Molding

There are some circumstances when you don't want to remove the interior casings. They may sit against expensive wallpaper or you may want

**Exterior view:
sill nailed up and
into casings.**

to limit the amount of interior repainting you'll have to do. In either case, you have some options.

Wood exterior siding often comes with wide casings, similar in size to your interior ones or even wider. Pry them off—careful, they might have nails coming up from the sill—and the whole pocket will be exposed. I particularly recommend removing them if they are weathered as they are easier to remove.

If you have brick molding (on either brick or stucco or other masonry buildings), you will have a blind stop about 3 ½" wide under the molding. This will necessitate drilling or cutting an access hole through the blind stop in order to install the ropes. You might find nails going through the sills and into the brick molding. Think twice before removing this molding as there is an alternative: cutting your own access holes.

Drilling Access Holes

Easier yet (with brick molding especially) is to drill an access hole into the jamb where the lower sash sits. With both sashes removed (or even just the lower if you are only replacing its ropes, although it makes little sense not to replace the upper ropes, too, if you're going to the trouble to cut an access hole), you will need to determine where the top of the weights are (their distance from the bottom of the pocket). How? Well, usually at least one of the ropes is intact. If so, and assuming the rope as it comes out of the pulley has a little slack, pull the rope so it is barely tight, pinch the section coming right out of the pulley, and pull it down until the weight is at the pulley. Where your fingers meet the jamb will give you an approximate location for the top of the weight (see diagram on page 48).

Drill two holes and chisel out area in between.

Completed cut-out

Sheet metal covering nailed over cut-out

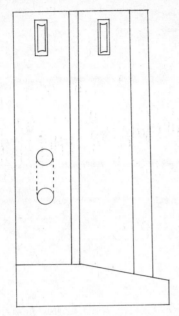

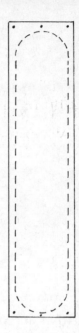

When the ropes are tight at the pulleys and have no slack, it means that their length does not allow the weights to hit the bottom of the pocket and even if you pull the ropes out and measure to the jamb, you will have to guess as to where to drill your hole. In either case, drill an inch or two higher than you expect the top of the weight to be found. If you have two different sizes of sash, drill for the top of the heavier, and thus taller, weight.

How to drill? You can use a 1″ to 1 ¼″ spade bit or a hole saw. Drill one hole and feel around for the top of the weights. If the weights have jammed up on top of each other you'll have to free them by prying them apart with a large screwdriver or other tool.

The first hole will determine where to locate the second hole:

- Too high (above the top of the weight), drill one lower

- Too low, drill higher

- If you have a space between these holes (this should be two inches or so), remove this section of the jamb by chiseling it out or sawing it. You will now have a rough oval-shaped opening through which you can attach the new ropes.

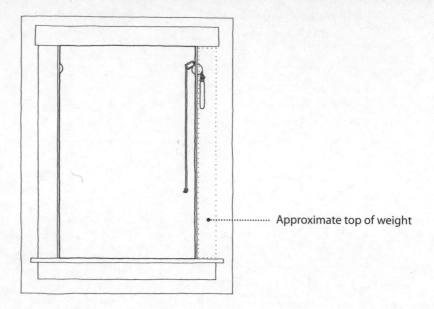

Approximate top of weight

Q **Hold on, Mr. Window. I did this and the hole is small and a nuisance to deal with and nuisances frustrate me and when I get frustrated, I revert to my elusive childhood full of sunshine, lollipops, and rainbows and then I never finish the window repair.**

A *Your reversion beats a childhood full of darkness, lima beans, and hail the size of golf balls, doesn't it? Stop complaining; this just takes longer than using real pocket covers. If you're trying not to tear off the casings, though, and cannot access the weights from the exterior, then you haven't much choice. I find that a small piece of baling wire or a section of a metal clothes hanger is useful for moving the weights around and hooking the rope after it's been dropped down through the pulley. Bending the end of the wire or hanger into a small hook allows you to grab stray ropes and the tops of the weights. You can force a narrow screwdriver or awl*

into the hole at the top of the weights, raise them, and then hold them still while inserting the rope. Frustrating? Sure, but it can be done.

After the ropes have been attached, cover the hole with either a small piece of spring bronze weather stripping, nailing all four corners, or a similar piece of thin sheet metal. This allows future access if needed. If you feel particularly talented, you can square off the hole in the jamb and insert a custom-cut wood cover, similar to a regular pocket cover. This cover can be held in with small, countersunk screws installed at an angle through the cover and into the jamb. You can also mortise a metal connector, such as a flat corner iron, into the cover and into the jamb so they lay flush to the jamb and then secure with screws, but that's a lot of work. For me, the sheet metal is faster and accomplishes the same purpose. And remember, since it's behind the sash, the hole and its cover will never be seen.

Small holes are a nuisance to deal with. One option is to drill a larger hole:

- Use a 3″ or 3½″ hole saw, centering your hole on a scrap piece of parting bead stuck in the dado above the top of the weight as shown in the diagram.

- The section of jamb you remove might split in half at the dado, but can easily be glued together.

- Because of the saw cut, the section or plug will now be slightly smaller than the hole where you need to reinstall it. Build up the edge by wrapping it with several layers of narrow masking tape, apply some wood glue to the tape, and reinstall in the hole. Keep a

small piece of parting bead in the plug's dado so the two sections on either side of the dado don't start to move towards each other.

- Line the plug up, let the glue dry, remove the parting bead scrap, cut away any excess tape—including the tape that is now in the way of the parting bead—with a razor blade, and caulk or otherwise fill the seam (Bondo works well here). This section will not be removable for future access unless it's sawed again.

Ultimately, the more room you have for roping the weights the easier the job, so remove the casings whenever possible if you don't have pocket covers and if removing the casings isn't unacceptably disruptive or causes you more work than drilling access holes.

Removing plug with hole saw

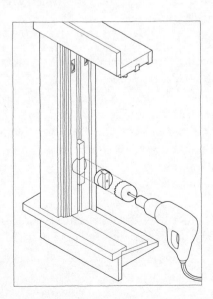

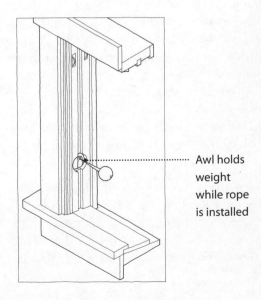

Awl holds weight while rope is installed

Duplex Pulleys

Duplex pulleys or spring sash balances contain spring-wound cables that have small corner irons or brackets at the cables' ends; small nails fasten the brackets to each sash. Small windows will often have only one duplex pulley. Larger windows will have one in each side of the jamb.

If your cables have snapped or look unreliable, the pulleys should be replaced since the cable cannot be repaired. Otherwise, pulleys in acceptable condition should be handled carefully. Remove the brackets from the sashes by pulling out the nails and slowly let the cables retract. Clean the paint off the cable with a bit of steel wool, lubricate them with a few drops of oil or bicycle grease, and move them in and out a few times.

How will you know if your duplex pulleys are in good shape? You won't! Other than the obvious rust or deterioration, you won't know when a cable is going to snap. That said, I can't necessarily recommend that you do a wholesale replacement of them; they can last for years as long as the cables don't corrode.

As I mentioned earlier, duplex pulleys are not a common hardware item and normally have to be ordered or purchased at a wholesale hardware supplier (see Resources).

To remove and replace duplex pulleys:

- Remove the stops and loosen the lower sash. Raise the sash up and insert a small pry bar under the corner bracket.

- Pry the nails out while holding the corner iron in place. Pull the iron from the sash and slowly let the cable wind up, releasing the corner iron when it reaches the duplex pulley. If you know you're going to replace the pulley, go ahead and cut the cable(s) with a wire cutter.

- With the lower sash removed, loosen the upper sash. Note that the section of the parting bead which fits over the pulley has been partially cut away to accommodate the pulley. If you replace the parting bead, you will have to cut this section away in the new parting bead. Alternatively, you can also run this section against a belt sander and grind it down, a technique that works quite nicely and more smoothly than using a chisel.

- Remove the cable(s) from the upper sash and then the sash itself.

- The duplex pulley is installed with four nails, two at the top and two at the bottom. Pry it off and scrape or remove any paint from the steel casing, which will have printing on it including a number (like #8 duplex or #10 duplex, etc.). THIS IS IMPORTANT! You have to replace it with a pulley with similar tension. The outer metal casing may be the same dimension, but the inner workings vary according to the size of the sash.

Reattaching sashes to duplex pulleys is much easier with two people doing the work. The cables are taut and are difficult to hold onto while balancing the sash. Mr. Window has done them alone, of course, since he is generally too cheap to hire any help, but doesn't recommend this approach since it's annoying.

To install a duplex pulley:

- Nail the pulley to the jamb. The cables should come out at the bottom of the pulley.

- Carefully pull the cables from the duplex pulley and coat with a bit of oil. Nail the appropriate cable corner irons to the upper sash.

- Lower the upper sash to the sill and install the parting beads in the same manner as roped windows, noting the section to be cut away in order to fit over the pulley.

- Install the cables on the lower sash and then install the sash.

NOTE: Don't let the cables slip from your hands while attaching to the sash. There isn't a terrific chance that they'll snap since they're new, but treat them gently.

After each sash is installed, check for operation. If the sashes don't move or close properly, the tension of the pulleys might have to be adjusted. See the directions enclosed with the pulley for this procedure. You will insert a screwdriver into a slot in the pulley and turn it to adjust the tension. Adjust one turn at a time and only after both sashes are installed! With two different sized sashes, perfect tension will be elusive.

NOTE: There is at least one brand of nonadjustable duplex pulleys on the market, but don't use them. You want the option to adjust the tension if you need to.

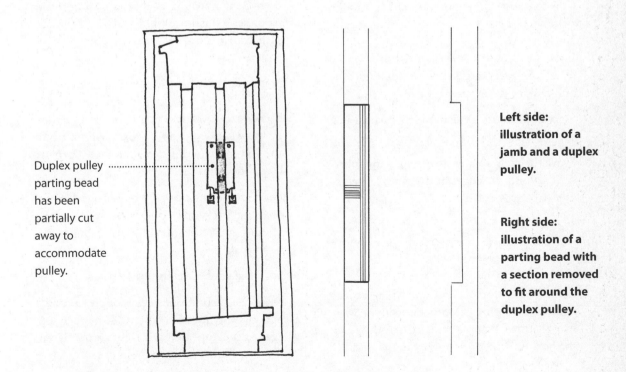

Duplex pulley parting bead has been partially cut away to accommodate pulley.

Left side: illustration of a jamb and a duplex pulley.

Right side: illustration of a parting bead with a section removed to fit around the duplex pulley.

Be concerned with the upper sash; you can always adjust the stops on the lower if you need to tighten the fit.

Removing Interlocking Weather Stripping

This is such fun. Interlocking weather stripping is almost always salvageable and worth keeping if it's forming a decent seal. Interlocking weather stripping requires a very precise fit with each sash. Other weather stripping, like spring bronze or vinyl, can be more accommodating, especially if a sash doesn't fit well.

Interlocking weather stripping is located on the vertical sides of both the upper and the lower sash, at the meeting rail, at the sill, and at the top of the jamb where the top rail of the upper sash locks into it.

How to remove it? It's not as hard as it looks (easy for me to say):

- First, if the lower sash is painted shut, break all of the paint around it, inside and out, and remove the stops.

- Place a stiff putty knife between the sash and the sill and push upward.

- Move the sash up and down, spraying lubricant around the edges at the jamb, if necessary (trust me, it will be).

Stuck closed and you cannot get to the exterior? All right, now it's harder.

- Remove the stops. The lower sash vertical weather stripping should be held in with two to three nails: one at the top, one at the bottom, and one roughly in the middle.

Find the top nail for each section of weather stripping (they will be on the top corner of the weather stripping as it faces inside to the room). Either drive the nails into the jamb with a nail setter and hammer or insert a small (5″ or so) pry bar under the outer corner of the weather stripping and pull each piece out slightly until the head of the nails stick out enough to grab with a pair of pliers or wire cutters. Don't worry if you mangle the corners of the weather stripping a bit (but avoid if you can); they can always be trimmed later with metal snips.

- Place the putty knife between the jamb and the sash and press against the sash, working up and down its height on both sides.

- Work the stiff putty knife between the bottom of the sash and the stool, but only press gently. You're only trying to pop the paint seal. Push too hard and you dent the sash and/or the stool, both of which can be patched.

- Insert the knife at the meeting rail as well, and bend towards you; it won't move far because the two sashes are locked together by the weather stripping installed here, but the lower sash can move enough to help break the paint seal.

- Keep moving the putty knife around while pressing back and forth against the sash. It can take a few trips around to break the paint seal.

- Soak the jamb with spray lubricant.

- Once the sash loosens up enough to move, pull up on the sash lifts and/or push up against the upper left and right corners, even if the sash only moves a few inches.

- Close the sash and open it again, moving it a little further. You'll now have to work it up and down repeatedly until it's in or close to a full open position.

Weather-stripped sashes are tougher to loosen up because the interlocking material doesn't allow you to pull the lower sash forward very far after the stops are removed. What happens if you simply can't budge it, despite all your putty knife tricks and bending at the sash and you can't get to the exterior?

You dig in with a crowbar, put some holes in the sash and stool, and force it up, that's what you do. I call this "the Alexander the Great and the Gordian knot" approach. At the time—333 BC

give or take—Alexander and his homeboys came upon the Gordian knot; legend had it that anyone who undid the knot would be the conqueror of Asia. Never mind that "the Al" was in the process of doing that anyway. None of this intricate untying for him; according to most writers, Alexander sliced the knot in half with his sword. Think of your ever-stuck bottom sash as the Gordian knot of the window world. If you have to dig into its face with a large screwdriver or the straight end of a pry bar, go ahead and dent it and the stool (put the blade of a putty knife on top of the stool first, though). You can always patch the holes later. This isn't a license to maul it, just put enough pressure on the sash to get it moving and then start pushing it up and down until it moves freely.

What if you have beautiful varnished sashes that are both weather stripped and painted shut and you don't want to dig into the lower sash to get it loose? You can pry up on the sash lifts, but they can break if the sash is really stuck shut. Instead, remove the lifts and screw blocks of wood in their place using long drywall screws. Place a wide putty knife on the stool, rest your pry bar on the blade, and pry up against the wood blocks and the sash should move. You'll have to fill the holes with toothpicks and glue or similar filler so they'll accommodate the smaller lift screws again. This method obviously works with painted sashes as well.

Moving a painted shut weather-stripped sash up and down when it would rather be left alone is tough on your hands. After raising it a couple of inches, it doesn't want to go down again. Get it down, and it doesn't want to be opened. Wear some heavy work gloves as you'll have to pound down the corners of the upper rail in order to get a reluctant sash to move downward. These can really be tough! Be sure to use plenty of spray lubricant on the jambs.

Once the sash is opened:

- Remove the remaining weather-stripping nails by prying under the weather stripping until you can grab the nail heads with pliers or end of the pry bar. You only need to do one side of the weather stripping at this point to get the sash out.

- Lower the sash a bit and move it and the weather stripping upward and then in towards you. You may need to put a putty knife under the weather stripping to ease it out.

- Place the weather stripping aside. The ropes are almost always nailed to the side of the sash when interlocking weather stripping is installed.

- Cut the ropes above the nails and knot the ends, easing them towards the pulleys. Set the sash aside.

- Remove the other piece of weather stripping. If you find a cardboard shim under either or both pieces, save these as you will need them during reassembly. It's a good idea to tape them to the weather stripping so they don't get tossed away.

The lower ends of the weather stripping at the upper sash are held fast with two nails that are pried out in a similar manner to removing nails from the lower weather stripping, using a small pry bar and pliers or wire cutters. Only one section of material has to be removed in order to remove the sash except in the occasional instances where the sash will open, drop down below, and clear the ends of the weather stripping (don't count on it, it doesn't happen very often). I remove the right-hand section, but it makes little difference which one you remove first. Well, OK, if you're a member of a radical left-hand advocacy group it probably makes a huge difference.

The upper sash will have to move in order to remove all of the nails holding the weather stripping. To remove the upper sash:

- Break all of the paint seal inside and out. DON'T GET TOO AGGRESSIVE! Why not? Because when the side of an upper sash is routed or sawed to receive the weather stripping, the edge that slides against the parting bead can break at the dado or saw kerf if you pound against it too forcefully, especially if the sash has been sealed shut with paint. This is true when the parting beads are removed as well. If it does split, and there's a decent chance that it will, you'll have to repair it with glue and small wire nails.

- If you can salvage them, remove the parting beads carefully. Their lower sections often have a narrow kerf or saw cut; the edge of the lower sash weather stripping is inserted into this kerf. Unless you want to duplicate this kerf in a new parting bead (see Weather Stripping Reinstallation), you can try and salvage the originals and reuse them. By breaking all the paint at the parting beads' edges and slowly easing them out with a small pry bar, you can sometimes work them out and around the lower corners of the upper sash (they can get a little splintered doing this), remove them, and sand the excess paint off before reinstalling.

- Spray a lot of lubricant on the jamb and at the edges of the sash where it butts up against the parting bead and exterior blind stop.

I've never tried this, but it was suggested to me by a very inventive glazier. He claimed if you wanted to get a painted-shut upper sash open, you only had to break the paint seal, attach weights to both sides of the sash, and let nature take its course. By screwing in either an eye or a hook at the bottom of each stile and then attaching, say, a suspended gallon can of paint or a gallon milk jug full of water to each side, the sash would open by itself if left alone overnight. Well, say, that sounds pretty cool to me. Normally, my repairs have to be done the same day so I could never apply this method. If you don't want to be drilling into the sash, use a G-clamp on each side, screwing them in until they're very tight. Be sure any weights hanging on second story or higher sashes use long enough cords to reach a foot or so above the ground—you don't want them suspended overhead endangering anyone walking below.

- Insert a stiff putty knife between the top of the sash and the header section of the jamb on the exterior side and try to force the sash down.

- After it moves an inch or so, force it back up (pounding upward on the corners of the bottom rail works well so wear gloves) and then down again.

- Continue to do this until it moves more or less freely. Usually, it has so much paint on it that it will move only quite stiffly. Scrape the paint from the jamb or take a heat gun and strip the paint from the jamb if it's really built-up.

- If the sash moves beyond the bottom of the weather stripping and will clear it, then you will not have to remove any of the weather stripping.

- Planning on replacing the parting beads? Go ahead and split them and don't worry about keeping them intact as you remove them.

Once you have the upper sash moving:

- Close it and remove the lower two nails of either section of weather stripping. This section will be gunked up with paint and will bend a little when you pry the nails out, but don't worry about it. Just get a stiff putty knife or small pry bar under it until the nail heads are accessible and can be grabbed with pliers.

- Lower the sash and remove the upper weather-stripping nails which will be near the pulley.

- Raise the sash a foot or so and move both the sash and the loose weather stripping down towards the sill, moving the weather stripping down and around the pulley.

- Remove it and the sash from the jamb and install your new ropes.

While the sashes are removed, run a file or stiff putty knife through the weather stripping at the meeting rail. Inevitably, this channel fills up with gobs of paint that prevent the sash from locking together tightly. You can also run a wire wheel attached to a drill for a thorough cleaning, which I recommend. Run a file, an old screwdriver, or a folded piece of heavy-grit sandpaper inside the kerf cuts in each sash. This not only cleans out any paint, but slightly enlarges the kerf for easier movement. Before reinstalling the sashes, rub a candle stub or piece of paraffin inside this kerf for some slick sliding.

Q I'm telling you, Mr. Window, this interlocking weather stripping is for the birds. It's hard to work around, the piece at the meeting rail is full of paint, and I hurt my pinky pounding on the sashes trying to get them open. Is this stuff really worth keeping?

A *Sorry about your pinky. Put some ice on it and take a cookie break and you'll feel better. Interlocking weather stripping is a lifetime material and does an acceptable job of sealing up old windows. Once it's cleaned, lubricated, and reinstalled, you'll be glad you kept it. This stuff is a throwback; very little of it is retrofitted onto old double-hung windows these days, and for that alone it can be worth keeping.*

Weather Stripping Reinstallation

This is more fun:

- Adjust and install the ropes for the upper sash. You may have noticed that the old ropes were nailed at the sash instead of knotted. The thinking was to avoid having the

knot jam up against the weather stripping. I have usually been able to force the knot deep into the knot hole, secure it with a nail, and have the knots clear the weather stripping. If the hole is too shallow or the groove for the weather stripping cut too close to the hole, then without knotting the rope, nail it in three or four places with nails similar to the ones you removed (wire nails with small heads or weather-stripping nails). If you nail, the end of the rope must be above the knot hole. Be sure to test the length of the ropes before installing the weather stripping.

NOTE: There are copper-plated nails made specifically for weather stripping, but they aren't available at all hardware stores. If yours doesn't carry them, you might find small copper nails at a marine boating shop. Their heads should not corrode like those of steel nails if they get exposed to moisture. Usually, it only happens with the nail or nails near the bottom of the weather stripping at the lower sash. They can also corrode at the meeting rail (spring bronze application) if too much water drips down on them from window washing or even latex paint.

- Place the section of weather stripping you removed into the kerf cut on its side of the upper sash.

- Insert the other side of the upper sash against its weather stripping still nailed at the jamb and move the other side of the sash, with the weather stripping inserted, against its section of the jamb.

- Lower the sash, and push the loose weather stripping section up and around the pulley, nailing it in place. For accuracy, try to use the old nail openings and holes.

- Spray the weather stripping with WD-40 or other lubricant.

- Move the sash up and down to assure it's working smoothly and that it closes completely at the top.

- Close the sash and nail the weather stripping at its bottom. Test the sash for movement again.

- Install the parting beads as usual.

NOTE: Often, with interlocking weather stripping, the lower half of the parting bead has a very narrow channel cut into it to receive the edge of the weather stripping. Look closely at the old parting bead for signs of this. You can duplicate this channel in a new parting bead by cutting into the parting bead with a hand saw or running the edge of a sharp chisel into it after the parting bead is installed. Or, you can cut along the edge of the weather stripping with metal snips, removing 1/8" or so and running this cut edge on a belt sander or smooth it with a metal file. The resulting edge will not be as smooth as the factory-finished one, but by cutting down the weather stripping it will fit correctly with the new parting bead. You must either cut a kerf in the new parting bead or reduce the size of the weather stripping for the sash to line up correctly. Line the weather stripping up with its old nail holes to be sure it's back where it belongs.

To install the lower sash:

- Lower the upper sash a few inches. This gets the meeting rail out of the way so its weather stripping doesn't latch onto that of the lower sash.

- Nail one side of the lower weather stripping to the jamb; be sure the bottom end of the vertical piece locks into the piece attached to the sill (they will be notched where they connect).

- Attach the ropes to the sash.

- Install the other piece of material and the sash in the same manner as the upper sash, inserting the weather stripping into the side of the sash and moving the two together into the jamb.

- Line up the sash and the loose section of weather stripping and fasten with weather stripping nails.

- If for any reason you cannot insert a nail in the existing top nail hole when installing the second piece of weather stripping, then pre-punch a small hole through the weather stripping first (use a small finish nail to make the hole) and nail as close as you can get to the original hole. You'll need to hold the nail with a needle-nose pliers and toenail it in, setting it with a nail set.

- Check the lower sash for movement.

- Spray the jamb with silicone or WD-40.

- Close both sashes together and check for fit. They should lock together if there isn't any paint buildup getting in the way.

What? They don't close? You'll have to adjust them. How do you adjust the weather stripping at the meeting rail?

- Close the window and look out and up through the lower sash at the meeting rail weather stripping. You should be able to see if each piece is clearing the other properly and coming together. When they don't meet and lock into each other, it means one has gotten bent out of alignment and needs to be moved back into its correct position.

- If the sashes aren't meeting, try and determine which section of weather stripping is out of alignment. Open that sash and gradually spread the weather stripping outward with a wide, stiff putty knife. Slip the knife under the lip of the weather stripping and move it just enough to bend the weather stripping. You shouldn't need to spread it out very far.

- The weather stripping could already be spread too wide, in which case you will have

to tap it back to a narrower profile. Do this by placing a small file or stiff putty knife against the weather stripping and tapping it inward towards its respective sash with a hammer.

- Check also that the vertical weather stripping is aligned properly so the sashes are close enough to lock (one reason I recommend using the old nail holes, you're assured everything is lined up unless the original installer was a dope). This sounds like more of a nuisance than it really is, but this is unforgiving material. It expects order and straight lines, something like the military, although without the uniforms and salutes.

Carefully bend the meeting rail weather stripping as needed.

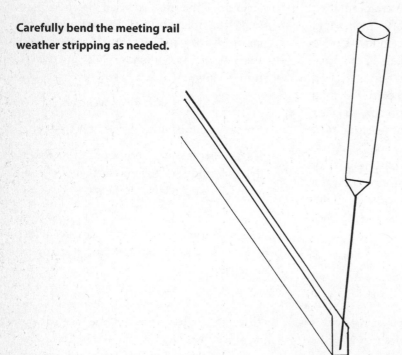

NOTE: If the weather stripping on the stiles is just trashed or pieces are missing, go ahead and replace it with spring bronze. Be sure to cut a small V-shaped notch at the bottom of the spring bronze so it will slip around the section of interlocking weather stripping that's nailed to the windowsill.

Alternatives to Pulleys, Weights, and Ropes

There are various pulley, weight, and sash replacement systems available in the form of jamb liners (contact Intek Plastics, Inc., www.intekplastics .com for one example) that either secure your existing or new sashes in place by friction or various spring or cable arrangements.

Replacement window kits by Marvin (Marvin Tilt Pac Window Sash Replacement Kit, www .marvin.com), among others are sold at lumber stores and home improvement centers everywhere. They consist of new sashes and jamb liners that install in your existing window openings once the sashes, parting beads, and pulleys are removed.

These kits work best in square openings for a tight fit and square openings don't exactly rule in old homes. In a sense, pulleys and weights are primitive, but they always work and can always be repaired. If a track replacement system breaks or the tension gives out, good luck repairing it. Plus, you have the issues of compatibility (will the new sash look like your old ones?) and cost. As I said earlier in this book, I'm not a purist about old windows, but you have a lot to consider before replacing them.

However, replacement windows are very tempting and in one sense, what's not to like? They're new, insulated, no layers of paint to strip off, and they offer sound insulation, too. Life would be grand if these decisions were so simple. Before replacing your windows, you should consider:

- New windows come in generic styles and kits as well as exact duplicates of your existing windows, these latter ones being the most expensive.

- The problem with using generic replacements for your worst windows is that they won't match the old ones you keep. You might feel compelled to replace everything which can be costly.

- Local building and energy codes vary. If you replace all your windows with matching wood windows, you might have to replace with insulated windows (existing old windows are single-glazed, that is, they have one piece of glass; insulated windows have two or even three panes of glass with an insulating space between panes). If you replace individual windows or sashes, single-glaze will better match your existing windows.

- When you replace a single sash of a double-hung window with a new, matching sash with insulated glass, the sash will be too heavy for the weights and you will have to adjust them accordingly. The bulk of energy savings from insulated windows does not come from the glass, but rather the jamb with its factory weather stripping and seal. Simply adding insulated sashes to your old double-hung jambs can improve your heat bill, but not as significantly as with whole new windows. Attempting to replace single-pane glass in existing operable sashes with insulated glass simply does not pay off unless you've got

LOTS of time on your hands. Most residential size sash, normally 1⅜" thick, will not easily accommodate the added thickness of insulated glass. So much wood gets routed away that the interior detailing of the sash is lost or diminished. I never met anyone who recommends going this route.

Look carefully at any and all replacement options. Unless you're willing to spend on a first-class product, the mix of new and old might not go over very well.

CHAPTER 2

— · —

Casement Windows, Awning Windows, Hopper Vent Windows

THE DETAILS

Casement windows open out like doors using one of two types of hinges: butt hinges (found on most doors) or friction hinges (also called scissor hinges). Butt hinges are visible on the exterior of the sash and require an opener or adjuster (an adjustable "arm") to control how far the sash will open and keep wind from slamming it around. The friction hinges are self-locking and are routed into the top and bottom rails of the sash.

You may have operable casements and not realize it if they have been painted and caulked shut and the hardware removed. Or, the original casements may have deteriorated and fixed

Casement with friction hinges

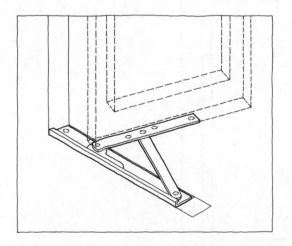

Casement with butt hinges

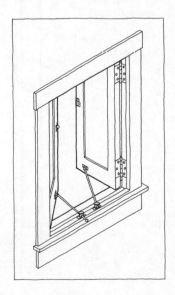

sashes installed in their place. The easiest clue if all the hardware is gone (and you don't have butt hinges, which will be very visible on the exterior of the window) is any sign of an old lock. When removed, the screw holes were filled and you can sometimes see the filler under the paint. The locks were almost always located at the center of one of the vertical stiles. Look carefully for a depression or outline from the lock. If you suspect there was a lock, scrape the stile and look for either two or four screw holes filled with Spackle. To its side, on the jamb, look for a slight depression. This is the former location of the lock strike and will also be filled.

Which side will the lock be on? Typically, with windows installed side by side, the sash to your left (looking from the inside) will open right to left; the window on your right will open left to right. Left to right opening is more common with single windows.

GETTING THEM OPEN

Casement windows are easier to deal with than double-hung windows. There are no ropes or parting beads to replace and you're only repairing one sash per opening. They also offer fewer ventilation options than double-hung windows. For instance, unless you have screens, you wouldn't open a casement all the way if you had an adventuresome cat whereas with a double-hung you can open the upper sash and feel confident your feline friend won't be wandering outside. Casements present their own repair and restoration challenges.

BEWARE: If the window has been sealed shut, it may have also been nailed shut from the outside. This means it will have to be gradually opened from the inside to force the nails out.

Insert putty knife between casement sash and the jamb

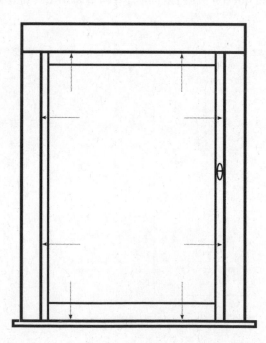

Q OK, Mr. Window, just how do you open a stuck-shut-forever casement window? I'm thinking a small, remote-controlled nuclear device since I already build these as one of my many hobbies.

A *I can't wait to hear about your other hobbies. Meanwhile, put the plutonium away and follow these steps:*

· *Break the paint between the sash and the jamb (at the point where it's closed) with a stiff putty knife and a hammer or use a heat gun. Remember, heat guns leave a mess so stick with the putty knife if possible. If you can break the outside paint seal, all the better.*

· *After the paint seal is broken, force the knife along the bottom corner of the stile opposite the hinge side, bending the putty knife inward and pushing the sash out more forcefully. The sash should spring out a bit.*

· *Work the knife up the length of the stile. Do the same at the top and bottom of the sash along the rails. You may need to push at two different points at the same time with two putty knives.*

These can be quite stuck, like they're squeezed into an opening too small for their size. Push out slowly so you don't break the sash or glass or loosen the bottom rail. If you have friction hinges, they can really be stuck so work them back and forth gradually once you get the sash open, spraying the hinges with lubricant. Forcing the sash open too abruptly when the hinge is frozen can stress the joints too much and damage the sash.

Look out for rusted hinges, loose glass, and loose bottom rails. Sometimes these rails are so loose that they will fall off as the window is opened, so hold onto them as you open the sash.

Now that you've gotten the window open, try to close it! See Chapter 4 for everything you always wanted to know about casement window repair but, with three college degrees, never thought you'd have to ask.

REMOVING THE HINGES

Your casement will have either butt hinges or friction hinges. Butt hinges are almost always salvageable while friction hinges, mostly those attached to the lower rails, can be rusted beyond repair.

As an alternative to chipping old paint out of screw heads, you can try a small wire brush attachment to an electric drill, something like a Dremel 1/2" Carbon Steel Brush DRE 442 or similar. It might not be worth the trouble and it's hard to judge how soon it will get clogged up with paint, but it should really clean out the slot in the screw.

To remove butt hinges:

- Take a hammer and putty knife and lightly tap around the edge of each half of the hinge to break the paint seal. Otherwise, when you remove the sash and force the hinge out, it can splinter the jamb and/or the sash.

- Unscrew the hinges at the jamb and put the screws aside. Even though it's unlikely the sash will fall out, hold onto it anyway as you remove the final screw.

- If the screw slots are filled with paint, use your screwdriver like a chisel (a highly recommended practice for ruining screwdrivers, by the way, so use a cheap one) and tap it with a hammer until the paint is chipped out.

- Watch for any shims (thin pieces of cardboard that help square up the window) under the hinges on the jamb side. THESE ARE IMPORTANT! The sash will not close properly unless these are reinstalled with it. I often leave the shims attached loosely to the jamb with the hinge screws so I'll know to reinstall them. Even with the screws removed, the hinges can still be stuck. With the sash completely open and one hand on the outermost edge or stile (where the lock is located), hit the now exposed edge on the hinge-side stile with the palm of your other hand. This should break it loose (remember to break the paint around the hinge first with a putty knife and hammer).

To remove friction hinges:

- Unscrew the hinges at the header (upper jamb) and at the sill. If the sash won't open all the way, spray a ton of lubricant on the hinges and keep working the sash back and forth.

- If the screws will turn but not remove, (usually at the lower hinge) loosen them completely and slip a tool, such as a small pry bar or stiff putty knife, under the hinge and pry against it. Let the hinge return to the sill or header and the screw head should be sticking out enough to grab with pliers.

- Remove all the screws; the sash should stay in place. I would say "will stay in place," but there is always one in a zillion that slips out. When you reinstall the window, replace the rusty screws with longer screws of the same diameter. Use brass or zinc-plated screws, as they are corrosion resistant. Be sure the heads of the screws are the same size as the old ones! Larger heads won't allow the hinge to slide past them.

- Gradually ease the sash away from the jamb, pushing out at the bottom first (this isn't critical, it's just easier to start at the bottom). You might have to slip a stiff putty knife under the hinges to force them out of the jamb or put the knife between the hinge and the stool and push it out there.

- Watch for cardboard shims! Friction hinges have them, too. Save these and use them when you reinstall the sash.

Are the hinges still pretty stiff and ugly looking? The bottom ones can be if water washes in under the sash and the hinge is slow to dry out. With the sash removed:

- Spray the hinges with more lubricant or penetrating oil and work them back and forth.

- If they're really stuck, remove the hinges from the sash and heat them with a propane torch or hold them with a channel locks or large pair of pliers over a gas stove burner. The heat does wonders for loosening corroded hinges. No torch or gas burner? Soak them in oil overnight. It's not the same, but it helps.

· Once the hinges are moving more easily, run any corroded or rusty hinges against a wire wheel attachment on a bench grinder and really clean them (wipe any oil off first). This will also remove any house paint gumming things up. Observe how the hinge slides and look for paint or dirt caught in the track and be sure to clean this out, too.

· If the hinges are salvageable, but are corroded, spray them with Rustoleum or similar rust-preventing spray paint after you've cleaned them. Once the paint is dry, spray them with silicone lubricant or rub with a little machine oil (automotive oil will do just as well).

· When working freely, friction hinges allow a casement sash to open fully to the point that you can wash the exterior of the sash from the inside.

WEATHER STRIPPING

Your casement might be weather-stripped with either spring bronze material or interlocking weather stripping. Interlocking weather stripping on a casement window consists of a piece routed into the sash on three sides with intersecting pieces nailed to the jamb. One piece locks into the other. On the hinge side, (butt hinges or—if you have friction hinges, where butt hinges would otherwise be located—the stile opposite the lock) a channel or kerf is cut in the sash which fits into a corresponding piece of weather stripping on the jamb.

Out-swinging awning window

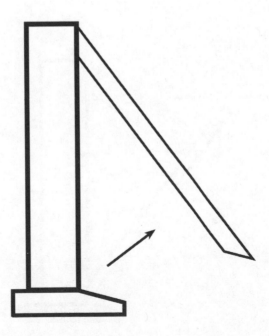

Like double-hung windows with interlocking material, casements require a precise fit of sash and weather stripping in order to close and lock properly. It can often be reused or portions of it replaced with spring bronze. Please see Chapter 4 for details.

AWNING WINDOWS/ HOPPER VENT WINDOWS

An awning window is similar to a casement except it opens horizontally rather than vertically. That is, take a casement, turn it on its side, and open it. Voila, an awning window.

Awning windows:

- Will have either butt hinges on the top rail or friction hinges at the stiles.
- Normally swing out from the bottom.
- Some awning windows are hinged at the top and swing inward from the bottom, requiring a casement opener or even a stick of wood to keep it open.

A hopper vent or a hopper light is hinged at the bottom (or has friction hinges) to swing either in or out at the top, just the opposite of an awning window. Sometimes a small chain is attached to the jamb and to the sash to control how far the sash will travel (in either direction depending on how it opens).

With either hinge, a lock will be present at either the top or bottom rail, again depending on how the sash opens.

Simple awning and hopper windows can be found in basements and closets. They were also occasionally installed over very tall double-hung windows. They are opened and are repaired in the same manner as casement windows and are fairly easy to work on. These are utility windows, not exactly fit with a violin maker's precision, with plenty of room to spare in the jambs. I have never found one that was weather-stripped, although colder climates can call for it.

In-swinging hopper vent

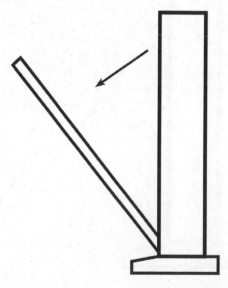

CHAPTER 3

— · —

Fixed Windows

THE DETAILS

No, a fixed window does not imply a window that can no longer reproduce baby windows. Fixed means the window does not open. A single sash can be fixed or a double-hung window without pulleys can be considered fixed. As these are inoperable, there is little reason to remove them or do any repairs other than caulking, reglazing, and repainting if they're in good shape.

BUT…You might have some problems, such as:

· Deteriorated wood sections
· The whole sash pulling away from its opening
· Loose glass

Or you might want to remove the sash in order to completely sand and repaint it.

See if you can first repair your fixed window without removing the sash(es) before you go mucking around and yanking things out. Large fixed sashes are a real nuisance to remove so better to leave them if you can. Even rotted sections can be dug out and filled with the window intact. Yes, I know, a true artisan would insist on removing that 8' x 5' oversize sash and carefully splice in new wood to the bottom rail and coat it with home-brewed preservative and apply four coats of paint and primer and plane down the edges for a perfect refit because now that it's out it won't fit back in the opening and woe to those lacking sufficient preservation righteousness who don't do the same. I mean, why take the easy and practical way out and dig out the deteriorated wood, brush on some preservative, pack it with epoxy, sand it smooth, prime, paint, and walk away when you can make a huge production out of it instead? Trust me, better to save the productions for the theater.

A large fixed window with a single pane of glass provides an unobstructed view. Smaller fixed windows, especially double-hung style, were probably installed to meet a budget. Why go to the expense of installing an operable window as long as some standard of ventilation was already met? Showing up decades later, you might want it to open, but future owners are not the main concern of homebuilders.

FIXED SINGLE SASH

A fixed single sash is either installed from the outside of the opening or from the inside. If installed from the inside, the sash:

- Rests against parting beads or similar stops
- Is secured with finish nails toenailed (hammered at an angle) through the stiles and rails into the jamb
- Is additionally secured by interior stops, although these mostly serve to present a more finished look

To remove this type of fixed sash:

- Break the paint around the stops. You'll have to find the space between the edge of the stop and the casing and insert a flexible putty knife to begin loosening each stop. Start with the vertical stops and do the upper horizontal stop last. With the stop partially loose, insert a stiff putty knife or small pry bar and gradually ease the stop out. Take your time as the edge of the stop is very narrow and it's easy to chew it up if you're too aggressive.
- With all three stops removed, hammer a couple of nails about halfway down the jamb where the stops were removed. Only insert them partly in and a couple inches away from the sash. Why? So they'll act as stops when the sash starts falling in as you pry it loose. The sash will most likely be so caked with paint and caulk that it will move very slowly once you break the paint bond, but put the nails in as a precaution.

- Insert a stiff putty knife between the outside edge of the sash and the parting bead or stop it is pressed against. If your fixed window is too high up to comfortably reach from a ladder and if it has opening side windows, you can break various OSHA (Occupational Safety and Health Administration) safety regulations by hanging out these side windows and doing your work with the putty knife. (PLEASE note: The word "can" implies hypothetical, as in, "You can enter the Nathan's Famous Fourth of July Hot Dog Eating Contest at Coney Island and you could try and beat the current record of 66 hot dogs eaten in 12 minutes, even if this is a dumb idea." Mr. Window is simply pointing out one way to loosen your windows and wants it made abundantly clear you're on your own safety-wise.) It's a bit of a stretch reaching for the top rail, but can be done, not that Mr. Window—now on a permanent sabbatical from highly visible commercial work and its safety inspectors— would ever consider doing this, either. And even if he did, not that he's admitting it, he can always resort to the "do as I say, not as I do" ruling used by anyone who dispenses advice and is the number-one implied value behind every parental admonishment ever uttered. Break the paint all around and force the sash inward.

- If there are no nails holding it in, lucky you! Push the sash in until it hits the nails you put in as stops.

- While holding the sash, remove your nails, push and pull the window in further, and work the sash back and forth until you can lift it out.

- If the sash has been nailed in place, locate the nails by running a putty knife between the sash and the jamb. You can then attempt to cut them with a hacksaw blade or drive a stiff putty knife into them with a hammer until they're broken off (as mentioned earlier, this isn't a tool-friendly procedure so use an old or cheap putty knife if you have one). You can also just force the sash out, taking the nails with it.

- After removal, clean all the gummed-up paint and caulking from the jamb prior to reinstalling the sash.

To remove a sash installed from the outside:

- The sash will be nailed against the jamb from the exterior side and then caulked or otherwise sealed around its edge.

- Break the paint on both sides with a hammer and stiff putty knife.

- From the inside, force the knife between the sash and the jamb and slowly push it out (it is unlikely an exterior-mounted sash will have interior stops).

- Obviously, it helps to have a second person helping, but removal can be done alone, even if from a second story or higher. You will have to restrain the sash to keep it from falling all the way out by screwing a piece of chain or wire to the top rail and then to the jamb. If it's a large sash, you should really have two people. There are some solo methodologies that even Mr. Window frowns upon. The sash shouldn't move very fast because it's been painted shut and the paint buildup acts as a brake.

- As the sash loosens and falls outward, move it back and forth to loosen it and lift it up and out. The ease with which it loosens is strictly dependent on the number of nails and their locations. If the upper rail has been toenailed into the header, for instance, you'll find yourself removing the sash from the bottom up and then pulling or prying down on the sash to finally free it. This is not a fun activity with large fixed sashes.

- After removal, clean all the gummed-up paint and caulking from the jamb prior to reinstalling the sash.

Any fixed sash that's been intact and installed for years might need some minor trimming when reinstalling. If you're having trouble fitting the sash back in its opening, remove it and sand or plane down the sides until it fits back in without resistance. You only need to remove a small amount of wood, if any! Removing the caked-up paint is often sufficient. I saw the results of one contractor who fed all the casement sashes from one house through a table saw for trimming. They opened and closed just fine and they all had nice, big gaps between the sashes and the jambs, enough to show daylight and let in the wind. The contractor's comment to the client: "Well, you wanted them to close easily, didn't you?"

DOUBLE-HUNG FIXED WINDOWS

A double-hung fixed window disassembles and reassembles the same as an operable double-hung window. The only difference is the upper sash and occasionally the lower sash can be nailed or secured shut. When you reinstall a fixed double-hung, consider keeping the upper sash closed with a small block of wood underneath the bottom rail, screwed into each vertical section of the jamb. This will allow for future removal if needed. The paint and caulk will also keep the sash closed and prevent it from opening. For extra security at the lower sash, in addition to the window lock:

· Screw a small block of wood to each side of the jamb and butt the blocks against the sash's top rail.

· Alternatively, screw a small block of wood to the upper sash stiles right above the lower sash's top rail or meeting rail. This helps prevent either sash from being forced open.

Q Yo, Mr. Window. I know you said the guys who built my house way back when weren't thinking of me—a definite case of shortsightedness I take very personally and thanks to the Internet, I can track down their relatives and give them a piece of my mind, such as it is—but I want to get some of these fixed windows to open. What do I do?

A *Any number of fixed windows can be made operable, especially double-hung fixed windows. Please see pages 138–143 in the next chapter for the complete scoop.*

CHAPTER 4

— · —

Repairs, Refinishing, Repainting, Weather Stripping, Redemption

A SHORT INTRODUCTION

All right, redemption may be pushing things a bit. However, it is possible to repair even the most deteriorated window. You'll have to decide whether it's worth keeping or replacing. The criteria usually involves:

· Time and money
· Historic or architectural accuracy
· The challenge of doing the work
· Time and money

More time than money? By all means repair. Enough money to replace? Then you have the option to do that or repair. Tons and tons of money? Move to Paris or buy a small winery in California and forget about your windows.

Old windows that are painted shut, broken, inoperable, leaky, and rattling can be greatly improved. THEY WILL NOT BE NEW WINDOWS! They will be quite serviceable, secure, and sealed to the weather, offering a long functional life. Look at it this way: If your house is eighty or one hundred years old and has the original windows that have survived years of indifference, don't you think that after they're repaired they'll be good for a few more decades?

Are there cost savings to repairing them yourself? Sure, but they shrink if you could be working elsewhere making a lot more money after taxes than you're saving by repairing your windows. This isn't entirely realistic because the time spent saving money on window repair is usually time you wouldn't be working for money somewhere else. True, it might be time you could be lying on a beach or enjoying long, leisurely breakfasts with the love of your life, not that either choice could possibly compare to tearing windows apart and getting splinters in your fingers.

You repair old windows because you want to keep them, they look good with your house, and there's some satisfaction to restoring and preserving the past when it makes sense to do so. There's also personal fulfillment from doing work that's new to you and doing it well, especially if your day-to-day job is spent at a desk. I have had attorneys as clients who would occasionally comment on dealing with briefs and legal minutiae all day and thought how satisfying it must be to end a workday and see a finished task in the form of an operating window. Sure, it was. Unfortunately, I couldn't bill out at several hundred dollars an hour as they did. Personal satisfaction is great and desired, but so is a pile of money. I don't expect to see an exodus of lawyers from the legal profession to the field of window repair any time soon.

In some neighborhoods that are part of a local historic district, restoration is expected and replacement not readily permitted. Besides, you can save enough money by doing your own repairs for a trip to the islands.

SAFETY CONSIDERATIONS

Be forewarned: The world of window restoration, chemistry, and abrasives will expose you to fumes, dusts, odors, noises, and solvents. A few precautions are in order starting with a few words about lead-based paint.

LEAD!!!!

Current and proposed legislation address the removal and disposal of lead-based paint. Some paint stores sell testing kits to determine the presence of lead in paint, water, soil, etc. I do not propose to explain legalities here. Think again if you believe Mr. Window will provide guidelines that could later be used against him in court. I suggest you go to the EPA's Website (www.epa.gov/lead/), the Office of Healthy Homes and Lead Hazard Control (www.hud.gov/offices/lead/), or contact your state or local public health departments regarding local and national laws. There is plenty of real concern over lead-based paint mixed with paranoia, legal issues, and dubious science.

I can say this: Basically, the guidelines call for the paint to be removed with the least disruptive method possible and disposed of in a prescribed manner. Given that even removing a sash can produce chipped paint and therefore lead contaminate, some regulations, such as those in San Francisco and Boston, make window restoration difficult to carry out. The regulations can vary depending on the amount of contaminate produced and whether you're a homeowner doing your own work. If a contractor removes lead-based paint on your property in an improper manner and the neighbors let fly with a lawsuit, you could be on the receiving end. They can let fly if you remove it improperly, too.

I would suggest that you do the work in an empty garage (for loose sashes and trim) in which you can contain the contaminated dust and debris and later clean and decontaminate your work area, following acceptable guidelines. Keep yourself and your clothes clean, too. Wear a disposable Tyvek suit (see below) and launder your clothing separately. Wash your hands before eating or smoking. I know, this last caveat sounds strange, wash your hands of lead before you fill your lungs with smoke, but that's what the government guidelines say.

One guideline is paramount: You don't want young children anywhere near lead-based paint dust and debris (keep pets away, too)! Lead dust and kids are a bad combination, both physiologically and perceptually. Children are still developing and are more affected by inhaling or ingesting lead so keep them far away from it. Justified or not, lead is the asbestos of the current decade and trial lawyers are testing the waters with lawsuits. For more reading, see "Appropriate Methods for Reducing Lead-Paint Hazards in Historic Housing," Sharon C. Park, AIA, and Douglas C. Hicks, at www.oldhousejournal.com/notebook/npsbriefs/brief37.shtml.

Restoration work goes on every day with good lead-based-paint management practices. Contain it properly, wash your hands and clothing regularly, and keep your kids away from the work site and you should be fine. To do this, you'll need to invest in some safety equipment, which you should wear even if you're not working around lead-based paint.

Basic safety equipment includes:

· Respirators (for smoke and fumes)
· Heavy dust masks (for sanding dust)
· Safety glasses
· Heavy work gloves
· Ear protectors
· Disposable Tyvek suits

Respirators and Masks

Respirators, gas masks, and dust masks have been around in one form or another since the 1820s. Modern versions include everything from throwaway paper dust masks to full hoods with separate air supply. You won't need anything quite that elaborate, although walking around in one would give the neighbors something to talk about and gives you an automatic Halloween costume. Your choices of respirators and masks come down to:

· Half-face reusable respirators with disposable filtering cartridges

· Full-face reusable respirators with disposable filtering cartridges

· Disposable dust masks

· Disposable respirators for dust or vapors (fumes)

Various manufacturers, including Wilson, North, and 3M, sell reusable silicone or neoprene (synthetic rubber) half-face respirators. Half-face means the mask or respirator doesn't protect your eyes, but covers your nose, mouth, and parts of your cheeks. A full-face respirator comes with a clear plastic shield to protect your eyes. Both versions attach via adjustable straps that wrap around your head. Neither is particularly comfortable to wear and you will regularly be tempted to tear them off and gulp in fresh air. The air won't be fresh—it will be filled with fumes or dust—but it will seem preferable to wearing an uncomfortable mask. Such are the drawbacks to lung preservation. Also, respirators do not form tight seals around beards so this is a great excuse to find someone smooth-shaven to do any tasks requiring respirators (good luck).

Safety equipment suppliers, listed in the Yellow Pages and the Internet, are a good source for respirators as are paint, hardware, and home improvement stores. For at-home viewing, do an Internet search on personal safety equipment to get a look at available products without the rush. If you go to a local safety equipment supplier, explain the type of work you will be doing in order to get the appropriate mask and filters for the job. Filters containing activated charcoal protect against organic vapors (solvents, chemical paint removers, etc.), while others protect against fine particulate (smoke, dust). The cheapest paper masks are for nuisance dust only and not recommended for window restoration work.

Dust masks are a little trickier to choose than organic vapor respirators. When you're removing sash and trim, you'll disrupt paint and dust and dirt. It could be argued that almost any decent dust mask will do under these circumstances,

3M Respirators

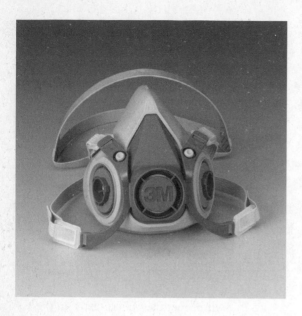 

but since you're likely to be dislodging some lead-based paint, it could also be argued you should only wear a mask or respirator rated for lead dust. This means a HEPA (High-Efficiency Particulate Air) filter, which removes over 99% of dust and other particles from the air passing through the filter. This is great and even desirable if you're sanding lead-based paint and the concentration of dust in your workspace is noticeable. Do you need to go this far if you're only pulling a few windows apart? Mr. Window assumes the Zen notion of silence in answer to this question, not because he is acknowledging the world of quietness in all its greatness, but, once again, he doesn't want to deal with any trial lawyers reading his book. Given the choice of masks and respirators available, Mr. Window further believes his readers will choose wisely. Maybe Mr. Window should have

been a lawyer himself. His own lawyer once told him he thought like one, which Mr. Window took as a mixed compliment.

Some half-face masks allow for a combination of filters if you're dealing with vapors and dust at the same time. As the filters get exposed to contaminants, they lose their effectiveness and require replacement. How will you know? You'll start smelling fumes in the case of organic vapor filters (the activated charcoal becomes clogged) or you will have trouble breathing through dust filters as they get clogged with dust. Don't be cheap about it! Replace the filters when they're no longer effective and keep your lungs clear so you can enjoy a fine celebratory cigar when the project is finished.

You don't necessarily need a half-face reusable respirator as disposable masks are available for both fumes and dust. There are dozens of models available, many of them from 3M, which offer disposable organic vapor respirators and a series of particulate (dust) respirators. At minimum, use a 3M 8210 Particulate Respirator for protection from dust. Buy a box of them (they run around a dollar a mask by the box). Its effectiveness, like any other respirator or mask, will be determined by the environment in which you're working (enclosed, outdoors, material being sanded, parts of particulate per million, etc.). If you're indoors and dealing with excessive dust, buy a HEPA respirator, such as a 3M disposable 8233; it runs around $6. Non-disposable respirators require filters, which are sold separately in pairs. The one advantage of a half-face neoprene or silicone respirator is that each accepts all types of cartridge filters so they're adaptable to multiple uses.

Safety Glasses

You will find safety glasses and safety shields at hardware and home improvement stores. A larger variety of eyewear is available at safety supply stores and glasses are easily viewed online. For less than $5, you can protect your eyes from flying splinters, dust, and broken glass. That's quite a bargain. If you already wear eyeglasses, a pair of safety shields can be worn over them. Safety glasses have become increasingly stylish, come in clear, yellow, and dark lenses, and non-prescription bifocal versions are available for around $20.

3M 8233 N100 HEPA Respirator

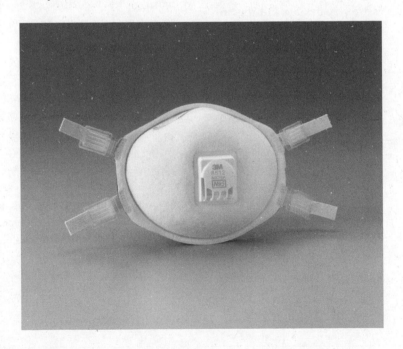

Gloves

Some people never wear gloves when they do construction or remodeling work and others wear them religiously. The right pair will protect your hands and provide you with plenty of flexibility. For window restoration, several types of gloves are appropriate:

· Inexpensive latex gloves for priming, painting, and applying glazing compound.

· Work gloves when removing and reinstalling sash.

· Rubber gloves to protect against paint remover and solvents.

Basic canvas work gloves, found at every hardware and gardening store, will do the job, but aren't the longest lasting or snuggest fitting. Cheap cotton gloves are very flexible, but the fingertips wear out. Leather or part-leather gloves can be longer lasting, but it depends on the manufacturer. I wouldn't turn finding the ideal pair of work gloves into any kind of pilgrimage, but do wear something if you want to keep the blisters down and protect your skin.

WARNING! Don't wear work gloves when using power tools with rotating parts, such as drills, disc sanders, belt sanders, or saws. When a glove gets caught in a spinning saw blade or drill bit or sanding disc, your hand will follow, often to its detriment and damage. Gloves are fine with speed-bloc finish sanders and hand tools.

Anytime you work with solvents, especially paint remover, you should wear rubber (neoprene) gloves (latex gloves won't hold up). If you're doing overhead work, buy a long pair of gloves (as close to elbow length as you can find) and wear a long-sleeve shirt or sweatshirt to protect the skin on your arms. The thicker the gloves the better from a protection standpoint, but the more unwieldy

Keep any old rubber gloves so you can cut off and salvage the individual intact fingers when you get a tear in a second or third set of gloves. Just slip the cut-off finger over the damaged or torn finger on the next pair of gloves and you can get a longer life out of them.

For hands unaccustomed to tearing windows out and sanding, renovation work can be tough on softer skin and long nails (you can kiss those good-bye). Do enough of this and your skin cracks and gets pretty rough. One way to counter this at bedtime is—bear with me, it sounds a little kinky—to heavily coat your hands with Vaseline, Corn Huskers Lotion, or your favorite medicated hand lotion or cream, and then put on a loose pair of latex dishwashing gloves, keeping them on while you sleep. Your hands soften and start to heal and your sheets stay clean.

from a practical standpoint (it's harder to grip tools and steel wool and such with thick-fingered gloves). Thinner gloves provide flexibility, but the fingers tear when you run across splinters in the wood. Find a medium-thickness industrial glove such as Chem Master and buy two or three pairs. They have other uses besides paint removal and they're handy (oh, bad pun) to have around.

Ear Protectors

For all you baby boomers and heavy metal devotees who never missed an ear-splitting live concert, wearing ear protection at this point in your lives might seem as useful as had Napoleon II looked back and said, gee, Dad, you really should have stayed out of Russia. Past or existing damage aside, you should still protect your hearing when using power tools or even hammering nails (the League of the Hard of Hearing—who else?—says hammering a nail can hit 120 decibels). The National Institute for Occupational Safety and Health (NIOSH) recommends limited exposure to any sounds louder than 85 decibels and certainly using hearing protection for those noise levels. (For the NIOSH lowdown on ear protection, log on to www2a.cdc.gov/hp-devices/hp_srchpg01.asp.)

Ear protection comes in several flavors:

· Inexpensive, disposable, expandable foam plugs are the most basic. These soft foam plugs are rolled between the fingers or across the palm of your hand and then inserted into the ear canals where they expand and conform to the shape of each canal, effectively blocking out damaging noise. Although disposable, these plugs can be washed and reused. They cost around 30–50 cents a pair and can be purchased by the box (100–200 pair) for a lower cost per pair.

· Pre-molded, reusable plugs are made from silicone, plastic, or rubber and available in several sizes. You might need a different size for each ear and some trial and error is necessary to find those that fit best.

· Custom-molded silicone ear plugs are also available; they are made from a mold cast from your ears for a perfect fit. Unless you're regularly exposed to high-decibel noise, these are overkill.

· Canal caps, which come attached to a flexible plastic or metal headband.

· Earmuffs, which resemble headphones, and completely cover the outer ear. These do not always form a complete seal if the user wears eyeglasses or has a heavy beard or sideburns. However, some models are available with built-in AM/FM radios that can be heard at normal volumes while the earmuffs block out high-decibel noise.

The best hearing protection is the device that you will regularly and comfortably wear. Personally, I like the convenience of earmuffs, but always keep a pair of disposable foam plugs on hand in case the earmuffs aren't close by. Wearing both foam plugs and ear muffs at the same time offers some additional protection. Regardless of which protective device you choose, you'll still be able to hear spoken communications, although not as clearly as when you're not wearing any protection. Depending on who's addressing you, this could be an unexpected bonus!

3M Hearing Protection Products

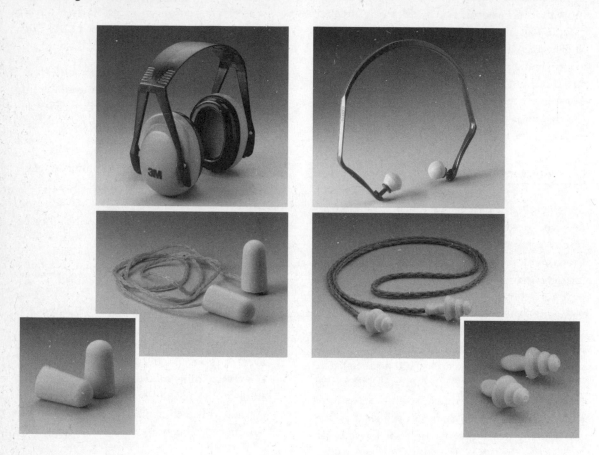

Disposable Tyvek Suits

Dupont Tyvek suits (www.tyvek.com) are inexpensive (about $6) polyethylene disposable clothing made to go over work clothes and protect the wearer from both dry particles and liquids. Painters wear them all the time when they spray paint. Basically, Tyvek suits keep you clean when dealing with lead-based paint dust. They are not impenetrable so don't expect them to protect you from solvents or paint remover. At just under $6, they're a pretty good deal and worth wearing if you expect to be in a dusty environment.

REPAIR PROBLEMS

The most common problems with old wood windows are:

· Excessive paint buildup
· Broken ropes
· Broken glass or loose glazing (putty)
· Loose corners
· Deteriorated wood
· Missing or broken hardware
· Sloppy fit

Paint buildup is inevitable with old windows. After all, a maintained house is going to get regularly repainted. Careful painters who keep windows moving are unusual. Once a window gets painted shut, few subsequent painters are going to go to the trouble to break the paint seal and open the window; they will add on another layer of paint, however. Sometimes windows are even painted in a slightly open position and kept that way for years. The other problem with paint is too little of it too infrequently applied. Regular painting is the single most effective and preventative protection for a home's exterior, but it's often enough ignored.

Old cotton ropes have a limited life. They deteriorate even if they're unpainted. Glazing compound can remain intact indefinitely if it stays painted; let the painting go and the glazing will deteriorate and allow water to soak into the sash.

After decades of use and inadequate exterior painting, corners loosen when the pins holding them together rust and the joints disassemble. Entire sections of wood can deteriorate, too, as water seeps in and the wood weathers or rots.

Hardware is hardy stuff and usually lasts the lifetime of a window, but lock springs can give out and lifts occasionally break. A lock that's caked with paint is difficult to operate and needs to be stripped down or replaced.

A properly operating window has a taut fit that's easy to both open and close. Some windows never worked all that well from the time of their installation and others develop problems over time. Like the other problems listed here, these can be solved.

Paint Buildup

This one's easy. You can figure that a maintained residence gets painted every eight to ten years on the exterior. Interiors will vary, but kitchens and bathrooms are typically repainted more often than other rooms. A seventy-year-old house has got, technically speaking, LOTS O' PAINT. Eventually you reach what a coatings (paint) chemist would call critical thickness, that is, the surface has too much paint and cannot guarantee intercoat adhesion (new paint won't stick very well). The more you build up the paint, especially on the exterior, the more often you'll have to paint because the paint will fail and begin to lift off, particularly on the weathered sides. It's a vicious circle that can end with paint stripping.

Old paint can be removed by various methods, including:

· Heat (torch, heat gun, heat plate)
· Chemical (various removers, liquid and semi-paste)
· Scraping
· Sanding (belt sanders, finish sanders, disc sanders, random orbit sanders)
· Steam

All these methods have their strong and weak points. No single one is particularly fast. Undoing years of painting is time-consuming, but then so was applying the paint.

Removing Old Paint

Paint stripping, regardless of the method, is a messy, smelly task, but a necessary one. Do it once and your windows are good for decades of painting to come. By the time they need to be stripped again, you'll be long gone, metaphysically and otherwise.

There aren't any fast, labor-easy ways to strip paint, but you do have several options.

Heat Removal

Heat removal is quiet, tedious, smelly, and produces solid chunks of paint refuse for easy cleanup. This method works best against many layers of paint (the more the better) and especially well if you have paint over varnish. The varnish seals the wood and provides a smooth surface for any subsequent layers of paint. They're easier to remove because the paint can't soak into raw wood. Removing paint over shellac, another clear sealer, is a gummy experience, however.

Heat softens the paint so it can be scraped off to bare wood. It has drawbacks and limitations you need to be aware of:

· It stinks! Not only that, the smoke is hazardous and not exactly lung-friendly. Heat removal should be done either outdoors or in a garage, preferably a detached one, with the doors open. You'll need to wear a respirator with HEPA filters (smoke is a very fine particulate, not a vapor). Any heat removal done indoors should be done in an empty room that's closed off to the rest of the house with fans running and all windows open. Why empty? Because the smoke will settle on carpets, furniture, and any pets wandering around.

· Lead-based paint will vaporize if the heat source is over 1100°F and this is prohibited by various regulations. You will need a heat gun that registers at a lower temperature. Of course, the lower the temperature, the longer it takes to soften the paint so it can be stripped.

· No propane torches or electric heating element type removers! First, they're both too hot (over 1100°F). Second, the torch is an open flame that brings its own problems if you're stripping the jamb and some wood inside the wall catches fire and you don't see it. More than a few house fires have been caused by painters and homeowners stripping houses with open torches. Too bad, because torching is fast and effective.

Heat guns are the slowest heat removal method, but they are also the easiest to control and are particularly good for intricate work. This is what you do:

· Turn on the gun and set to the highest temperature (under 1100°F if it's an adjustable temperature gun or maximum if it can't go that high).

· Strip the exterior of the sash first to familiarize yourself with the gun. There's a good chance some of the wood will get slightly charred from exposing it to too much heat so better to practice on an exterior that will be painted over.

· Hold the end of the nozzle an inch or so from the painted surface and keep it there until the paint softens and begins to smoke.

· Remove the gun, or move it to the next painted section, and scrape the paint off with a putty knife or sharp scraper. The paint you scrape off will be very hot, but will cool down in twenty seconds or so.

· KEEP THE HEAT AWAY FROM THE GLASS! Now that the statute of limitations has passed, Mr. Window is willing to admit he did not always follow this caveat and has cracked some glass on occasion. Just strip the flat areas of the stiles, rails, jamb, etc.

· If any paint remains, do another pass with the heat gun and scrape off the residue.

After cleaning the paint off with heat, some sanding or cleaning by solvent might be necessary to remove the residue and bits of finish you did not scrape away. The key is to let the heat do the work and scrape it as clean as possible. After some practice, you should be able to scrape all of the finish off and get down to bare wood.

Master Appliance (www.masterappliance.com), Milwaukee (www.milwaukeetool.com), and Makita (www.makita.com) all make quality heat guns in the $80–150 range. You can rent a heat gun at many tool rental stores as well. There is also a relatively new heat removal system, the Speedheater 1100 or Silent Paint Remover that uses infrared heat to soften paint for removal. I haven't tried it and cannot attest to it. The Speedheater 1100 can be purchased for close to $450 or rented from the manufacturer (www.silentpaintremover.com), whose product description seems to suggest it's the greatest thing since the invention of happy hour. A Web search brings up some enthusiastic users and others who were less than enthusiastic. It's marketed as being faster, neater, cooler (as in runs at a lower temperature), and less toxic than standard heat guns. Check this out for yourself at www.silentpaintremover.com. A competing infrared tool, the Paint Peeler, is available from the Scott Machine Tool Company, who can be contacted at www.paintpeeler.com or (800) 613-1557.

Chemical Removal

Chemical paint remover is the most expensive way to remove paint. Most standard removers will require at least two applications to strip paint clean, but can often strip varnish and shellac alone with one application. They are also one of the most practical ways to strip a sash near the glass where heat can crack the glass and aggressive dry scraping can cause a break if the tool slips.

Paint removers are available in several forms:

· Solvent-based liquid and semi-paste
· Water rinse-able "safe" strippers
· Sodium hydroxide (lye) paste
· Environmentally friendly/natural

There is no end to the discussion and claims of one type, brand, or application of paint remover over another. Some swear by solvent-based products while others swear at them. Each of these products is expensive, typically running over $20 a gallon. Some come as kits with neutralizers and special scrapers that aren't all that special. Still, if you want to remove excessive paint, you need to consider all the methods and materials available to you.

Solvent-Based

These are the most toxic, smelly, skin-burning, and potent removers in the group. A solvent-based paint remover consists of a main solvent, which is the active ingredient, surfactants for penetrating the paint film, thickening agents, especially paraffin, to reduce the rate of evaporation (the longer the stripper remains wet, the better the results), and additional solvents for more skin-burning properties. Working with these strippers calls for rubber gloves, a respirator for organic vapors, and long pants and sleeves.

The most common solvent in solvent-based strippers is methylene chloride, a suspected carcinogen, which is another way of saying if you exposed enough rats to a high enough concentration for a long enough period of time, they would become ill. This is also true if you fed these same rats a 24/7 diet of barbecue pork and chili dogs or forced them to watch an endless loop of certain reality TV shows, but I digress.

It's ill-advised for people with existing heart conditions to use methylene chloride products because it metabolizes in the blood to form carbon monoxide and forces the heart to pump faster. Too bad, because it's a terrific paint remover. Methylene chloride penetrates the paint or coating film and forces the paint to swell up to as much as ten times its original volume, causing internal pressure resulting in wrinkles and bubbles in the paint as it pulls off the wood.

Using solvent-based strippers is fairly straightforward. You will need:

· Paint remover
· Tarps, plastic, or drop cloths
· Protective clothing and respirator
· Some clean cans or thick plastic containers
· A heavy plastic squeeze bottle
· A throwaway paintbrush
· Medium-grade steel wool
· Rags

Here's what you do:

· Whenever possible, take the wood you're stripping outside or into a garage with the door(s) open.

· Completely cover the surrounding floor area with thick drop cloths.

· If you're stripping woodwork that is not being removed, tape off the surrounding walls, floors, etc., that you do not want to strip with several layers of wide masking tape. The tape will catch the overflow of the stripper and protect the surfaces you want left alone. There is still the good possibility you'll drip some on the wall under the window, however.

· Suit up with gloves, respirator, long sleeves, eye protection, etc.

· Pour a pint or so of your chosen paint remover into a clean can or heavy plastic container.

· Brush a thick coat of remover over the painted areas. Brush once without overbrushing back and forth as this disturbs the paraffin wax "skin" that forms at the top of the stripper to keep it from drying out. If the stripper appears to be drying out right away—this can happen when it's applied over certain varnishes—brush on another coat immediately.

· Cover the stripper with plastic food wrap. Just press it against the stripper and it will stick. The plastic further slows the stripper's evaporation and will leave it in a wet state for hours and even overnight.

NOTE: Check the stripper from time to time to be sure it isn't drying out as different brands will remain wetter for longer periods of time with or without the plastic covering.

· When the paint has wrinkled and loosened, remove the plastic wrap and carefully scrape off the gunk using a flexible putty knife. Dispose of said gunk in a plastic container or cardboard box.

· If a second application is needed, apply it, repeating the steps above.

· Pour some lacquer thinner into a thick plastic squeeze/squirt bottle, such as a shampoo bottle (place the bottle inside a steel can and let it sit for ten minutes or so to be sure the thinner doesn't dissolve the plastic).

· When the final paint removal is done with the putty knife, squirt a small amount of lacquer thinner on the stripped area and clean up with medium-grade steel wool. Do a final wipe and rinse with more thinner and a clean rag. The stripper and residue need to be thoroughly cleaned off before painting or refinishing.

· If you're stripping a sash and don't want to strip the paint near the glass, run masking tape around the inner edge/ogee of the sash to prevent the stripper from dripping down towards the glass. You can also tape the outer edge of the sash, just outside the painted rails and stiles, to keep the stripper from dripping down the sides.

· Lightly sand the wood before applying any finish.

If you think the paint remover smells, wait until you open the lacquer thinner. So why use it? Because it's the best solvent for quickly and cleanly removing the residue from the stripping. Paint thinner doesn't do the job as well and water . . .well, forget water (more below).

Which brand paint remover should you buy? Let me put it this way: Jasco Premium Paint &

Epoxy Remover (www.jasco-help.com/products/prod_rem.htm) always works and is sold everywhere. It shares the messiness, odors, and toxic properties of its competitors, but it's reliable. Although it can be rinsed off with water, stick with lacquer thinner. If your painter friend or neighbor or cousin has another brand they recommend, by all means give it a try.

Other Solvents

Methylene chloride, in all its toxic nastiness, is the best solvent for solvent-based paint removers. Next up, and nowhere near as good, are acetone, toluene, and methanol, which are the primary ingredients in lacquer thinner. Throw some wax and thickening agents in and you have a runner-up stripping material; these strippers work OK with varnished and lacquered finishes. In fact, these are the main solvents in so-called refinishers that are sold to consumers for stripping furniture. They're pretty useless on paint and require the same safety and ventilation standards as methylene chloride paint removers.

Water Rinse-able "Safe" Strippers

If I were really cynical, as opposed to highly skeptical, I'd say "safe" is another term for "doesn't work," but that would be untrue. These strippers do work—eventually, sort of, a little. These strippers do not contain methylene chloride, but can contain various lower-level solvents. Some products claim you don't need to wear gloves and there are no harmful fumes with their use. Wear the gloves anyway and pay attention to the fumes. These products are much slower working than methylene chloride strippers and require more applications to soften multiple coats of paint, but you can use them indoors with less trepidation than methylene chloride. I'm not a fan, obviously, but you might feel more comfortable using them. Try 3M Safest Stripper, but be prepared to wait while it works on the paint.

Sodium Hydroxide Paste (Lye)

Lye in paste form is an effective paint stripper. Homemade mixes of lye, cornstarch, and water have been around for years. Lye works because of its high alkalinity and is known as a caustic stripper. I suppose that term could also be applied to certain clothing-challenged professional men and women after they've worked one too many bachelor/bachelorette parties and begin commenting on the party guests.

Caustic strippers:

· Work slowly.
· Irritate and burn exposed skin.
· Produce no toxic fumes.
· Remove multiple layers of paint.
· Darken most hardwoods so are inappropriate for furniture and veneers.
· Discolor softwoods.
· Must be rinsed with a neutralizing agent such as a water and vinegar mix.

The biggest name in caustic paste stripper is Peel-Away (Dumond Chemicals Inc, New York, NY; 800-245-1191; www.dumond.com). Peel-Away is sold in plastic buckets and comes with a coated paper used to cover and seal the stripper after it's been applied. The paper prevents the Peel-Away from drying out. There is never enough paper and it's expensive to buy separately. However, you can use all kinds of substitutes such as coated butcher paper for a much lower cost. In fact, when working on sashes with their narrow rails and stiles, I found that wide duct tape makes a great cover material and it's already the correct width, unlike the Peel-Away

paper that comes in a large sheet and has to be cut down to size. The very cool feature of this system is when you remove the paper, most of the Peel-Away and old paint come up with it for easy disposal.

When using Peel-Away or similar strippers:

· Wear rubber gloves, long sleeves, long pants, and eye protection.

· Apply a thick coat with a putty knife or the tool (a plastic spatula) that comes with the material.

· Cover the stripper completely with paper as per instructions.

· Allow twelve to twenty-four hours before removing the paper and stripper.

· Always neutralize the wood surface after removing the stripper.

· Lightly sand the wood before applying any finish.

The problem with lye as a caustic remover is it can soak into the wood and dry, forming salts that draw in moisture. Eventually, the salts can seep out and break down any new coats of primer and paint. Mr. Window found this out the hard way when he last used Peel-Away and despite rinsing and sanding, the fresh primer on almost one in ten windows began foaming once the masonry contractor showed up to wash the building. Mr. Window did the mature thing and blamed the mason. The mason then aimed his pressure washer at Mr. Window and wondered aloud if Mr. Window might reconsider his comments, which I did, blaming instead the city water department and its obviously contaminated water.

Peel-Away sells a separate neutralizing agent, although plain vinegar should do the job. Of course, I was using plain vinegar on the above-mentioned foamy sashes, which says something about the efficacy of vinegar. Whichever you use, you must scrub diligently to get all the remover, well, removed. Peel-Away is considered a very effective product for lead-based paint abatement and has been used on a number of high-profile historic landmarks, including President James A. Garfield's house in Mentor, Ohio. Close to 1,500 gallons of Peel-Away removed up to eighteen layers of paint during the $2.5 million restoration. Needless to say, Dumond Chemicals, Inc. was one cheery supplier on that job.

Environmentally Friendly/Natural

There are some paint removers made, respectively, from soy beans and citrus fruit and they are about as effective as using tofu or orange juice for your paint-stripping purposes. What's next, pureed salad greens? I'd love for these products to work and prove that nature trumps whatever coating concoctions wayward humans come up with, but lemons and soy are no match for high-gloss oil enamel paint. The chemical and coatings industries sold the paints you're trying to remove so let them now sell you the strippers to remove them. This isn't Mr. Window's giving in to industrial control, just reality.

Tank Dipping

An alternative to hand-stripping is tank dipping, which uses either solvent-based stripper (cold tank) or caustic stripper mixed with hot water (hot tank). The item to be stripped is dipped in

A great hand tool for removing paint is a Shinto Saw Rasp, which combines saw blades with a rasp type design. One set of saw teeth are coarse; flip it over and you have a set of fine teeth. The blades cut through layers of paint without causing a lot of dust. Different models run from $20–30 at fine woodworking stores or on-line. The Shinto Saw Rasp works especially well for limited paint removal of really gunky areas, such as meeting rails.

a large tank of stripper, removed, scrubbed, and rinsed off with lacquer thinner or water.

Hot dipping really raises the wood grain and discolors the wood. I wouldn't recommend it for your sashes or much else. There is also the real possibility of cracking the glass, against which the tank operator won't offer any guarantees. Cold dipping is more benign, but costly. If you're considering either type of dipping, have a sample done first so you know what you're getting into.

Scraping

Scrapers, if kept very sharp, can cut through many layers of paint, but the process is haphazard. Dependence solely on scrapers usually results in gouging the wood. If the paint is really flaky and loose, you'll have a better degree of success. Also, if the paint was applied over varnish it can scrape off more easily, "easily" being a relative term here. Scraping does produce paint dust, although nowhere near as much as sanding produces. It's hard work, but if you can isolate the debris and use a good scraper, this approach might be the right one for you.

Despite scraping's drawbacks, I recommend Red Devil's (www.reddevil.com) carbide paint scraper. It runs under $20 and it does wonders, especially on varnish and paint over varnish; it is less successful on paint over paint. Unlike most paint scrapers, this one offers both a high degree of control when cutting through finishes and a long-lasting carbide blade. It isn't commonly available and will probably have to be ordered from your Red Devil dealer or online. Sweden's Sandvik scrapers are also terrific. You can get by with less expensive scrapers, but they're not as easily controlled and the blades lose their edge much faster than carbide blades. Warner Tools (www.warnertool.com) makes a complete line of carbide and standard scrapers and putty knives.

Some scrapers, such as those made by Bahco, a division of Sandvik, accept various blades shaped for moldings and intricate woodwork. Warner also makes a molding scraper. Scrapers are available with straight blades measuring from one inch to five inches. After scraping, you should do some sanding of the scraped area to smooth it out. Keep a HEPA vacuum running to clean up the paint chips and dust as you work. Any gouges—there'll be some, there always are—can be filled with Spackle, wood dough, or automotive body filler.

Sanding

The advantage of sanding is that you have some control over how much paint is removed. You may only need to spot-sand rough areas, whereas with heat or chemicals you have less control over the degree of removal. I like sanding for removing paint and smoothing out old wood, but you run into all kinds of problems with controlling lead-based paint dust. For the most part, it's prohibited unless the sanders have HEPA vacuum attachments that capture airborne lead dust.

When sanding, you have a few options:

· Disc sanders, which have a revolving disk (5″ or 7″ commonly) that accepts a variety of sandpaper grits, from fine to coarse.

· Random-orbit sanders.

· Finish sanders, also called palm sanders or speed-bloc sanders.

· Belt sanders.

So many choices, so much dust. To get a look at and feel for all types of sanders, take a stroll through the power tool section at any home improvement or tool store.

Disc Sanders

A disc sander has a rotating disc that moves in one direction. This tool can be either a single speed (really fast) or variable speed so you can adjust the speed and the cutting power to the material you're sanding. Variable speed disc sanders are also used as polishers. Electric drills accept disc sanding attachments, but they don't work as well as real disc sanders.

Disc sanders cut fast and deep if you're not careful and throw dust everywhere with three exceptions: Fein, Festool, and a modified Makita disc sander from American International Tool Industries, Inc. (see Dust-Friendly Sanders below). The circular motion of the disc leaves disc marks on the sanded surface that can be removed with finer sanding paper.

Random-Orbit Sanders

With a random-orbit sander, the round pad moves in an oval-shaped loop at the same time it spins, allowing for a gentler more controlled sanding with fewer swirl marks. These sanders are normally variable-speed and allow for some dust collection. Both the sanding discs and the pad to which the disc is attached have holes for removing sanding dust to a small dust collector (or you can attach a vacuum cleaner). Random-orbit sanders are not thorough dust collectors, even with a vacuum attached, so don't figure these as a solution to airborne lead-based paint dust. They are handy sanders, though, especially for finish work.

Finish Sanders

A finish sander is often called a palm sander because the small ones, which take either special round sandpaper or one-quarter sheet of full-size sandpaper, fit under the palm of your hand. A larger version takes one-half a sheet of sandpaper. These sanders cut fast, but not as fast as random-orbit sanders. Some have small dust-collection bags, but they don't meet any kind of lead abatement standards.

Belt Sanders

Belt sanders are two-handed tools. They come in different sizes requiring corresponding sanding belts that run between the sander's front and rear rollers. 3″ x 21″ is a common size and handles well. Smaller sanders, such as the Bosch 1278VSK Compact Belt Sander Kit, come with narrower belts under two inches wide, but the belts are an uncommon size and not always readily available. A 3″ x 24″ or 4″ x 24″ sander is heavier to handle and probably more heft and power than you need for sanding window sashes. Belt sanders almost always come with dust bags to catch some of the larger particles, but you'll still have plenty of other dust and grit floating around.

A belt sander does not work as fast as a disc sander, but with a heavy grit paper it will cut fast enough and offers precise sanding, especially on flat, straight sections of wood. Also, there's less chance of digging into and gouging the wood when using a belt sander as opposed to a disc sander, although you can leave a depression if you let the tool run too long in one place.

Dust-Friendly Sanders

Most dust-collector bags and compartments that come with power sanders miss a reasonable amount of dust, even with vacuum cleaners attached. They certainly won't pass any lead abatement standards, but there is hope.

American-International Tool Ind. Inc. (1116-B Park Ave., Cranston, Rhode Island, 02910, 401-942-7855) offers a S344 Sander Vac 5″ disc sander ($259 current price) with dust collector, which, according to their literature, meets Massachusetts lead abatement standards. The collector consists of a circular, transparent plastic shroud that attaches to the sander around the disc. The outer edge of the shroud has a short continuous brush attached to it that bends when pressed against the surface being sanded. The shroud catches the dust, preventing it from blowing off, and allows it to be removed through a hole to which you attach the hose of a vacuum cleaner. This system works, but has a couple of drawbacks:

· The dust collection is more effective only if the entire area of the disc is engaged or sanding an area larger than itself.

· When sanding a sash rail, you would have to place a board next to it so the disc and its shroud never have open space under them for the dust to escape. This is haphazard at best and allows dust to escape.

Better systems, but more expensive, are offered by Fein Power Tools, Inc. (800-441-9878 or www.feinus.com for local dealers) and Festool (888-337-8600 or www.festool-usa.com), both German companies which are not commonly known in America. Fein offers an MSF-636 Six-Inch Random Orbit Sander combined with their 9-55-13 Turbo II Dust-Free (HEPA) Vacuum claiming up to 98 percent dust-collection capability. Boat repair yards in the Seattle area and elsewhere swear by these tools when sanding down fiberglass and wood boat hulls because they do such a terrific job of dust collection, a critical factor for EPA compliance. Online comments from www.oldhouseweb.com (www.oldhouseweb.com/ourStore/tools-228318B0000223PI.shtml) are very favorable except for a lack of instructional material and a specialized vacuum connection available only from Fein (it's inexpensive, about $3). The Fein MSF-636-I Kit 6″ Random Orbit Sander currently lists for over $700, but their sales rep assures me the "real world" price is just over

$500. Figure that one out. An 8″ sander is also available from Fein as well as straight rotary models in the same sizes. Fein dust extractor vacuums with available HEPA filters can also be purchased or you can attach other makes of vacuum cleaners to Fein tools (be sure to buy the adaptor from Fein to connect to a different size vacuum hose).

Festool sells competing sanders, but offers one specifically for stripping down paint: the RAS 115 E Rotary Sander, listing for $310. This is a small sander with a 4½″ pad and weighs only five pounds. It has a rear dust-extraction port that connects to a vacuum hose and a dust extraction hood to catch any dust that might escape the vacuum. Festool also makes vacuum cleaners and expects to have a HEPA option early in 2005. Each company also sells sanding discs, whose hole configuration (the dust is sucked through the holes in the paper and in the pad) are not that easy to find, although 3M makes similar discs.

Both Fein and Festool are more expensive than your standard sanders, but offer dust extraction that neither their Japanese nor American competitors can match. If you decide to buy either company's sanders, but not their vacuum systems, be sure to compare the vacuum you do purchase—it should be a HEPA model—for power and suction capacity, even hose size. All these criteria affect performance. One advantage to sanders with dust extraction is the sanding discs last longer because there is less sanded material to clog them.

Sandpaper

Sandpaper consists of a paper or cloth backing, adhesive, and abrasive particles that cut through wood and old finishes. There is cheap sandpaper and there is better sandpaper; better will last longer and is worth the extra cost. Garnet is a cheaper paper that's appropriate for a final finish, not for cutting through paint, old varnish, or rough wood. Aluminum oxide paper is much tougher, lasts longer, cuts through anything, and can be used for deep cutting as well as finish sanding.

Sandpaper is identified by number (36, 40, 50, 60, etc.) and that number refers to the grit of the sandpaper. An 80-grit paper, for instance, has 80 abrasive particles—aluminum oxide, silicon carbide, or other—per square inch of paper. And, no, I don't know who counts this stuff. The higher the number, the smaller the particles, the finer the paper, and the smoother the finish it will produce. For windows, I use 50- or 60-grit on stripped or scraped wood to smooth it down, eliminate splinters, and remove any remaining primer or varnish. After that, 100-grit is fine for the final smoothing, although you might want to go further (120- or 150-grit, for instance) on the interior side. Coarse paper will also remove paint on its own, but this causes too much dust dispersal unless you're using a sander with dust extraction.

Hardware stores will often carry both types of paper. Paint stores always have aluminum oxide, especially the 3M brand, which is sold just about everywhere. Sandpaper is sold by the sheet, by small packet (five sheets or so), and by the sleeve (50 or 100 sheets). Consider buying your sandpaper by the sleeve if you have a lot of windows to do or future projects (there are always future projects on an old house). Sleeve prices are discounted versus buying individual sheets.

A sheet of sandpaper can be cut or torn into four smaller sheets for a palm or finish sander. You can figure one of these smaller sheets per two sashes depending on how much old finish remains. If all the old finish gets removed before sanding, a single smaller piece of 50-grit paper will last for several sashes. Change the paper when it gets too clogged, deteriorated, or torn to do any further sanding.

Sanding belts are also sold by their grit and by dimension (3″ x 21″, 3″ x 24″, etc.) so be sure to buy the correct size for your sander. If you have a lot of belt sanding in your future, buy your belts by the box (ten to a box). Stores that sell power tools as well as tool rental businesses should have sanding belts both individually and by the box. The same is true with sanding discs and usually sheets of sandpaper.

Be sure to buy the correct type of sanding disc for your sander! Most disc sanders secure the sanding disc with a center locking nut while many random orbit sanders use a hook and loop system (Velcro) and thus special adhesive sanding discs. Buy plenty of paper, regardless of what type of sander you're using. You can return the unused paper or keep it for another project. It beats running out to the hardware store in the middle of your restoration work.

Steam Cabinets

If you have a lot of windows to restore and you like building things, a portable steam cabinet might be for you. Olde Window Restorers, of Weare, New Hampshire (I never heard of Weare either, but it is known for the famous Pine Tree Riot of 1772, which no doubt rings a bell.) sells a set of plans for constructing your very own steam cabinet. Steamers are not the latest thing, but late enough when it comes to sash stripping. The idea is to place several sashes inside an enclosed cabinet pumped full of steam, slowly cooking the paint and the glazing compound until it softens for easy removal. Sounds great, but having experienced a manufactured unit first hand, it's not perfect. For one thing, if you cook glass panes long enough, some will crack. You never know which ones will withstand the heat intact.

After removing the steamed sash from the steam cabinet, the putty is so soft it does scrape off easily as does the paint, but as the sash cools, the paint and putty harden up again and it's goodbye easy street. That said, this is a non-toxic process, it works reasonably well once you adjust the timing for your windows, and the plans are inexpensive—about $20 as of this printing—the materials are extra, including the Portable Steam Paint and Putty Stripper, the steam unit, also conveniently sold by Olde Window Restorers for just over $300, including shipping. I haven't used this equipment nor built one of these steam cabinets. I suggest you watch the videos available on Olde Window's Web site and judge for yourself. The cabinet seemed to make sense, but using the portable unit on its own did not. For further information, go to the company's Web site at www.oldewindowrestorer.com or contact Dave Bowers, PO Box 542, Weare, New Hampshire 03281, telephone (603) 529-0261.

Disposing of Debris

Your state and local regulations will determine how you should dispose of any lead-based paint debris, including sections of woodwork. An EPA-proposed ruling allows for homeowner- and even contractor-generated residential lead debris to be disposed of with any residential trash. The idea behind this ruling was to make lead abatement more affordable, but it upset any number of people opposed to such casual disposal. In some states, you can legally place this debris in with your normal trash and in others you cannot. Contact your trash hauling service for the lowdown. They should know the regulations and will give you a fast answer, which can be better than wading through the sticky waters of the state environmental affairs offices.

Once you have addressed the paint and varnish removal issues, there are other repair and restoration issues to consider, including glass replacement, wood repair, painting, and refinishing. With the sash removed, it's an ideal time to repaint and even clean the glass.

BROKEN GLASS AND LOOSE GLAZING

I try not to replace glass myself. Sometimes I crack it or mismeasure and get mad at the world and regret not going into Microsoft Windows instead of real windows (even if the latter have fewer bugs). That's why there are glaziers in the world and who am I to upset this natural balance and order? You have four options for replacing broken glass:

- Do it all yourself.

- Call a glazier to do the work on-site.

- Take the sashes in to a glazier or a hardware store which does glass replacement.

- Remove all the broken glass and old putty yourself and then call a glazier or take the sashes out for glass installation.

 If you are required to treat lead-based paint debris as toxic waste and take it to a special facility, consider saving your debris in a sealed 5-gallon bucket until your window repairs and any additional future restoration work is finished. There's no point in making multiple trips for disposal.

Keep in mind that glazing, like leaded paint, can be a source of hazards, including lead and a minor amount of asbestos which was used as a binder in some products. Your method of removal will determine your degree of exposure. Given the Draconian measures regarding asbestos, I'm surprised window glazing has gotten so little attention.

When removing broken or cracked glass with the sash removed:

- Place the sash on either a flat workbench or brace it in an upright, vertical position.

- Wear eye protection and work gloves.

- If the glass is badly cracked or loose but cannot be pulled out, tape the cracks so the glass won't fall out as you remove the putty.

- As much fun as it might be to take a hammer to the glass and break it all out, leaving a jagged edge of glass under the putty, don't do it. It just makes your job harder. It's easier to remove large pieces of glass then chipping out a million little bits of glass.

- The glass is held in with glazing points, small, flat, sharp triangular or diamond-shaped fasteners between the glass and the putty. These will have to be pried out before the glass can be removed.

- To remove large pieces of glass after the putty and points have been removed, turn the sash over and insert a putty knife between the glass and the sash, gradually prying the glass out.

NOTE: If you're removing the glass from the lower sash of a double-hung window, be sure to remove all the putty and glass bits from the dado or kerf (also called a rabbet) in the upper meeting rail (also called the check rail). The glass slides inside this rail as opposed to sitting flat like it does on the other three sides of the sash, although on some older windows and some less expensive ones this rail resembles the other three and does not have a rabbet.

- Once the glass is removed, place it in a trashcan or box and then break it into small pieces. Window glass cannot be recycled and must be treated as trash.

After breaking the glass into small pieces, place the debris in some kind of sealed throwaway container.

With the glass out, you'll need to remove any remaining putty, including the bedding, a thin layer of glazing putty the glass is set in and sits on, before installing the new glass. Sand the cleaned-out areas with a folded piece of heavy grit sandpaper until the wood is smooth. Be sure to sand down the rabbet in the check rail or upper rail of the lower sash as well.

Replacing the Glass Yourself

Well, it will be a learning experience. ALL the old putty has to be removed and you have a choice of removal methods:

- Chopping it out with a hackout tool, stiff putty knife, or chisel and hammer
- Heat gun or propane torch and a putty knife
- Grinding wheel on a drill
- Prazi Putty Chaser

Chiseling out old putty with a hackout tool or chisel is the toughest way to remove old putty. Heat is the easiest, but raises lead-based paint issues. Grinding it out or using the Prazi Putty Chaser produces a nice, clean result at the expense of a dusty mess in your work area. There are no neat tricks here although you might feel like making your windows disappear by this point.

Hackout Tools, Chisels, and Stiff Putty Knives

A hackout tool, which you'll only find from a supplier of glazing tools (e.g.,www.crlaurence.com/Productpages/showline.asp?GroupID=282), resembles a stiff blade putty knife but the cutting edge is on the side rather than at the tip. This allows you to whack at the blunt side of the blade to loosen the old putty, offering control and speed. Homeowners, painters, and even some restorers who only occasionally do glass repair never see these tools, but they're quite handy; you can make your own by grinding down the side of an old chisel. Regardless of what tool you use for hacking out old putty:

- Unless it's very weathered, old putty is often rock-hard and resistant to hacking.

- Chip away carefully so you don't splinter the wood.

- Wear a dust mask and be aware the putty can contain trace amounts of asbestos as well as be covered with lead-based paint.

- After removing all the outer putty and the glass, there will often be additional putty under the glass (the bedding) that will have to be removed.

Chipping away at tough putty is frustrating and time consuming. For a professional glazier, this accounts for much of the labor cost when replacing glass. Keeping the putty wet with a spray bottle of water while you're working will decrease any airborne dust.

NOTE: Want to try a power approach to hacking? Look at the Fein MultiMaster with a saw blade attachment. Think of it as an electric pizza slicer that chops through old putty. The Multi-Master also takes sandpaper, polishing, scraper, and grout blade attachments for a host of other fun jobs around the house. The MultiMaster VS XL Kit with all the above-mentioned goodies currently lists for $399 at www.feinus.com.

Heat Gun and Propane Torch

Now we're talking. Take a propane torch—it's faster than a heat gun—to old putty and it softens up remarkably. Place the tip of the torch or gun right up to the putty and hold it until the putty softens; then push the putty off with a stiff putty knife with the knife resting against the glass. It will come off clean and with little if any damage to the wood, although you will char the wood some and bubble the edge of the paint. However, it will heat any lead-based paint on the putty to an unacceptably high temperature if you're concerned about lead vaporization (although this is a small amount of paint). For that reason, you might be more comfortable with a heat gun's lower temperature. The heat gun is definitely a better choice if you are removing putty from an installed window or one that you cannot remove.

The heat will release nasty fumes from the burning paint and putty so wear a respirator with HEPA filters and do the work outdoors or in an open garage. Replace the glass after you do any paint removal on the rest of the sash. You don't want to install new glass and fresh putty only to mess them up while stripping the rest of the sash. You can go ahead and prime and apply a first coat of paint to the sash as well, although you'll have to prime and paint the glazing, too.

Grinding Wheel

Hardware stores sell a variety of small grinding wheels that attach to electric drills. These will grind out hard putty and even grind down the glazing points, but you'll have a fine white dust everywhere as the putty pulverizes. I can't really recommend it even though it's wonderfully convenient. If dust isn't an issue for you and you don't like heat or hacking methods, this will remove most of the putty (it can't get into the corners).

Prazi Putty Chaser

Another drill attachment, the Prazi Putty Chaser (www.praziusa.com/puttychaser.html) is a steel shaft with a carbide cutter at the tip. The cutter rotates and cuts through the putty. You control its movement by a guide sleeve attached to the cutter. Dust is still a problem and the price ($20 give or take) is more than a grinding wheel attachment. Given its smaller size, some will find the Putty Chaser more awkward to control.

Next Steps . . . Removing the Glass

With the putty removed, take out the small glazing points which secure the glass to the sash. They can be pried up with a putty knife or a screwdriver or pulled out with a pair of pliers. Your glass might lift out easily in one or several pieces depending on its size. If not, flip the sash over and insert a putty knife between the edge of the glass and the sash and force the glass outward. Remember that the upper rail of a lower sash normally does not have glazing points holding in the glass. Rather, the glass sits inside a rabbet or dado and will have to be pulled out after the other three sides of the glass are free.

A lot of older glass installations involved bedding the glass in a small amount of glazing compound. You'll find this under the glass after it's removed. This bedding will have to be completely cleaned out before installing new glass. Use heat or a sharp paint scraper to do the job and then sand down the wood until all residue of the bedding is gone. Take your time with the scraping; it's easy for the tool to slip and gouge the wood.

Measuring for New Glass

Correctly measuring a sash for glass replacement has sent many an innocent homeowner down the road to frustration (and back to the hardware store). Sometimes you measure correctly, but the sash is not square and the new glass, which is very square, won't fit. Other times the check rail isn't figured in or the exact measurement of the sash is used instead of cutting it back some to allow the glass to set into place.

You can measure from the inside or the outside of the sash:

· On the outside, measure from the cleaned-out bottom edge (also a type of rabbet) to the cleaned-out top edge/rabbet. If it's a lower sash with a rabbet at the top rail (most common), measure up to the rabbet itself and add a quarter of an inch. I'm hard-pressed to state a universal figure here since rabbets can vary. You can confirm the measurement, however, by turning to the inside of the sash. Next, measure the width between the cleaned-out right and left stile rabbets.

· On the inside, you measure from the beginning of the top ogee detail at the top rail, where the detail begins and meets the flat area of the rail, to the corresponding point on the bottom rail. Do the same with the stiles.

Want to take the easy way out? Take your sash to the hardware or home improvement store and let them measure it. They'll then fit the new glass into the sash which makes a dandy carrying case until you get home and bed and glaze it (unless you have the store do it). With large panes of glass, this can be a little awkward as you still have to slip the glass out again in order to bed it so you might want to carry these separate from the sash until you're ready to install.

Measuring glass between the stiles (subtract $1/8$" from this measurement).

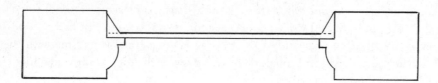

Measuring glass between the top rail/lower sash—the dotted lines indicate the rabbet/ check rail—and the lower rail/lower sash (use this measurement and then subtract $1/8$").

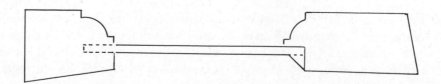

NOTE: What's an ogee? It's the interior curved, often S-shaped, wood detail, routed into the rails and stiles, at the edge of the glass.

One edge of the ogee meets the glass and the other meets the flat sections of the stiles and rails. The glass rests against the exterior side of the ogee.

· Subtract ⅛" from your height and width measurements. Why? Because the glass won't fit if you measure exactly; you need some room for negotiation here. Give the final measurement to whoever is cutting the glass.

Q Hey, Mr. Window, I measured my glass and thought I had it right, but forgot to subtract an eighth of an inch and now it won't fit. Besides blaming my parents for my math anxiety and attention deficit disorder, what can I do?

A *I say do the mature thing and blame the hardware store for wrongful cutting, but they probably have it all on video as part of their Homeland Security measures, so that won't fly. You could return the glass and ask to have the eighth of an inch cut off, not the easiest task for a hardware clerk who doesn't cut glass all day, but only occasionally. Your other choice is to take a very sharp scraper and shave the rabbet down until the opening is large enough to accommodate the glass. This is perfectly legitimate and beats a second trip back to the hardware store unless it's close by or your measurement is way off.*

Buying the Glass

Glass is sold in various thicknesses and priced by the square foot. Single-strength glass (SS) is approximately ³⁄₃₂" thick; double-strength (DS) glass is ⅛" thick. A lot of older residential glass was single-strength, but broken panes are typically replaced with DS glass. Often times the added weight of DS glass makes no difference at all, particularly with multi-lite sash. Sash weights don't have to weigh exactly as much as the sash they support to still operate properly. When the increased weight of the glass does affect the sash—it tends to drop down and won't stay up—some minor adjustments to the stops or adding weather stripping usually takes care of the problem.

In a few elegant homes and somewhat more often in commercial buildings ¼" thick glass, sometimes referred to as plate glass, was used. This stuff is heavy! You can't get away with DS glass here, you need to replace with ¼" again or the sash won't be heavy enough for the weights. Uncertain about your glass thickness? Take a small piece of the glass to be replaced to your glass supplier so you'll be sure to purchase the right thickness.

Glass can be purchased from a glass company or a hardware store, the latter often being the more expensive of the two sources. When you transport your glass, stand it on edge, not lying flat, unless you like buying more glass after your first batch has cracked.

Installing the Glass

Some glaziers dry-set their glass in old sashes, that is, they don't bed it in either glazing compound or latex caulk. I think bedding is a good idea, as you can't always expect a new pane of glass to sit entirely flat in an old sash.

Another good idea is to brush either oil-based primer or plain linseed oil (available at paint stores) on the rabbets before applying any glazing compound to prevent the glazing from shrinking. I've never seen a glazier do this, but it's understandable that a glazier can't take the time on a job for this added step due to the oil's drying requirements. For the most part, modern glazing compound performs well without sealing the wood first, but I would still seal if time permits.

Speaking of glazing compound, unless you have a brand you prefer working with, oil-based DAP '33' is available everywhere and always does the job. It's manufactured in white and in gray, although the gray isn't as readily available as the white.

WARNING! Some products advertised as glazing are more like Spackle and terrible to work with. DAP '33' always works if you have any doubts about buying another product.

NOTE: If you're going to sand or otherwise remove the exterior paint, do so before replacing glass or glazing. Otherwise, the new glazing gets full of dust and dirt from your work and it's just generally messy looking.

To install new glass:

- Brush on a coat of linseed oil or oil-based primer onto the rabbets all around the sash. A fast-drying (under an hour) oil-based primer allows you to install the glass the same day. Sealing the wood first prevents it from absorbing any oils from the new glazing which can result in the glazing shrinking and pulling away from the sash. Allow your chosen sealer to dry according to the directions on its container. Again, this isn't a critical step, but there's no harm in doing it and if the wood is bone-dry, it can be helpful.

- If you buy new oil-based glazing compound, have it put in the paint can shaker at the hardware, paint, or home improvement store for a thorough mixing. Ignore the strange looks from the sales clerks. Otherwise, remove the contents from the can and completely knead the glazing compound until it's soft and pliable. In cold weather, placing the can in hot water or near a heater will also soften it and keep it pliable.

- Apply either a thin ribbon of glazing compound or a line of latex caulk to the rabbets. Lay the material down very flat with a glazing knife or putty knife (glazing knife is easier). At the meeting rail rabbet, pack some glazing compound in with a putty knife or glazing knife.

- If you bed the glass in glazing, it has to be even bedding. Otherwise, the glass won't sit flat when you press it against the bedding and it can crack.

- Carefully pick up the glass and lay it on the bedding. In a lower sash, insert the glass into the upper rabbet first. Don't drop the glass onto the bedding, but place a hand underneath and slowly lower it down.

- Press the glass into the bedding, but don't force it; just push enough until it stops moving further. If your bedding is even, but the glass won't sit flat, then the rabbets themselves aren't quite flat. This is to be expected after hacking and scraping out old putty. Don't worry about it; the bedding will make up the gaps. Any remaining gaps can be filled by pressing more glazing compound/caulk between the glass and the sash later after the glass has been secured.

· With the glass flat and resting on the lower rail, install the glazing points. Unless you're doing a lot of glass—in which case it could be worth investing in a point setter (around $80), a stapler-like gun for setting points— you'll be using some kind of push-in point. The triangular and diamond-shaped points can be pushed in by hand instead of with a point setter, but I'm not a big fan of this because it's easy to put pressure on the glass and crack it. Sometimes (too many times), the push-in type are longer than the original points and stick out beyond the glazing, but you'll have to live with it. With a screwdriver or stiff putty knife, push the points in slowly without forcing them against the glass, but be sure they secure the glass. For small panes, twelve or fourteen inches per

If you want to keep your hands clean when applying glazing compound, wear some latex gloves. Glazing is an oily material and takes some time to wash out. Another trick is to wipe your hands off with a dry towel and work out most of the gunk before washing them. I wouldn't plan on keeping the towel, though, so use a rag.

Triangle, diamond, and push-in glazing points.

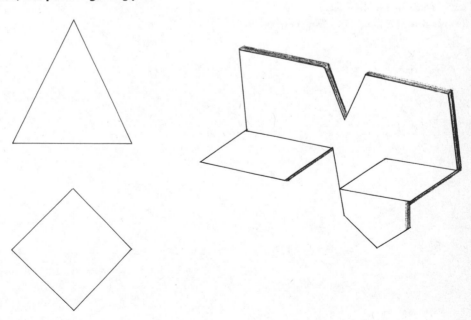

97

side, install two points per side, roughly two inches from the corners. With larger pieces of glass, install a point every eight inches or so. Points are not installed in the upper rabbet of a lower sash if it's a closed rabbet or dado, which is almost always the case in homes built in the twentieth century. Older homes sometimes had an open rabbet similar to the other three sides of the sash. These rabbets would receive glazing points.

· When replacing a single, smaller pane of glass in a sash with multiple panes, watch that the point you're using isn't so long as to go all the way through the muntin. It's usually not an issue, but watch for it anyway.

· After the points have been set, take a handful of glazing compound and knead it until it's soft. Some repair books say to roll it into

snakes to lay against the glass and that's fine, too. Using the palm of your hand or your thumb, force the glazing around the edge of the glass; don't worry about applying excess material, because it will be trimmed off. Putty doesn't hold the glass in (the points do that), but rather seals it to the weather. Trimming it to a nice straight line doesn't affect its performance, but leaves it better looking.

· Take the end of your glazing or putty knife and press the putty in further, working your way around the sash. Next, hold the end of the knife at a 45-degree angle with the handle parallel to the line of putty. Starting in a corner, run it down each line, beveling the putty. The putty might pull out in which case force it back in and run the knife again. You want to form a 3-D triangle of putty.

Glazing knife, unfinished glazing compound, and finished glazing compound.

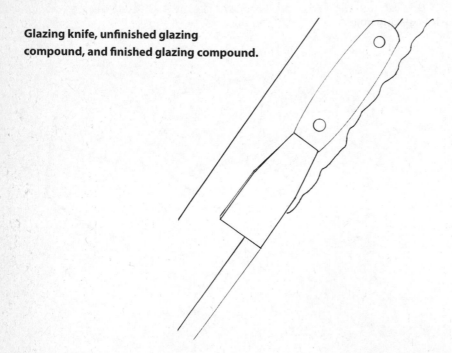

· Remove the excess putty you've knocked off and run the knife again, holding the bottom corner of the tip—the point that's against the glass—closer to the edge of the wood so when you run the knife down you'll leave less putty behind. When you get to the corners, tuck the end of the knife in towards the corner and lift the knife up.

· Keep the blade of your glazing knife clean and don't use it for Spackle or Bondo or plaster work. If any material dries on the blade, scrape it off or run it against a bench grinder's wire wheel. You can lightly sand it with 100-grit sandpaper as well, but avoid rounding off the corners. A clean knife is less likely to pull the putty off when you're smoothing it out.

· To check that you're getting a good, straight line of putty, look through the sash from the inside of it. Do you see the edge of the putty sticking out onto the glass? If you do, the line of putty is too wide and you need to cut it back. The idea is to never see the putty when you're looking out the window. Typically, as painters paint and patch up putty over the years, it all spreads further and further onto the glass, even though it shouldn't. You're starting fresh so keep the putty's profile narrow as it should be.

· Once you've trimmed down the profile, trim it down a bit further. Why? When the putty gets painted, the paint should also coat the very edge of the putty right onto the glass (a sixteenth of an inch or so), sealing it and preventing water from getting underneath and loosening it.

Q Uh, say Mr. Window, remember how I asked what to do when I brought home a piece of glass that was too big? Well, heh, heh, seems like I also ordered a piece for another window and it's too short. What now?

A *First, find someone else to do your measuring; you'll be happier. As long as the glass will seal to the upper rail, meaning it isn't so short that after it's installed there's a gap between it and the top of the sash, you can nail in some small wood blocks or an entire strip of wood at the bottom rabbet, set the glass down, and proceed with a normal installation. You can also use closed-cell (stiff) foam weather stripping instead of wood blocks. Too short even with the blocks? Well . . . not that Mr. Window would ever consider this (this disclaimer sounds vaguely familiar), you could raise up the bottom end of the glass on blocks or a wood strip and at the top, where it presumably isn't setting into the upper rail, run a thick line of caulk (use something with some heft, such as a urethane caulk, which is sticky to apply), and seal up the gap. Tape the inside of the top edge of the glass with electrical tape so the caulking doesn't run over to the ogee. After the caulking has set, remove the tape (electrical tape should pull away more easily than masking tape). After it's dried, check that the seal is complete by looking at the caulk for signs of daylight showing through.*

NOTE: If raising the glass on wood blocks or foam weather stripping puts the edge of the glass out of the reach of your glazing points, you can always secure the glass with a wood strip or wood blocks and glazing compound. It won't be the most even-looking line of glazing, but it will work.

Will it leak? Not as long as the caulk remains intact and given all the exotic caulks you can buy now, the seal will last for years and years. The strip of caulk will be noticeable from the inside, but you'll ignore it after awhile.

You're not creating another Sistine Chapel here; you're not even creating the Little Chapel in the Pines. You are trying to repair your windows, keep your costs down, and get acceptable results (and sometimes impressive results). Filling in a gap between the glass and the sash with a line of caulk will do the job and keep you to a budget. Think of it as creative window restoration.

Different brands of glazing have different curing times. If uncertain, allow at least a week before painting the glazing. A common error is to leave glazing compound unpainted after replacing glass. Unpainted glazing will shrink and fall out and lose its effectiveness as a seal. Then, you get to repeat this process all over again. You can paint new glazing compound the same day, but this isn't the best approach because it will take much longer to dry and harden. To paint glazing the same day as you apply it:

· You must use an oil-based primer!! This is really important. If you apply latex products over fresh glazing, the solvents from the glazing will try to pass through the latex film and cause both it and the glazing to crack. Once this happens, the glazing will have to be removed and new glazing applied again. Oil-based products will form a film that does not allow the drying solvents from the glazing to escape in such a way as to cause any cracks in the glazing. This is true with fast drying oil primers as well. The putty will remain soft for a longer time than if it was allowed to cure, but I've never found this to be detrimental. Sometimes you don't have

any choice so go ahead and use an oil primer and don't worry about it.

· After the primer has dried, coat with your choice of exterior paint.

NOTE: When you use glazing compound, you end up with oily fingerprints and smudges all around the glass. Don't try to wash them off without priming the glazing first! Water can get behind the glazing and loosen it or otherwise affect the seal. If the messy glass really bothers you, carefully wipe off the smears with a dry rag or with one dipped in a little paint thinner, avoiding touching the new glazing until the glazing has been sealed.

Limits of Glazing Compound

Glazing likes warm weather and although application below 40 degrees can be done, DAP says don't do it. Well, if it's December in Montana and you've decided to spend your holiday vacation repairing windows, you'll be lucky if it's 40 degrees in your kitchen. Also, DAP nixes the use of glazing compound on sashes longer than 48 inches. Residential windows this size in older homes are unusual and their glass is traditionally held in with wood stops that are often deteriorated, but salvageable. In fact, when you have wood stops that are intact, but worn, you can force glazing compound or latex caulk between the stop and the glass to fill in any gaps and seal the glass to the weather. Knife or smooth off the glazing the same way you would for sashes without wood stops. Smear either material into any cracks or pits in the wood and wipe them off with a rag. If the stop is too deteriorated to save, install a new one (look in the molding section of your lumber store for a similar type of molding) using galvanized finish nails and caulk the edge of the stop that rests against the glass.

The main drawbacks to do-it-yourself replacement are the glass cracking as you install or being the wrong size because your measurement was too optimistic and now the glass won't fit your slightly out-of-square sash. That's why I like glaziers. You, on the other hand, might find glass replacement is your forte and excel at it in which case you should ignore my advocacy for glaziers.

On-Site Glaziers

Not cheap! Their rates are likely to start at $35–40 per hour on up depending on where you live, plus the cost of materials. Any work done from a ladder, that is, the sash is not removed and the glazier is climbing around your house, will be the most expensive as it is the most time consuming. Still, the work is guaranteed and any glass breakage is the glazier's problem. Glaziers do not prime or paint new glazing compound (OK, I've never seen a glazier pick up a paintbrush, but I never thought I'd see people driving around in military vehicles disguised as family cars, either).

Taking the Sash to a Glazier or Hardware Store

The shop rate can be cheaper than the on-site fees (no travel or service charge, for instance). Hardware stores are convenient, but the cost depends on who's doing the work and if they're charging by the hour (some individuals may be slower than others). Some shops bill out at a fixed charge per square foot of glass replaced. A glass shop may be a faster and less expensive option for the glass than a hardware store.

Hacking Out the Old Putty Yourself and Having Others Install the Glass

This is the best of all worlds if you have budget considerations, but don't want to mess with installing the glass. Glaziers aren't fond of chiseling out old putty, even if they use power tools to do it. Many younger glaziers work primarily on new windows which use special caulking and metal stops to secure the glass and have little experience with older windows. Even with an experienced worker, the bulk of the labor fee comes from cleaning out the old glass and putty. Do the grunt work and provide the glazier with clean sashes ready for glass and you'll keep your cost down and leave the more fragile work to others. You may even want to do your own finish glazing and just have the glazier cut and install the glass with points. This is also a cost saver.

Missing or Loose Glazing

Your glass can be intact without cracks or chips, but when the exterior paint is in poor condition, the glazing usually needs some work as well, including selective removal. When partially removing old glazing:

· You'll need a hackout tool, chisel, or stiff putty knife; using heat can crack the glass.

· Take it easy. If the glazing is cracked yet tight, leave it. Otherwise, you're likely to crack the glass and then you'll get to remove all of the glazing.

· Reglaze with new putty and rub glazing into any cracks and gaps of the old but intact glazing. Seal the new glazing with oil primer and follow with paint.

Some restoration architects now call for all the old glazing to be removed from a sash if one or two cracks appear in any section of glazing. This is absurd and guarantees broken glass regardless of how carefully the glazing is removed. You can live with glazing cracks. When the glazing is tight and hard, just fill them along with any minor gaps near the glass and call it good.

STRUCTURAL REPAIRS

Wood windows are infinitely repairable. Entire sections can be replaced, filled with epoxy, braced, and tightened, extending the life of the window for years and years. Even the most deteriorated sash can be rebuilt, although it's a judgment call

as to the advisability of doing so in some cases. The following techniques will bring you windows that are intact, secure, and weather-tight.

Loose Corners

Older wood sashes are assembled with mortise and tenon joints at the corners and are held in place with two pins or thick nails per corner.

As the paint deteriorates, the pins become exposed to moisture and can rust and loosen. The bottom rails can even fall out. If the rails soak up enough water, they can rot away, especially at the corners. Don't worry, you can fix them—really.

NOTE: If the rail has dropped and the glass has been reglazed since the drop, you will not be able to push the rail all the way up into its correct position unless the old glass is moved up first. This

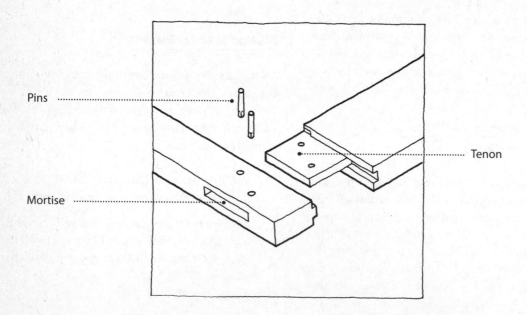

Pins

Tenon

Mortise

requires removing all or most of the glazing and, with the sash upside-down, gently pushing the glass back where it belongs. This can be a precarious job if the glass is well-sealed and there is the chance you'll break the glass (as the size of the glass increases, the better this chance). If it is a new piece of glass, installed to the new dimension of the dropped rail, you can't do anything unless you replace the glass with a smaller size.

Depending on the degree and cause of the damage, a loose sash corner can be repaired simply or it can require filling and reinforcement. These repairs, running from the simplest to the most elaborate, are the following:

· Installing corner irons (also called angle irons or corner braces).

· Reinforcing the corners with galvanized nails or deck screws.

· Removing deteriorated wood and replacing with epoxy and wood reinforcement.

Corner Irons

Installing a corner iron is the simplest repair for a loose sash corner. It's considered by some (all right, by many) to be the cheesiest repair as well because it's a quick fix that's very visible and doesn't always fully address the problem. Why bother with it?

· It's better than letting the sash continue to deteriorate and the corner irons will hold it together until a full future repair can be performed.

· You might be planning on replacing your windows in a few years and only want a temporary fix.

Galvanized corner iron.

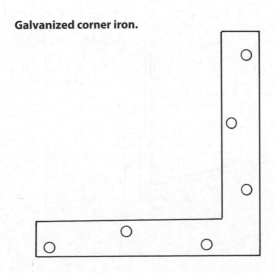

· If your windows are in bad shape and you can only do full repairs on some, this is a good way to stabilize the others until you get back to them.

· Some people are less interested in aesthetics and more interested in resolving the problem inexpensively. For an apartment building owner, for instance, looking at other maintenance problems, flat corner irons are a bargain and they do the job.

There are two types of corner irons, standard and flat. Flat irons are used for sash repairs as shown in the illustration.

Flat corner irons are typically installed on the outside of the sash and are visible even under paint, although I did run across one pair that had been mortised into the sash and covered over with wood filler, thus rendered invisible. Again, this is a fast fix and can be done on sashes while they're still hanging or with the sashes loose.

Corner irons are available at every hardware store in the universe. A three- or four-inch zinc-plated Stanley or other brand corner iron will do the job.

To install a flat corner iron:

· Using a paint scraper and wire brush, remove any loose glazing, splintered wood, and flaking paint from the affected corner. Allow a wet corner to dry out before continuing with the repair (you can speed up drying with a heat gun or hair dryer).

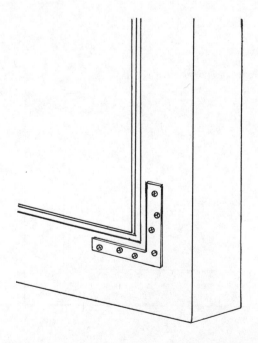

Corner iron installed.

NOTE: When the glass has dropped down along with the rail, it will have to be moved up to its correct position before installing the corner iron. If this is too much trouble or there's too great a chance the glass will break, you'll have to install the corner iron as is and fill any opening in the wood with appropriate filler.

- Push the rail and stile together. If you're working on an upper sash that's still installed, prop the bottom rail up with a piece of lumber wedged against the sill. Place a piece of cardboard or scrap carpet under the lumber to avoid scraping the sill. If the sash is loose and on a worktable, you can wrap some sash rope around the sash and twist it like tourniquet (see page 110) until the corner comes together.

- Prime any bare wood that will be under the corner iron.

- Poke around the corner with an awl or small screwdriver to check for rot or missing wood (you'll know when the tool passes through). Everything intact? Place the corner iron on the sash and mark the screw hole locations with a pencil. Remove the corner iron and pre-drill some pilot holes (small holes for inserting the screws, drilled to avoid splitting the wood). Return the corner iron and install (screws are included with the corner iron).

- Did you find soft, missing, or rotted wood (see page 107)? You can either do a full repair or a temporary repair (which can last a surprisingly long time). Since you're using corner irons, it's safe to assume you don't want to get into a full-blown restoration at this point (if ever), but you do need to address the deteriorated wood if for no other reason than to provide a stronger material to insert your

screws. The easiest approach is to gun in a big blob of filler like Liquid Nails Concrete Repair (www.liquidnails.com), which comes in a tube like caulk. Is this the intended use of Liquid Nails Concrete Repair? Of course not, but it will fill the void and provide some anchoring for the screws, although it never dries completely, remaining flexible indefinitely (flexible does not mean runny, it means rubbery). You could also stuff in some J-B Weld Marine Weld or Waterweld fillers (www.jbweld.net) or any of a number of quick-fix epoxy products available at your hardware store or home improvement center. These repairs will be functional and buy you plenty of time until you do a full repair. Keep them painted and they'll buy you years of time. However, you'll have to drill and dig them out later should you decide to do more work on the sash. Chances are, if you get used to looking at the corner irons, you'll leave the sash alone and go on to something else. It's amazing what a little stability and cosmetic fixes can do to the most ardent restoration mentality when other house projects call.

Nails and Deck Screws

If the sashes are removed and any rails are loose but the wood is undamaged, there is a very simple repair to tighten them up again. It isn't unusual to get some wobble in a lower corner. These corners are held together by pins and the taut fit of the mortise and tenon joint. After years of use, some wobble or movement isn't unexpected. Rather than driving more nails through the face of the sash, do this:

- Turn the sash on its side so you're looking at the end of the tenon.

- Drill two holes, at a diagonal, on both sides of the tenon.

- Then, either drive a 16-penny galvanized finish nail into each hole or use a deck screw (be sure to countersink the head).

NOTE: To countersink a screw after drilling a pilot hole, you can use a self-countersinking screw, a countersinking drill set, or take a drill bit whose diameter is larger than the head of the screw you're going to use and drill out the top of your pilot hole just enough that the screw head will drop into it.

- Repeat on the other side as shown in the diagram below.

This really tightens up the joint and the repair remains unseen. On the upper sash, there isn't much room for deck screws—the lower rail is small—so figure on using galvanized finish nails. If the joint has superficially weathered, scrape off the weathered wood and apply some waterproof automotive body filler or epoxy over it and sand flush when dry (see Fillers, page 107).

NOTE: Some really old sashes are held together in the corners with wood dowels or pegs instead of pins (nails). The dowels were either glued in or forced in for a tight fit. If you have dowels instead of pins and they appear to be loosening, you can drill them out and replace them with a slightly larger dowel secured with waterproof glue. Sometimes dowels loosen because the grain of the dowel is at a right angle to the grain of the surrounding wood and they move against each other. Dowels are sold packaged and precut or in three-foot lengths that you can cut to size.

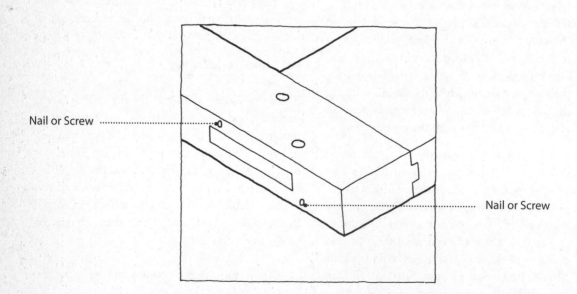

Nail or Screw ....

Nail or Screw

Rotted or Deteriorated Wood

Let's make a distinction between weathered wood and wood rot. If wood is kept sealed with paint or similar material and this seal is consistently maintained, then, in theory, the wood should never deteriorate due to moisture or weather problems. Why? Because Mr. Window says so, that's why. Aside from that, when wood "weathers," it absorbs moisture and expands; it then shrinks as it dries. As this process repeats, the wood begins to disassemble, in a sense; the surface gets rough or splintery, cracks develop, warping starts in, etc. Moisture penetrates wood if isn't kept sealed with some kind of coating. If the paint on a window is flaking or even non-existent, then the sashes will begin to weather and split and all those fun things. True rot is another issue.

Wood rot is caused by fungi, which are really itty-bitty organisms. They're even smaller than many celebrities' brains, which is difficult to believe. Fungi are everywhere and fungal wood rot organisms float around biding their time until they find:

· Wood fiber
· Moisture
· Limited air circulation

This triad is like hitting the biological jackpot for fungi. After moving in, they start munching on the wood and will continue to do so until the temperature or moisture level becomes unfavorable or they're destroyed with a fungicide. During your repairs, it's critical that you remove as much of the rotted wood as you can and kill the remaining fungi. Otherwise, spores will stay behind and can regenerate later.

How will you recognize rot? The wood will be soft, powdery, "punky," and easy to drive a sharp tool through. When a window rots, it's almost always one of the bottom rails and/or lower two inches or so of the stiles or it's the sill. These areas are the most likely to hold water once the paint deteriorates and an opening is generated in the wood. Rot is not as common as weathering, but can be repaired thanks to the wonderful world of chemistry.

Before going on to the repairs, we must (must!) discuss wood fillers as they play a prominent part in this work.

Fillers

Fillers include epoxies, wood dough, Spackle, patching plasters, caulking, fiberglass-reinforced polyester resin, and automotive body compound such as Bondo. Well, actually Bondo has become eponymous for automotive body filler like Kleenex has for tissue. Clearly, the Bondo people have no objection to this cultural identification at all.

Wood dough, Spackle, patching plasters and putty, and caulking are inappropriate for the repairs being discussed here. They are normally used for filling cracks, voids, and holes in wood and walls and not for structural repairs. Do they get used for structural repairs? Sure, all the time, and they often fall out when exposed to the weather, although caulking can hold its own against water and changes in temperature.

Q Hey, wait a minute Mr. Window. Earlier you said, and I quote, to "gun in a big blob of filler like Liquid Nails Concrete

Repair" if the wood was iffy and a corner iron had to be installed. What gives? Is this some kind of literary license famous authors such as yourself regularly take, much to the detriment of your eager and willing readers?

A *What gives is the corner iron is a quick repair and the Liquid Nails allows you to get on with it without doing a more elaborate repair. There are all kinds of fixes that will prolong the life of your windows until you have time to really take them apart and these fixes are fine and appropriate. Contemporary restorers of great art have to undo the work of earlier restorers who did the best they could with the then available materials and expertise (often considered inferior by present day standards). Had they done nothing, these works of art could have perished or deteriorated beyond repair. There's nothing wrong with temporary repairs if they stabilize the window. Literary license? I reserve that for letters to my publisher explaining why my manuscripts are late.*

The remaining wood fillers and repair materials generate plenty of opinions and choices. Every wood worker, boat repairer, and restoration junky has a favorite material and another to condemn. Mr. Window understands that nothing is permanent (the IRS would argue otherwise), even the best repairs can come undone if they're not maintained, and not everyone is willing to spend tons of money and time tracking down and ordering the self-proclaimed god of wood fillers because a manufacturer tells you so. Here is the information to help you make an informed choice.

Fillers perform several duties:

- They fill voids left after rotted or weathered wood is removed.

- They add structural integrity to a wood repair.

- When diluted, fillers penetrate, reinforce, and strengthen exposed wood fibers.

Many wood fillers are harder than the wood itself after they've dried and cured. This is a mixed blessing given that an overly rigid sash corner doesn't allow much movement or give and take as the weather changes. One reason these corners weren't typically glued when they were assembled was to allow such movement (which is unnoticeable) that would prevent a paint film from cracking. On the other hand, this hardness makes for a durable repair if the filler doesn't shrink and pull away from the wood it's bonding to. I've never found the hardness of some fillers to have any adverse effects on a sash.

When a wood window section has deteriorated, it's never a nice, clean, even break. It's choppy and splintered and uneven. Reinforcing these ragged sections is important. You can try to stuff filler into them with varying degrees of success, but better to apply a material that will soak in and bond and form a more uniform surface for the solid filler to butt up against. For this reason you sometimes need to have both liquid and solid fillers available for your repairs.

Automotive Body Filler

Bondo is the most recognized name here and it has a host of products for home, auto, industrial, and marine. Basic automotive body filler or compound consists of a polyester filler material and a hardening agent. It is quick drying, sands easily, and is an excellent choice for interior wood repair. For exterior repairs and repairs requiring structural properties, marine or waterproof automotive body filler with added fiberglass is a better choice. Bondo does manufacture a fiberglass jelly and other weatherproof products appropriate for this work.

For a more liquid filler, fiberglass-reinforced polyester resin can be thinned 25 percent with acetone allowing it to soak into weakened or deteriorated wood to strengthen the fibers, according to Robert J. Albrecht (*Old House Journal,* May/June 1993). He notes it is similar to soaking the wood with consolidant (see LiquidWood below) and yields excellent results. Polyester resin, which comes in liquid form, is available at automotive supply stores along with automotive body compound. It is also available at marine supply stores.

When used properly, these materials are suitable for many window repairs. Proper use includes using the material on dry wood, thoroughly packing the cavity or area to be repaired with the filler so you do not leave any gaps or voids, and allowing sufficient time for it to harden in a dry, preferably warm, area. You might have to apply the material several times to complete your repair if the cavity is deep.

Some repairers and restorers shun automotive body fillers and claim they are inadequate and eventually loosen and separate from the wood they are repairing. There is some truth to this, particularly if a corner of a sash has some flex to it (the stile working against the rail due to warping, for instance) and the material isn't properly applied or maintained. For the most part, I haven't found this to be a problem, but would always advocate waterproof material for your repairs.

Epoxy

The most foolproof material is epoxy. It is also the most time consuming and expensive. Marine suppliers and paint stores carry various brands of epoxy mixes. One product line with a decent work history and that shows up regularly in government restoration projects is made by Abatron, Inc. (800-445-1754, 5501 95th Ave., Kenosha, WI 53144 or www.abatron.com).

Abatron's LiquidWood and WoodEpox are whiz-bang materials that can repair even the most rotted wood. LiquidWood is a two-part (resin and hardener) liquid consolidant. When mixed and poured onto deteriorated wood, LiquidWood will penetrate and harden the existing wood fibers to the point that they can be sawed, drilled, or sanded, rendering it harder than the original material.

WoodEpox is a two-part (resin paste and hardener paste) structural putty used to fill large holes and voids, even to replace missing sections in windows, sills, doors, and so on. WoodEpox can also be sanded and tooled. In lieu of using WoodEpox, LiquidWood can be mixed with fine sawdust and used as a putty-type material. Both products work best in dry weather (they can take forever to dry in damp conditions). They can also cost 4–5 times as much as automotive body filler and may be a more exotic material than you really need. Two pints of LiquidWood (one pint of hardener and one pint of resin) currently cost $35.50 plus shipping; an equal amount of WoodEpox runs $32.25 plus shipping.

Abatron is popular with historic preservationists because it can repair even the most neglected wood. The company does have its competitors (every epoxy manufacturer in the rest of the world). One brand is West System (www.westsystem.com), whose products are sold primarily at marine and boat shops all around the country. Their prices are comparable to Abatron. Some restorers swear by West System, which has been around for years, as do many boat repairers.

NOTE: Do your epoxy and filler work in a warm room or during warm, dry weather. Otherwise, it will take it as a personal affront that you're trying to make it work in cold, damp conditions and it will respond by taking its sweet old time drying. In warm dry weather, epoxy and automotive body fillers have short drying times; have your area to be repaired all ready and work fast unless you want to end up with a chunky repair and wasted filler.

Rot and Weathered Wood Repairs

Let's start with a weathered sash with a bad bottom rail, one with missing or badly deteriorated tenons. This can be any kind of sash; the repairs are all the same. Here's what you do:

- Turn the sash on its side and dig out the entire deteriorated tenon. Use a screwdriver to get the bulk of it out and then use an electric drill with as large a bit as you can fit into the opening, moving it in and out while the bit is turning, grinding up the deteriorated wood.

- If the area is wet, dry it out with a heat gun or hair dryer.

- Does it look or feel like rot? Pour some wood preservative into the affected area and allow it to dry. There are a zillion preservatives available and you will need one that kills the fungi, accepts wood filler, and is paintable.

One example, JascoTermin-8 Preservative, protects against fungus as well as wood-munching organisms like termites and carpenter ants. Note the drying time which can run several days!

- Set aside some long splints of wood, maybe 6-8″ long. I like to use sections of parting beads split with a chisel or even a pair of wire cutters so they'll be roughly ½″ x ½″ at their thick end. The slivers will actually be long right triangles for the most part. You can also use dowels, but these seem to work better. Plus, the old parting beads are free and it's one less item to purchase.

- After your preservative, if any, has dried, mix the fill material of your choice, which might first include a liquid consolidant.

- Force the corner back together; if it springs apart, you can wrap a rope around the sash, knot it, and, inserting a small piece of wood or screwdriver, twist it like a tourniquet until the corner comes together. Be sure they line up flush and square. Secure the screwdriver or piece of wood to the rope with tape to keep the rope tight (see page 116).

- If your repair requires a liquid consolidant first, mix the needed amount and pour onto the damaged wood. Note the drying and cure time before going on with your work.

- Mix enough solid wood filler to generously fill the cavity until it's overflowing. Force it into the cavity with a narrow putty knife, moving quickly before it sets up and starts to dry.

- Next, hammer your wood splints into the space and into the soft wood of the bottom rail and/or up into the stile. If no liquid consolidant has been used, they'll go right in, but don't pound so aggressively that you split the wood. If consolidant has been used, predrill some holes before adding the filler to allow the splints to get past the consolidated wood, which will be harder than normal wood. There will be some natural resistance when you reach a stronger section of the wood.

· Clip off the ends of the splints until they are roughly flush with the edge of the sash and then smear some more filler over them. No need to be particularly neat about it, as it will all be sanded after it dries.

· You can also use 16d galvanized nails or even deck screws if you haven't got any splints or

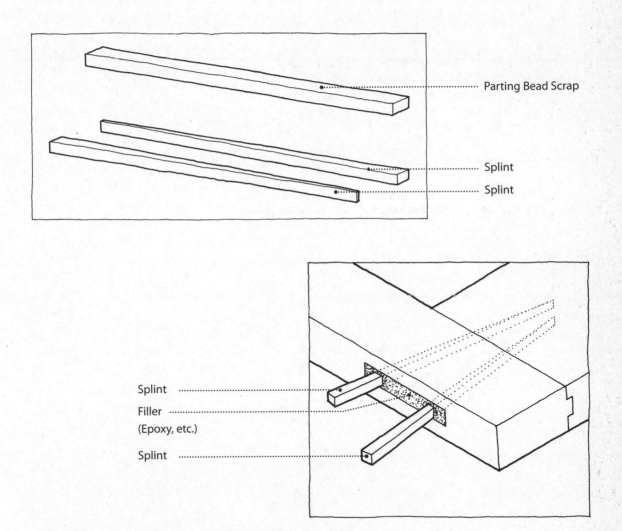

Parting Bead Scrap

Splint

Splint

Splint

Filler
(Epoxy, etc.)

Splint

dowels. Insert them in the same fashion and force any needed additional filler around them. If their heads stick out beyond the edge of the sash, you can sand them off with a belt sander.

· When the material dries hard around the splints or dowels, the whole corner will hold together as they are now the new tenons (it will look a little funky, but reserve judgment until you're finished sanding).

· Repeat the procedure at the other corner(s) if necessary.

· When dry, sand smooth and flush with a power sander (a belt sander works very well here). Wear a dust mask and be prepared for fine dust everywhere!

· Fill in any remaining cavities with a second application of filler and sand when dry, using a finish sander to complete the job.

· Prime and paint the material as soon as possible in order to seal and protect it.

NOTE: It's easy to get aggressive with the belt sander and sand the corner down too far, thus losing some of the dimensional size you're trying to maintain. Take your time and pull the sander off now and again to be sure you're not grinding through too much of the filler. When you're close to the desired dimension, use a finish sander to complete the job.

Muntin joint; illustrating a stile and a muntin (with rounded edge).

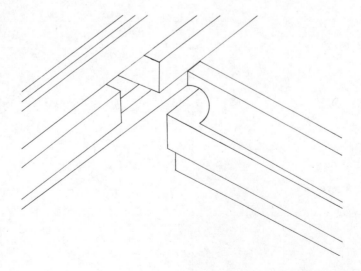

This always works, especially if you use an epoxy. You won't think so when you're first looking at this sorry excuse for a sash with its rot and splinters and holes, but you'll be pleasantly surprised with the finished product

Muntins

Muntins, also called muntin bars or sash bars, are the wood dividers between panes of glass. Glass is secured to the muntins the same as it's secured to rails and stiles. When someone—all right, a glazier or a window someone—uses the term "six over one," for instance, it means six panes or lites of glass in the top sash and one pane in the lower. The upper sash is also called a divided lite sash; the muntins are the dividers.

Muntin bars are glued and sometimes wedged or nailed into place. Their ends are rounded and coped to fit into and butt up against each other and the stiles and rails. The ends can loosen over time and deteriorate. And any horizontal muntin above a sash lock stands a good chance of having a chunk of it knocked or chipped out when the lower sash is opened if the strike (the movable section of the lock on the lower sash) is only partially opened and it gets rammed into the muntin. I saw this over and over and over. Repairing chipped muntins and loose muntins is another window restoration chore many people run into.

Chipped Muntins

A chipped muntin is an aesthetic issue, not a structural one. If it doesn't bother you, leave it and attend to something that does bother you (your cable company, your children, etc.). You can do a close enough repair with filler and some hand tools or a better repair with filler and a mold.

To repair with hand tools:

· Lightly sand the chipped section of the muntin. This will give a little more tooth for the filler to set on.

· Tape the glass near the repair so the filler won't stick to the glass.

· Mix a small amount of automotive body filler (this is a perfect job for standard Bondo, which dries quickly and can be hand-sanded).

· Let the Bondo set up for a minute. Take a narrow flexible putty knife and push the Bondo into the chipped area, just filling it until it's the size of the rest of the muntin.

· Drag the knife across the Bondo, shaping it to match the detail of the muntin as best you can. As the Bondo dries, it will hold the shape as you form it, but stop when it starts to stiffen.

· After the Bondo has dried, remove the tape and take a folded piece of 60 or 80 grit sandpaper and further shape it. Your results will probably be a little uneven, but after it's painted, who's going to notice?

· Apply one coat of primer and one to two coats of paint to your repair.

To repair using a mold:

· Lay some plastic food wrap across a 4–5-inch section of intact muntin and the glass next to it.

· Mix some Bondo or patching plaster and press it against the plastic and all the details on one side of the muntin. Be sure it's pressed in completely and neatly, a half an inch thick or so. Try and form the whole mess into a partial cylinder, with the smooth side facing you.

· Allow to dry, pick the mold off the sash, and pull off the plastic.

· Tape off the glass and surrounding area near the chipped muntin.

· Brush a thin, but thorough, coat of petroleum jelly inside your mold. Test that you've used enough petroleum jelly by placing a small amount of fresh Bondo on the inside of your mold, allowing it to dry, and removing it. If it doesn't stick, reapply more petroleum jelly and proceed.

· Mix more Bondo and spread just enough onto the damaged area to cover it.

· Press the mold against the Bondo on the muntin and leave it there until the Bondo has dried.

· When you remove the mold, the repair should be more detailed than one done with hand tools. Some light sanding will probably be needed to even it out.

· Remove the tape, prime and paint your repaired section.

· You can also use patching plaster if you don't have any Bondo.

If you found you used too little Bondo and your finished product isn't quite complete enough, repeat the process. You shouldn't need much additional Bondo so apply lightly. Wipe the inside of the mold with more petroleum jelly before using it again.

Broken Muntins

Muntins are not especially robust members of the sash family once the ends deteriorate. You can patch and secure them, but they won't be as tight and taut as a new muntin; however, it's not that critical that they be so. A loose muntin will wobble when you work it back and forth with your hand. Short of replacing it—we'll get to that shortly—the best tactic is to force some glue between the end(s) of the muntin and whatever it's attached to and toenail a very small nail or brad to help fasten it. If there's a gap between the end(s) and the attachment point(s), try to squirt in some epoxy, shape it with the end of a screwdriver, and nail the muntin end after the epoxy dries. Sometimes you can fill the gap with the glue itself and call it good. After it's painted, who will be the wiser?

It's really unusual for the entire muntin to be missing, although a large section of it can be sheared off. To completely replace a muntin, you will have to:

· Have a new section run out at a millwork company, unless they have stock on hand. Having a piece run is an expensive proposition. There is a minimum set-up fee plus the cost of the wood. Unless you have a lot of material to run out, it isn't worth it. The new material must be cut to length and then cut with a coping saw before installation.

· Fake it—a favorite term of Mr. Window.

Faking a muntin:

· Look closely at the missing detail. It's often a flat section, against which the glass sits, and an ogee-type detail.

· You can duplicate the flat, plain detail with a section of lath or even narrow bullnose, both available in the molding section of a lumber store. Whichever you use will have to be cut to the correct width and length. Both cuts can be done with a handsaw.

· Take the piece you're going to patch in and nail and glue it to whatever remains of the old muntin or to the adjoining muntins, rails, or stiles. You could even drill some pilot holes and attach it with very small screws.

· If you need to repair on the interior side, a small piece of quarter-round molding, cut to fit, can be an acceptable replacement for the more ornate original detail.

· Pack a lump of epoxy into the rail or stile where a muntin had formerly been attached and a hole now remains. Stuff the new muntin end, fake or otherwise, into this epoxy. As the epoxy dries, it will secure the muntin. Further secure the muntin with small screws or finish nails.

This isn't going to be the perfect replacement, but as long as it's secure and watertight, it will blend in well enough after it's painted.

"Well enough" isn't exactly a running theme in this book, but it is a guideline. Let me put it this way: I remember seeing an old picture of Lyndon Johnson sitting in his White House office. Behind him was a double-hung window with a piece of parting bead missing, which most people wouldn't notice, but I am cursed to observe these details. If neither the United States government nor the president of the United States can be bothered with keeping the Oval Office windows in top-notch condition, rest assured no one will notice any minor imperfections in your bungalow. I know what happens in one house isn't nec-

essarily relevant to what happens in yours, but this does provide some perspective.

Let's assume the entire corner is gone. This is repairable, although it requires a small act of faith in Mr. Window as well as Mr./Ms. Epoxy Manufacturer. You'll proceed as above, but will have to contain the wood filler until it hardens into a corner.

· Dig out all of the deteriorated material and force the corner back into its proper position. Cross the sash in both directions with rope tourniquets if necessary.

· Pour in any liquid consolidant, if needed, and after it's dried, drill some holes to accommodate the splints.

· On one side of the now-missing corner, attach a piece of cardboard wrapped in plastic wrap to the adjoining rail and stile using thumbtacks. Wrap the edge of the cardboard around the bottom edge of the rail so the filler won't ooze out here. The plastic wrap will prevent the filler material from sticking so the cardboard can be easily pulled away.

· Lay the sash on the side with the cardboard. Cut two small holes in the cardboard so you can nail some splints up into the stile.

· Stuff some filler into the deteriorated ends of the rail and the stile, laying it on thick.

· Hammer some splints into both, cutting them roughly flush with the edge of the rail and stile respectively, and layer a little more filler into and over the splints. Don't try to fill the whole corner out at once.

· After your first application dries, apply a second or even a third until it fills out completely. You may want to wrap an additional

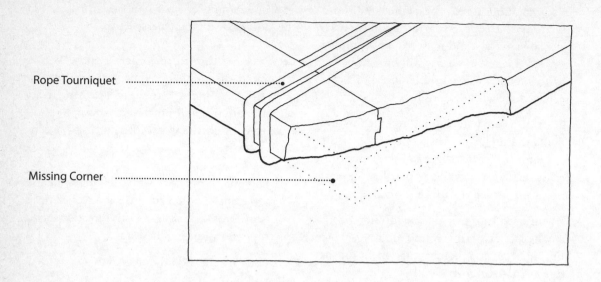

Rope Tourniquet ....

Missing Corner ....

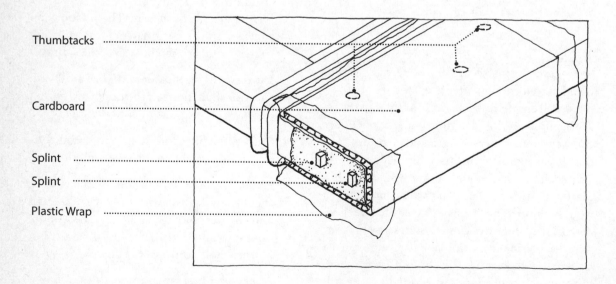

Thumbtacks ....

Cardboard ....

Splint ....

Splint ....

Plastic Wrap ....

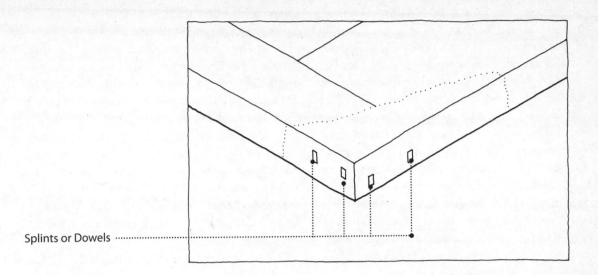

Splints or Dowels

piece of cardboard against the edge of the sash to prevent oozing there.

· After the filler has dried, remove the cardboard and sand everything flush and square. You will probably need one last application to fill in small voids.

Does this work? Well, I once had to fill an entire bottom rail with pieces of parting bead, construction glue, and filler, making repeated applications, until I had just about recreated the entire rail. All I had been left to work with was the interior face, about ⅛" thick. I mean, it was necessary, the window had to be reinstalled that day, and there wasn't any time to have a new rail milled. It worked quite well and the client was happy.

NOTE: If the rail is just too far gone to repair and you have budget considerations, consider replacing the entire piece. Take your old rail to a millwork shop and see if they have a similar piece available. Some will carry sash rail stock and some won't. Cutting a tenon using hand tools is doable, but unless you regularly do nineteenth-century carpentry demonstrations at county fairs, the result won't be as neat as a machine-formed tenon. Aside from the tenon, the rail should be coped to accurately fit against the stiles. For an excellent illustrated article on this type of construction and the use of wood sash power tools, go to www.woodmagazine.com and do a search on "window sash."

I've seen some homemade jobs where stock 2x4 material was used without much regard to matching the ogee detail; the repairer simply wanted to stabilize the sash and not replace it. The ends of the stiles were cut off and the 2x4 run all the way across the bottom of the sash and screwed up and into the stiles. This is perfectly legitimate and I recommend it if you don't need to look at the perfect window. Like other budget-restrained, cost-saving repairs that will not yield a fully restored window, you will notice the difference less and less after you've lived with it for a while.

One glazier I knew would disassemble old paneled interior doors because their stiles and rails had the same ogee detail as window sashes. He used these pieces to fabricate new ones when he needed to replace a sash rail. If you're especially talented with a table saw, you can cut new sections from stock framing lumber, reproduce a passable ogee detail, chisel out new tenons, and install. I could never do it very well, but I watched a carpenter who built theater sets do it. In his work, he had to fake all kinds of details and these skills served him well when he repaired windows.

Sill Repairs

The sill sits at the base of the window on the exterior. It is cut at a slope so water will drain off of it and away from the sash. The sill is nailed up and into the jambs to stabilize the window. When your double-hung window was originally installed, the sill, jamb, and header came as one section that was installed first; the sashes, along with the parting beads, ropes, stops, and weights, were installed next. Sills need more attention than most other exterior woodwork because of their drainage requirements.

When poorly maintained or left unpainted, sills will either rot or split due to weathering and water. Moisture is the ultimate foe. In masonry structures, moisture can even rise up from the bricks or stonework and affect the sill from underneath. In fact, a peculiar problem with sills and masonry buildings is the tendency for sills on the weathered sides of a building to cup (the front lip of the sill starts to lift), which prevents proper drainage. These often have to be replaced or at the very least sanded down to form a better slope.

While you're repairing your sill, find out what caused the problem in the first place and see if it's been resolved. A leaky gutter, for instance, might have been fixed, but the sill ignored. A rotted sill could simply have been the luck of the draw when fungi were being dealt out one day, but be sure any water problems have been repaired so your sill doesn't deteriorate after you've worked on it.

Q **Well, excuse me, Mr. Window, but I have a friend who restores Chippendale furniture—you know, the stuff named after famed eighteenth-century English furniture maker Thomas Chippendale, whose "chinoi-**

Do you have some cupped sills? Is it winter and raining and you don't have time to repair them and get rid of the puddles of water? Take a handsaw and cut some kerfs at a right angle through the width of the sill. These will act as troughs for the water to run off until you can repair the sill during warm weather. You only have to cut deep enough to get the water to drain off. Cover the sill with plastic after you've made your cuts, allow it to dry out, and then prime and paint the cuts, leaving the plastic over them if it's still wet out.

serie" designs just make my heart flutter. Anyway, my friend would never dream of using wood fillers or deck screws or any of the stuff you recommend. Just what do you have to say for yourself?

A Mr. Window wonders if your friend is visible to anyone besides you, but in the age-old Socratic manner, he'll answer your question with his own questions. Does your friend have a shop full of wonderful tools such as routers and joiners and planers? Do you think the average homeowner has any of these tools, let alone the expertise to use them? I don't, and I'm Mr. Window. Has your friend ever found the day coming to an end, the weather turning ugly, and the inside of his workshop exposed to rain and wind the same way someone's bedroom or dining room would be while repairing a window? You see, I write for people who could be complete strangers to tools and home repair, but want to learn. For those with more advanced skills and abilities reading this book, they are better prepared to do even more extensive repairs than I describe, but are in need of a reference book and clearer knowledge of how windows function. My recommendations produce solid, functional windows good for years of use if they are maintained. There's a huge difference between a Chippendale table all warm and cozy indoors all day, pampered with furniture oil and serving only as a resting place for, dare I say, imported delicate collectibles, and a working window, exposed to the weather, not unlike our pioneer ancestors, crossing the plains barefoot in four feet of snow, wondering why they forgot to pack their boots or pay attention to the weather reports but persevering nevertheless. These windows are still expected to open, close, and keep that same weather at bay. Mr. Window says fie on Mr. Chippendale.

If your sill is simply weathered and split, it can be filled with epoxy or one of the various fiber-glass materials and sanded smooth. Here's how you do it:

- The sill must be completely dry before you start the repairs. Scrape or sand off (keeping in mind any lead content) all loose paint. In damp weather or if the sill is wet, dry it out with a propane torch or heat gun.

- Cover the sill with plastic if you cannot finish the repair right away.

- If you have any concerns about rot, brush in some paintable fungicide wood preservative and allow it to dry before proceeding, covering it with plastic until it's ready for the remaining repair.

- Prime the sill with oil primer. Use a fast-drying primer if you're working in damp or wet weather, keeping the sill covered over with plastic as the primer dries. Tape the plastic to the jamb or make a tent out of it to keep it from resting on the primer.

- When the primer is completely dry, force your chosen waterproof filler material into the cracks and splits with a flexible putty knife and allow the filler to dry.

- Sand the filler smooth with a disk sander or random-orbital and finish-sand until smooth. Unless you want to hand-sand the filler, be prepared for a lot of dust!

- Immediately prime again and paint as soon as the primer has dried. Apply two coats of good quality paint of your choice. Cover with plastic as needed if the weather is questionable.

This is an easy and long-lasting repair and is much simpler than sill replacement.

Partial Sill Replacement

Sill replacement can be a real nuisance and I hate it. The sill is nailed up and into the jamb and it is impractical to try and remove the entire window unit and renail a new sill. Sometimes only a portion of the sill, maybe up to one half of its width, deteriorates and has to be removed. This results in splicing in a new section and filling the seam between the new and old wood.

If you're only replacing a portion of a sill:

· Remove the deteriorated section using a sharp, wide wood chisel and hammer. You can also cut this section away using a power circular saw, but be aware the teeth might cut against the underlying brick if you have a masonry building. Wood-cutting saw blade teeth and bricks mean you can toss that saw

blade away. Uncomfortable using a circular saw? Try a jigsaw or even a narrow grinding wheel attached to a drill. Better to be safe with a tool you're comfortable using even if the job takes a little longer.

NOTE: The sill might be nailed up and into the brick molding or exterior casings as well so be aware of these nails when you remove any deteriorated wood located here.

· You can use any number of sizes of standard dimensional lumber to splice into the remaining sill as long as you sand or plane the filler piece to match the slope of the original sill and bevel the front edge to match the original. Fir, cedar, or redwood are all good choices while hem/fir and cheap cuts of pine are not.

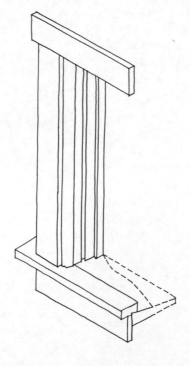

Sill repair: Remove deteriorated wood, fill, and sand smooth.

· Cutting the bevel is a lot easier if you have a table saw. If not, you can adjust the blade of a circular saw to make the cut (there's an adjustment on these saws to move the blade to different angles), but you'll need a decent saw, which means one with some power to it, not the $39.95 special at the hardware store. Another choice is to use a belt sander to form the bevel or angle at the edge of your replacement section. It's more time consuming, but safer than using an unfamiliar circular saw for such an awkward cut.

NOTE: Cut a drip line on the underside of the sill if your replacement piece runs the length of the sill. A drip line is a narrow channel or kerf, about ³/₈″ deep, cut into the sill about two inches from the outer edge and along its entire length. It allows water to drip off before it flows back under the sill and into the wall. Cut your wood to the approximate shape of the section that has been removed and prime the underside.

· Prime the entire sill section, including the underside. You can first coat it with a paintable wood preservative if you wish.

· Fit your replacement section against the existing sill.

· Secure it to the undamaged section of the sill (see below for replacing large sections) with glue and either galvanized screws or finish nails inserted from the front beveled edge. Be sure to predrill your holes, especially if you're using screws, and countersink the nails/screws so the heads aren't visible.

Above: Drip line.

Below: Saw kerf (bottom of new sill) cut as a drip line.

- Especially with masonry buildings, you might (probably) have to pound some wood shims (cedar shingles cut into strips work very well) under your replacement section to support it from underneath as well as bring it up level with the rest of the sill. Pound the shims in far enough so they are not flush with the edge of the sill, but under it. These shims will tightly wedge the new section against the jamb and brick molding.

- Fill in the nail/screw heads and the gaps between the new and old wood with epoxy or other appropriate filler. Sand smooth when dry and prime the sill again.

- Caulk the bottom edge of the sill, especially if you have shims under it, with a paintable urethane caulk so there's no visible gap between it and the underlying masonry or wood.

- Apply at least two coats of paint to finish the job.

As with any exterior wood repair, maintaining the painted finish is the key to its longevity. Trees have bark for protection from the elements. We strip off the bark and replace it with inferior paints and stains that need regular recoating, a chore often ignored because it's expensive and time consuming. Maintaining a painted finish is especially important on repaired sills because of the amount of water they come in contact with.

Q **Geez, Mr. Window, you're not the most optimistic guy in the world; kind of a restoration fatalist if you ask me. Anyway, is there an easier sill repair than filling or replacing, you know, like covering it with weatherproof contact paper or something?**

A *Mr. Window, who views himself more as a restoration realist than fatalist, applauds your creativity, but he doesn't know of any weatherproof contact paper, which is too bad because you could choose paper with pretty flowers or kitties on it and wouldn't that be fun. You can cover an eroded sill with sheet metal and get an acceptable result if it's done neatly. Purists will scoff and scold, but a thin sheet of aluminum will hold up better than neglected wood. Mr. Window has no problem with this, but he does recommend you do some basic stabilization to the underlying damaged sill before covering it up with metal. Why? Because it can continue to deteriorate, albeit slowly, once it's covered up and some simple intervention can stop this.*

Here are the steps for covering your sill with sheet metal:

- Scrape off the worst of the deteriorated paint and choppy looking wood.

- Apply wood preservative and allow it to dry.

- Gun in a caulk of your choice, such as a good urethane and smooth it out with a flexible putty knife, wiping the knife clean afterward. Allow the caulk to dry and brush the sill with a paint of your choice.

- Cut a paper template to fit your sill, including the underside of the beveled edge if it's accessible. Include the ins and outs around the parting beads and nailing stops as best you can. Follow all the details closely, keeping in mind you'll have to cut the sheet metal to match these details.

- Purchase the sheet aluminum at a home improvement center or sheet metal supplier (they might have scraps or ends that will be large enough for your job).

· Place the template on the metal and trace it.

· Using a good pair of tin snips or metal shears, cut out the pattern.

· Test fit the sheet metal and trim it as needed. Check again for fit.

· Remove the sheet metal and caulk the edge that will sit on the sill near the stool. Apply some caulk to the beveled edge of the sill and to its underside, if accessible.

· Insert the sheet metal starting at the stool and lay it flat; nail the edge of the sheet metal with one-inch shingle nails or galvanized roofing nails.

· Take a piece of wood as long as the sheet metal and bend the edge of the metal over the beveled edge of the sill.

· A second set of hands is helpful at this point, but not critical. You now want to bend the sheet metal under the beveled edge (if accessible) and nail it there. This is easier if someone else is holding the sheet metal taut to the sill with another piece of wood. Otherwise, nail the metal to the face of the beveled edge.

· Once the sheet metal is nailed, determine if it needs any nails around its edge (it probably will). After all nailing is completed, touch up any needed caulk around the edge of the metal.

· Scuff the sheet metal with fine sandpaper, prime, and paint.

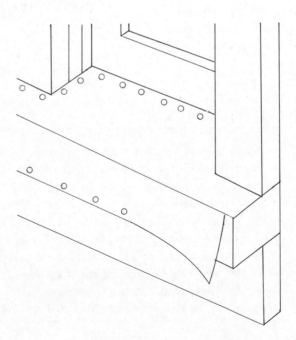

Sheet metal fitted and nailed to the sill.

If the sheet metal is cut and installed cleanly, it will blend in well enough with the rest of the window to render it unnoticeable to most observers as long as most observers don't include historical perfectionists. I've seen sloppy jobs that just looked bad and neat jobs that looked terrific. You might buy some extra sheet metal to practice your bending in case your first efforts aren't to your satisfaction. You can also take your template to a metal shop and have them cut and bend the metal to fit, but it's probably not worth the fee given that this is a straightforward job.

Sill Replacement

A trashed sill will be pretty obvious to you. The wood will be soft to the point where you can sink a screwdriver into it and break the sill apart in large pieces. About all that remains is some wood under the stool and the brick molding or exterior casings and the jamb. There isn't anything here to fill or patch—it will have to be removed and replaced. New sill stock is available in several styles and fitting it in is a pain.

Here are the steps:

- Remove all the loose, trashed wood with a hammer and chisel or circular saw.

- Completely clean out all pieces of the deteriorated sill that run under the jamb and exterior trim or brick molding. You will have to saw off or pull out any remnants of nails sticking into the jamb from the sill.

- Purchase new sill stock to match your existing; prime both sides and all edges.

NOTE: In a pinch, you can use a section of 2x6 as long as it will sit at a slope.

- The only way to remove the entire sill is to remove the interior stool, too, as this rests on and is nailed into the sill. To remove the stool, you have to remove the interior casings and stops. If you want to skip these steps, and you will, you can chisel the old sill out until the remaining section under the stool has a clean edge to it. You will then butt the new sill up to this remaining section, although

Note about caulk: It's tempting to just keep gunning caulk into deep crevices and cracks until they're filled, but caulk isn't truly a structural material. It can be a filler and an adhesive and a sealant. If you have large gaps, say, under a sill, apply DAPtex Latex Insulating Foam Sealant first or as the only sealant, although I'd use it as a filler and apply urethane caulk as a final sealant because I think the urethane would be less maintenance over time. It's either that or use backer rod, which is like solid foam rope, sold in rolls, that you cut to size and stuff inside of crevices. You'll never need a roll of it unless you're a professional mason so stick with a spray can of foam, which is more fun to use anyway.

you might have to trim down the width of the new sill and caulk the seam between the new sill and the remnant of the old one.

· Unfortunately, you can't just tuck in a new sill piece and smugly say to yourself, what's the big deal? There's nothing to this sill replacement stuff. Mr. Window must have lead dust on the brain. This might be very true, but the new sill has to be trimmed before installing. Because of the angle of the sill and the framing on which it sits, the ends of the new sill have to be thinned down in order to slip under the jamb and brick molding or casings. You can grind them down with a disc sander or chisel them out; neither way is spectacularly precise, but there isn't much choice.

· Trimming the sill to fit results in gaps at its ends and a gap at the stool where the remnant of the old sill is still under the stool. Since you can't nail up into the jamb, you have to pound some shims under the sill to form a tight fit against the jamb. Especially on masonry structures, this will hold the sill with such force that you won't need any kind of fastener or even glue to secure the new sill, although you can toenail some small galvanized finish nails through the brick molding or casings into the sill.

· Fill the gaps at the stool and the areas that were trimmed under the jamb and exterior casings or brick molding with appropriate filler such as epoxy and sand flush to the sill when dry. Caulk under the sill with urethane caulk.

· Prime the sill again and, when dry, apply two coats of paint.

As I said, I hate replacing sills, but you haven't got much choice if one of yours is too deteriorated to otherwise repair.

MISSING OR BROKEN HARDWARE

Locks and sash lifts (handles) are available at hardware and home repair centers. The least expensive are made from aluminum and come with several finishes including bright brass, antique brass, nickel, and bronze. Solid brass hardware is very expensive and doesn't offer any clear advantages over the aluminum in terms of function. It certainly feels heavier and more substantial and the finishes are better, but at a price.

Your existing hardware is usually quite usable despite the paint buildup.

Q **Says you, Mr. Window. You probably have some kind of super hydrogen-powered hardware cleaner. Stripping and cleaning all that paint off is a real mess for mere mortals.**

A *Actually, it's really easy.*

Cleaning Window Hardware

To clean painted window hardware the easiest way possible:

· Remove all of the hardware, which isn't as easy as it sounds. With enough paint in them, painted screw heads are impossible to grab with a screwdriver. Chip out the paint using a hammer and the edge of a stiff putty knife or an old, cheap screwdriver as you can mess up the head doing this (if your screwdriver is already bunged up, grind down the head on a bench grinder or with a metal file until it's flat again). Once the paint is out of the screw's slot, unscrew it with a better screwdriver. You might have to try to move the screw forward, tightening it, in order to loosen it. This sounds counterintuitive, but it works. Use a screwdriver whose head completely fits the slot; using a small one will just damage the screw head and make it tougher to remove. You might not be able to remove the strike part of the lock, which is screwed into the upper sash, by unscrewing. These screws can be so deteriorated that you can do little except pry the lock out. The best way to do this is to take a large slotted screwdriver and place it under the screw from inside the strike. Give it a good twist until the strike loosens, then do it to the other screw. Watch that you're not putting so much pressure on it that the rail starts really twisting. When you reinstall the strike, either use longer screws, since you've now messed up the hole, or stuff some toothpicks or bits of wood and some glue inside the holes to fill them out.

· Discard the screws and replace them with new Phillips screws. Buy them by the bag or box from a fastener supplier if you can. If you have bronze-colored hardware, you can use small, black drywall screws that are inexpensive and install quickly. Absolute historical accuracy calls for slotted screws, however, like the ones you removed. Some people notice these things; they should not be invited to your home under any circumstances.

· Take all your now-removed hardware and toss everything into an old coffee can or similar container along with a cup of granulated dishwasher detergent. Fill the can with boiling water, cover it, and let it sit for a day or two. The paint will loosen and slip off. An even better approach is to keep it all simmering/boiling in an old pot on a hotplate outdoors (if you put it on your stove, your kitchen will smell like boiling rust and really dirty socks and your family will demand you take them out to dinner, which pretty much kills any big savings from my cheap stripping methodology). This is a very nifty tip and is good for cleaning paint off of any small metal objects. TSP (trisodium phosphate) can be used instead of dishwasher detergent, but it's more expensive. The waste water from this stripping will be full of paint, some of it lead-based, so don't pour it down the drain or into the toilet. Call your garbage/disposal company or water department for proper disposal information.

· Remove the hardware from the cleaning solution and rinse in another container of clean water. After the hardware has dried, you can clean it by hand with steel wool, but it's a million times faster and more effective to use a benchtop grinder/polisher. These are great tools and useful for all kinds of polishing jobs as well as grinding down metal and sharpening tools. Prices start at under $50 (the money saved by reusing your hardware will pay for the grinder). With a fine wire wheel attachment, your hardware will look like new. With additional buffer attachments, you can get your brass hardware to look like small mirrors.

· Although a lot of old window and door hardware were brass-plated or even solid brass, some were plain steel and all the polishing in the world won't prettify it very much. I

(1) Hook lift.

(2) Sash lift.

(3) Casement lock.

(4) Double-hung window locks.

I'm a big fan of two sash lifts on most windows. Many come with just one because the builders saved twenty cents a window or some equally parsimonious amount (I know, I know, it all added up, even a hundred years ago). Wide windows are easier to open and close with two lifts, especially for kids or anyone who might not have the strength to easily open the windows. I'm also an advocate of installing sash lifts on the upper sashes at the upper rail, corresponding to their location on the lower sashes, so they can be moved by pulling down without pushing on the bottom rail. In Europe, they address this by installing the lifts on the outside of the upper sash; you open the lower sash and reach out to the handles that are attached to the lower rail of the upper sash, which makes a lot of sense.

recommend applying bronze-colored spray paint (Rustoleum Dark Bronze is very good). It's an inexpensive solution and the hardware looks great. Simply spread all the hardware out on cardboard in the garage and spray on three or four light coats until covered. You'll have to change the position of any lock catches or latches (the section of the lock that twists open and closed) to paint the entire lock. I've done this dozens of times with excellent results. And for even better results, spray a final coat of clear polyurethane on the hardware.

Replacing Hardware

There are plenty of hardware suppliers and manufacturers so you'll never lack for options when it comes to replacing your vintage window hardware. Most hardware and home improvement stores carry major hardware lines from the utilitarian and more modern-looking Stanley to Ives, whose lines include inexpensive coated aluminum to all-brass in a variety of finishes. Ives products are very close matches to hardware manufactured after the Victorian era. Victorian reproductions and twentieth century styles are available from specialty suppliers such as Rejuvenation of Portland, Oregon (800-787-3355, www.rejuvenation.com).

The difference in price between a coated aluminum and an all-brass sash lift is substantial: a little over a dollar for the former to $6–7 or more for the latter depending on the suppliers, size, and quality. Hardware costs can really mount up if you have a lot of windows.

Fixed Pulleys

Fixed pulleys are simple pieces of hardware: small spinning wheels held in a metal casing. They usually last forever, but breakage occasionally occurs and the wheel no longer moves. Pulleys come in several flavors:

· Those that are held in by screws.

· Those that are held in by tension or friction and often have a nail driven through each pair of pulleys' wheels to keep them from falling out.

· Most pulley casings have rounded tops, but some are square; Victorian pulleys can be more ornate with multiple half-circle styling.

· The sizes of the pulleys vary.

Replacement pulleys are still made, ranging in quality from inexpensive stamped metal to heavier ones more closely resembling some of the originals. These are not common hardware store items and can be ordered online and found at some hardware wholesalers, salvage companies dealing in historic hardware, and restoration businesses such as Rejuvenation. You can also contact a company that installs new retrofit windows and ask if you can salvage some pulleys from one of their jobs. Normally, the pulleys are hammered into the jamb to make room for the new window, which fits inside the jamb as a single unit.

Pulleys held in with screws are installed flush inside a mortised-out section of the jamb. This is a taut fit especially after it's been repeatedly painted over. To remove this pulley:

· Back out the screws.

· If the jamb has been painted, take a putty knife and hammer and tap the end of the blade around the outline of the pulley; this will help prevent pulling any wood splinters loose when the pulley comes out.

· Place the end of a screwdriver or small pry bar inside the wheel and gently pry it out on one side.

· The pulley should now be loose and easily removed.

One option to buying a new pulley is to find one in an unused window in the house, perhaps in the basement or a closet, and swap the pulleys out.

Pulleys that are held in by tension—via small teeth at the top and bottom of the pulley that embed into the jamb—have been around at least since the 1920s. They were installed to sit on the jamb surface and are usually harder to remove than screw-in pulleys. Removing the screws was a money-saver for the manufacturer as well as the window manufacturer installing the pulleys, but these were lower in quality and weight to the older pulleys. This is nothing unusual in the history of home building—this drive to keep prices down and speed up production. In addition to being wedged into the jamb, these pulleys often had 16d nails driven through each pair of pulley wheels to help secure them and keep them from falling out. If you have these nails present, you'll have to remove the casing, remove the nail, and then push the pulley through from inside the pocket.

Too much trouble? The sash will function with only one working pulley, but it just won't move as smoothly. If it's a choice between tearing a casing off and an underperforming window, just assume a post-modern deconstructionist attitude and declare it doesn't make any difference.

Pulley held in by teeth.

Problems with the Weights

Sometimes, the weights will get wedged in the pocket. There may have been a little shifting in the framing (unlikely), thus restricting the space, they may have always been tight and never worked properly (more likely), or the weights have corroded over time and no longer smoothly pass each other inside the pocket (always a possibility). If they are only a little tight, you might try spraying a lot of lubricant down into the pocket from the pulley. Soak them with spray silicone or WD-40. This might work, but if they're truly too tight to pass each other, you'll need to put a narrower weight in to solve the problem. Sometimes just swapping with another weight in the opposite pocket will work.

Haven't got any scrap weights lying around? Who does? You have some alternatives:

· Buy some steel flat bar from a scrap yard or metal dealer and bind together some short sections with tape to approximate the weight you need. To attach the rope, wrap some baling or copper wire around one end of the steel, twist it tight leaving ten inches or so available, and form a loop coming out of the top of the bars with this other end of the wire. Form a small loop and twist this end around the flat bar and tape it and the twisted wire to the flat bar (the more layers the merrier).

· Fill a pipe with concrete or plaster, packing it in tightly, and let it stand upright on a piece of foil or plastic until the filler dries. Place a four- or five-inch steel eye in the drying material on the open end of the pipe. This provides a place to tie the rope. Don't have a spare eye and getting tired of trips to the hardware store? Take a metal hanger, cut

out a section, and form it into a U-shape; stick the open ends well into the drying concrete. All bets are off as to when, or if, the ends will corrode and rust.

· Call an architectural salvage yard for scrap weights.

· See Resources for suppliers of sash weights (an expensive option).

Be sure your new weights clear the old ones before you install the sashes again by pulling on the ropes and moving both weights up and down several times.

Casement Hinges

Casement butt hinges are generally problem free other than moving stiffly from excess paint buildup. I've never seen a rusted-out casement butt hinge because water doesn't collect near or on them, but they can corrode if the paint wears off and the outer knuckles are exposed.

For better working butt hinges:

· Remove the hinges from the sash and jamb.

· Soak the hinges in boiling water mixed with granulated dishwasher detergent to remove any paint.

· When the paint has softened and fallen from the hinges, rinse them with water and dry them with a clean rag.

· Clean any remaining paint with coarse steel wool or with a wire brush attachment on a benchtop grinder/polisher.

· Once the hinges are moving freely, spray them with a rust-inhibiting paint such as

Rustoleum. When the paint has dried, lubricate the hinges with a few drops of oil or a spray lubricant and reinstall.

· If you reuse the old screws, run the heads of the screws against the wire brush attachment on the bench grinder/polisher to clean off the paint.

Friction hinges are more problematic than butt hinges. The bottom hinge has plenty of opportunities to rust or corrode as rainwater washes in and wets the hinge. Sometimes they're almost frozen and very difficult to move. If your hinges are giving you fits and have paint slopped on them, follow these steps:

· Remove the hinges and soak in boiling water and granulated dishwasher detergent until the paint falls away.

· Rinse the hinges in clean water and pat dry with a rag.

· Clean the hinge using the wire wheel on a bench grinder/polisher, being sure to get inside the tracks.

· If a hinge just refuses to budge or barely moves, take a propane torch to it or, using channel locks or pair of large pliers, hold it over a gas flame. The heat from either source usually loosens things up.

· Work the hinge back and forth until it moves more easily.

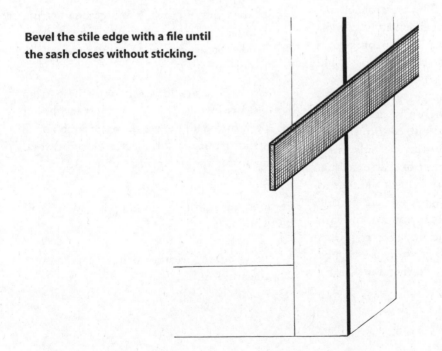

Bevel the stile edge with a file until the sash closes without sticking.

- Squirt some penetrating oil on the hinge and then soak it in a shallow pan of motor oil overnight.

- Work the hinge some more the next day. When you're satisfied with its "action," wipe all the oil off and spray it with Rustoleum or other rust-inhibiting spray paint and lubricate again before reinstalling.

If a hinge is just too corroded to reuse, you'll need to replace it and the other hinge as well. Why both? Because a new single hinge will affect the way the sash opens, even if it is the same size as the old hinge. I don't know why, though it could have something to do with different manufacturers.

Be sure to replace it with the same size hinge! Measure the hinge in its closed position (it will be 8″ or 10″ or 12″ in length or some such derivation). Whitco hinges (www.vincent-whitney.com or 800-332-3286) are probably the most common replacement casement hinge. The Vincent Whitney Company also manufactures double-hung window locks, casement locks, and casement openers.

After installing new hinges, you might have to trim the sash down slightly so it will close properly. Usually you only have to trim the vertical inward-facing edge on the lock side to get the sash to close. Take a piece of coarse sandpaper or a wood file and rub it down the edge at a 45-degree angle as though you were putting a bevel on it. With the edge trimmed, the sash should close easily. If the opposite edge hits the jamb when closing, file it down as well, just enough to clear the jamb, allowing a little extra for a coat of paint.

SLOPPY OR TIGHT FIT

Double-Hung Windows

It's a good idea to check for fit before installing the parting beads. Do this by:

- Roping the upper sash, without nailing the ropes, and raising it completely.

- Tap small scraps of parting bead into the jamb. Rope the lower sash, without nailing the ropes, and observe how well the sashes match up at the meeting rail and how well they slide.

- If the upper sash is tight as it slides down, remove the paint from the exterior jamb. If it's still tight, or if the lower sash is tight, then it's a matter of taking a belt sander to the sides of the sash and gradually trimming away. Don't get carried away with the sander. Sand some and then test the sash in the opening.

- Does the sash slide easily until the parting bead is installed? The parting bead hasn't been forced all the way into the jamb and is sticking out too far. Place a block of wood against it and hammer it in further.

For loose sashes that slide sloppily and don't fit tautly in the jamb:

- See if adding weather stripping will resolve the problem.

Sashes way loose?

· Add a wood shim to one of the stiles. Measure the size of the gap and slice off a shim by running a piece of lumber through a table saw. Or, go to a lumber store and buy a bull-nose stop or a piece of lattice the same width as the thickness of the sash and close to the additional size you need to add.

· Cut a slot in the section of wood you're adding to match the cut in the stile to accommodate the rope. If the material is wider than the sash is thick, trim it down.

· When you've sized the material accurately, nail it to the side of the sash with small finish nails or some of your weather-stripping nails.

· You can also build up the stile with narrower material, such as two lengths of screen molding. Cut them to length and line each one up with an edge of the stile and nail them.

For sashes that do not meet properly at the meeting rail:

· You may have to shim or trim one sash. It's easiest to add to or plane down the upper rail of the upper sash.

· If the sections of the lock don't meet because the catch on the lower sash is lower than the strike on the upper sash, then add a shim to the upper sash to bring it down so the meeting rail will be flush.

· Sashes that bypass each other, that is, the catch on the lower sash rises above the strike on the upper sash, means that one sash is too big and needs to be trimmed down. A substantial gap of one-quarter inch or more is best dealt with by trimming some from each sash.

· Sashes that are only off slightly (or, if noticeably off, but you do not want to do any trimming) can be made to lock by adding a small

The shim.

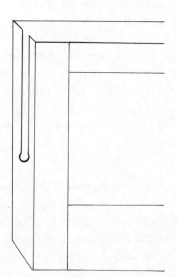

There is an easy way to adjust an upper sash that needs shimming so the meeting rail actually meets and like all of Mr. Window's quick fixes, it works just fine. It's especially convenient if you need an odd-sized shim, something you'd have to cut on a table saw (which most people, including Mr. Window, don't have) and can't just buy off the shelf at a lumberyard. Instead of adding a shim to the top of the upper sash, screw half a dozen or more drywall screws into the header of the jamb where the upper sash closes. Screw them in just enough so when the sash is closed, it will meet the lower sash evenly at the meeting rail. Next, nail a section of parting bead to the outside header blind stop, the horizontal section at the top of the jamb that the sash closes against. Doing this will create a seal since the sash no longer closes tightly against the jamb because of the screws. This will keep the sash weather-tight. If the gap between the sash and the top of the jamb is noticeable on the interior, nail another section of parting bead to the existing horizontal parting bead already installed at the jamb's header. You'll never notice the built-up parting bead or exterior trim and your problem is solved.

shim under whichever section of the lock needs to be raised to resolve the problem. You can use Popsicle sticks, screen molding, or other flat, narrow sections of wood or stiff plastic cut to size and predrilled for the lock screws (you'll need longer screws to accommodate the shims). You can also use small metal washers (you might need a small stack of them for each screw) if you want to be really tacky about it.

There is nothing wrong with adding shims under the locks to accomplish your goal of tight-locking windows. It's all very nice to shim and build up the sashes or trim them down until they precisely meet at the meeting rail on their own, but a lock shim is much simpler if your time or talents don't

allow for trimming and shimming the sashes themselves. When you're old and looking back on your life, I can guarantee you perfect windows will not be your most pleasurable memory. If it is, I can also guarantee you you'll wish it wasn't.

Casement Windows

Like humans, even those with televised makeovers, casement windows begin to lose their shape as they age. They can sag against the hinged side, particularly with butt hinges. As their shape changes, casements will no longer open and close properly, often sticking against the jamb. A contrasting condition occurs when they have been shut for years and are then sprung open and often will not close without being trimmed down.

Before doing any extreme hacking:

· Remove the sash and all the paint from its sides and strip the paint from the window jamb. This combination is often sufficient adjustment for the window to close easily.

· When reinstalling, be sure the hinge screws are tight. A small amount of play can throw the sash off and prevent it from closing completely. Reinstall any cardboard shims that were under the hinges when you removed the sash.

· If stripping the paint isn't sufficient, try to close the sash and note where it is sticking out beyond the edge of the jamb. This is almost always on the stile opposite the hinge side, that is, the edge with the lock. Look up and down the length of the sash as you close it. On the interior face of the sash, mark the sections that need trimming with a pencil. To do this, close the sash as far as it will go without forcing it closed and run the pencil down the jamb drawing a line on the face of the sash.

· After marking, trim the side of the sash with a plane, a scraper (a regular paint scraper, not the Red Devil carbide scraper), or a sander. Do this a bit at a time and close the sash after each trimming. You only want to remove a small amount of wood. Eventually, the sash will close tautly.

· Trim enough so it will close easily and not scrape any paint from the jamb. There should be enough room between the sash and the jamb, after painting, to insert a business card or a flexible putty knife from the outside. You might need more room if you are installing weather stripping.

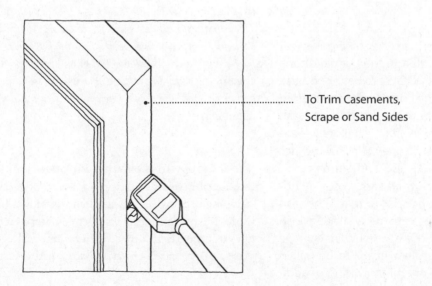

To Trim Casements,
Scrape or Sand Sides

Sometimes the hinged edge or the stile opposite of the lock will stick on the inner edge of the jamb, before you can close it. It would seem to work OK if the whole sash could be pushed outward another ⅛″ or so, but if you did this it would not sit well in the jamb. If this is the case, you will have to trim this edge of the sash at a 45-degree angle until it will pass freely (See page 131). Usually, a piece of coarse grit sandpaper or a file will do the job. Just run either the sandpaper or file up and down the edge until you put a slight bevel on it. Casement adjustment is more an art than a science. I recommend less Jackson Pollock and a little more Raphael when you trim these.

Occasionally a casement will stick at the upper rail. If so, sand it lightly until it closes. More often, though, the bottom rail will not clear at the sill so strip any paint buildup from the sill first and then check for fit. To trim the sash, run a belt sander against the bottom edge of the rail, doing a small amount at a time. Be careful; it's easy to distort the edge if you get too aggressive with the sander. Close after each sanding and check for clearance.

NOTE: Almost all old casement windows feature a single lock, located in the middle of one of the side stiles. TWO LOCKS are better because they would prevent the bottom of the sash from migrating out away from the jamb as the sash ages. Once again, those clever builders saved maybe twenty-five cents per window by not installing a second lock. Also, without a second lock near the bottom of the sash, you may not be able to determine how far to trim if the sash sticks. What may appear to be a sticking sash that will not close all the way could actually be a slightly warped sash that needs to be pulled in near the bottom. I'm a big advocate of addi-tional locks, especially on tall casements. You can either locate a second lock near the bottom rail or remove the original lock and locate it and the other lock at equal distances from the top and bottom of the sash.

Another way of pulling in the sash at the bottom is to install a handle or hook lift, although these are not as elegant-looking or as useful as a second lock.

Q **Yoo-hoo, Mr. Window. I trimmed my casement just like you said and it seems to have enough clearance, but it still sticks when I close it and goes "sproing" when I push it open. It sounds like a cartoon sound effect. What bright ideas have you got now?**

A *You can keep trimming, but I have a feeling you wouldn't like the sound effect of wind whistling inside your house. Rubbing the lower rail and the lock side stile heavily with an old candle stub does wonders for sticking windows and doors, too. Really rub it in. The sash might well be trimmed enough, but may also be slightly warped or may bend a little once it's shut. The wax from the candle allows for smoother movement. You can't expect paint to stick over wax so either paint first or clean all the wax off before you paint and then wax again.*

If Your Casement Is Weather Stripped

Interlocking weather stripping was the weather stripping of choice with casement windows. Like its double-hung counterparts, this material must line up properly in order to close and seal completely. If the casement has malformed over the years, the weather stripping, or some sections of it, may no longer line up and should be removed.

To adjust existing casement weather stripping:

- Renail any loose weather stripping using small wire nails (with heads) or copper weather-stripping nails; ¾″ size will do nicely. Be sure to use a nail set so the heads are flush with the weather stripping.

- Set any loose nails.

- Observe where the weather stripping is binding and bend its opposing pieces outward with a wide putty knife a bit at a time. Conversely, you might have to bend it inward. You can rub some automobile paste wax on the weather stripping, allow it to dry to a haze, and then close the sash, looking for any areas of the wax that get excessively scraped off by the other piece of weather stripping. This isn't a perfect way to observe, but it helps if you can't tell otherwise.

- If the weather-stripping sections simply will not lock together regardless of your adjustments, remove the offending section from the jamb. You can pry it off or drive the nails through with a nail set or punch.

- Install spring bronze or vinyl weather stripping to replace the section you removed (see Weather Stripping, pages 143–152).

It isn't often that you have to remove interlocking weather stripping in order to get a casement to close. There's also no reason to drive yourself crazy trying to adjust the weather stripping if it simply won't fit. Pull it out and replace it with something more forgiving, such as spring bronze, and get on with your work.

FIXED WINDOW PROBLEMS

Fixed windows have some peculiar problems. Let's start with single fixed sashes.

The larger the fixed sash, the more likely it will migrate out away from the jamb (if it's installed from the outside), most noticeably at the bottom rail. Typically, as the space grows, painters or homeowners fill it with caulk or Spackle or other fun fillers. The glass can migrate out at the bottom from the sash itself. I don't know the reason for either of these phenomena other than some shifting or movement in the building itself, the effects of gravity, weather, or possibly alien antiwindow rays being directed at us from outer space. Large windows on the weathered sides of a home are more likely to suffer these phenomena.

If this separation bothers you or is extreme, remove the sash and reset. Clean out all Spackle or other filler material formerly placed between the sash and the jamb and reset the sash. You could set the sash with countersunk screws on the side stiles for added measure to prevent it from moving again.

The glass is another matter. It can be removed and reset, but old glass is fragile so it has to be removed carefully. Removing a large pane can be precarious; sizable panes need to be removed with glazier's suction cups. Unless it's really loose, leave it alone. As long as it can accept a bead of glazing compound to keep water out, and it's secured by glazing points, it's all right. Another option is to remove any glazing at the lower rail and install a wood stop (try a small quarter-round molding from a lumber store) for extra security. After nailing the stop, force some glazing compound or latex caulk between the stop and any gap with the glass as well as the nail holes. Prime and paint the stop so it doesn't deteriorate.

Be prepared to replace the glass if you try to remove it. A hired glazier won't guarantee against breakage, either.

Turning Fixed Windows
Into Operable Windows

Double-Hung Fixed

A fixed sash installed from the outside can often be turned into an operable window. The same is true for a fixed double-hung window without pulleys. Either type of window is disassembled the same way as its respective operable version. To make a fixed double-hung window operable:

- For traditional weight and pulley operation, remove the casings and confirm that you have space for sash weights.

- You'll need four sash weights, four pulleys, and sash rope.

- Install the pulleys in the same location as your other operating windows with pulleys.

- Drill a series of vertical holes large enough to accommodate the pulley wheels so they can spin freely. After drilling the holes, file down the opening until you have a smooth, even rectangle.

- Test-fit the pulley and adjust the hole size and shape as needed. Be sure the opening is straight and level.

- Either mortise the jamb to accept the pulley or let it install flat on the surface of the jamb. Some replacement pulleys are thin enough to sit on the face of the jamb and not need any mortising.

- Drill two pilot holes for each pulley's screws and install.

- Install the ropes and weights as you would an operating window.

- It is unlikely the sashes will have knot holes in them to accept the sash ropes. You can either rout out a path for the rope with a router and drill a knot hole (at a slight, downward angle), or drill the hole first and, using a handsaw, cut a series of kerfs deep enough to accommodate the rope and then chisel out the wood remaining from the kerfs. Never heard of a router? Mr. Window has heard rumors about them, but has never owned one so you're in excellent company.

- Install the sashes and test for fit and function.

An alternative to ropes and pulleys are duplex pulleys, which call for a midway section of each jamb to be mortised out deep enough to house the pulley. Be sure to order pulleys that can accommodate the specific size of your window.

The simplest methods are to use sash controls or sash pins, although the sashes will not move as smoothly as they will with pulleys. It really depends on how often you expect to use the window and how important smooth movement is to you. For only occasional use, pop in a couple of sash controls.

Outswinging Casement/Butt Hinges

To convert a fixed casement sash installed from the outside into an operable window with butt hinges:

- Remove the sash from the jamb as you would any fixed sash. It should have at least four finish nails securing it.

- Prime and paint all four edges of the sash and let dry.

· A butt hinge consists of two leaves and a hinge pin that sits inside the hinge knuckles.

· Look at an existing operable casement window for guidelines. Measure the size of the hinges and purchase a matching pair for exterior use. Also measure the location of the hinges from the top and bottom of the sash to the top and bottom of the respective hinges. You will install the new hinges in the same location on the fixed sash.

NOTE: Be sure all sashes are the same height!

· You will be cutting a mortise (a notch or slot) into both the sash and the jamb so each hinge can be recessed according to its thickness and install flat and flush. For this you'll need a sharp wood chisel.

· Take your hinge location measurements from the operable casement sash and mark them off on the fixed sash.

· Take one hinge and with the knuckles facing out and resting flush against the outside edge of the stile, trace an outline around it. You can trace with a pencil or, better yet, a very sharp knife (you won't have to dig in too far; the cut from the knife provides a better starting point for the chisel than a pencil line). Do this for both hinge locations.

· Lay the edge of one hinge leaf against the edge of the sash where the knuckles were resting and line it up with the traced outline of the hinge on the face of the stile. You're doing this to determine the depth of your cut. Trace the edge of the hinge with a pencil or knife.

· These markings and measurements and cutouts should be done carefully! If the hinge goes in crooked, the sash won't operate properly.

· Lay the sash flat on a work table and find the hinge outlines on the stile. Cut the width of each hinge first. Place your chisel on your markings with the beveled edge facing inward towards the mortise, not away from it. Strike the chisel firmly for these first cuts, but don't go crazy. You're only cutting in ⅛" or so. Use the marking on the edge of the stile, the one noting the thickness of the hinge, as a guide. Finish cutting the length of the hinge in the same manner as the width.

· After the outline has been cut, hold the chisel at a 45-degree angle and make shallow V-channel cuts (two cuts at opposite angles), no deeper than the thickness of the hinge, midway across the length of the mortise.

· Make a series of smaller V-channel cuts about ⅛" apart and perpendicular to the first cut. These cuts should be to the edge of the mortise.

· When these cuts are completed, chisel out the chipped wood by inserting the chisel at the marking on the edge of the stile. Make short, even, flat strokes.

· Clean out all the wood and get your cut as flat as you can. Lay one hinge leaf in the mortise and check that it's flat and flush with the rest of the stile. Cut deeper if you need to.

· Did you cut too deep? No problem, you can cut a cardboard hinge (a business card works well) and place it under this side of the hinge.

· Once the hinge sets flat and straight, mark the screw holes and remove the hinge. Your pilot holes for the screws must be straight so drill carefully. You can purchase a self-centering drill bit if you feel the need for one.

· Attach the hinge and tighten the screws. Keep one hinge loose for measuring on the jamb.

· Go back to the operable casement and measure the location of the hinge mortises on the jamb. Carefully measure and mark the jamb of the fixed sash and mortise out for the hinges using the loose hinge as a guide.

· Attach the second hinge to the sash and then screw both hinges and sash to the jamb.

If you don't have an operable casement to use as a guide, you can safely figure on installing the hinges four inches from the top and bottom of the sash. This doesn't mean you can cut into the jamb using these same measurements! Remember, the sash is slightly smaller than the opening. Measure both and adjust the jamb measurements accordingly.

After installing the hinges and hanging the sash, you'll need to install an opener or control arm and one or two locks (I prefer two). Here's what you do:

· A single lock is installed in the middle of the stile opposite the hinges; two locks are installed equidistant from the top and bottom or equidistant from the top and bottom ogee details depending on your preference. Find this location and mark it with a pencil line.

· Close the sash and place the casement lock catch at your halfway mark and hold the strike to the jamb; the catch has to clear the strike, but be close enough to lock into it. Draw a line at the top and bottom of the catch with your pencil.

· Open the sash, hold the catch inside your pencil lines, and mark the screw holes.

· Remove the catch and drill one pilot hole.

· Attach the catch with one screw and check that it's straight before completely tightening the screw.

· Drill the remaining pilot hole(s) and install the screw(s).

· Grab the catch, pull the sash closed and place the strike against the jamb where the catch will insert into it. Open and close the catch against the strike to be sure it will be taut, but easy to open and close.

· Mark the screw holes for the strike and drill one pilot hole.

· Insert and tighten one screw to hold the strike, checking that it's straight before completely tightening.

· Drill the second pilot hole and install this screw.

· Using your power drill and a drill bit just smaller than the opening in the strike, drill a series of holes into the jamb. With the drill running, move the bit up and down through the holes, cleaning out any remaining wood between them. Hold the drill at a slight angle in each direction while running it up and down. Avoid running the drill bit against the strike.

· Check that the catch will comfortably engage the strike.

· The opener or control arm is installed approximately at the center of the sash; its base is installed in a corresponding location on the stool with the movable arm pulled in away from the sash as far as it can comfortably go. This way, you get the maximum opening distance for the sash. Before installing the control, place the base and the end of the arm where you expect to install them, hold the arm against the sash, and push the sash open, keeping the arm against it. This will tell you how far it will open and whether you need to adjust the location. Be sure the arm is level when you screw it to the sash. Mark all screw holes with a pencil and drill pilot holes before installing the screws. The end of the arm that attaches to the sash will be screwed in first.

· Your control arm will also come with rudimentary, but illustrated instructions, on the package.

Hinge pin between the knuckles.

Use hinge to outline measurements.

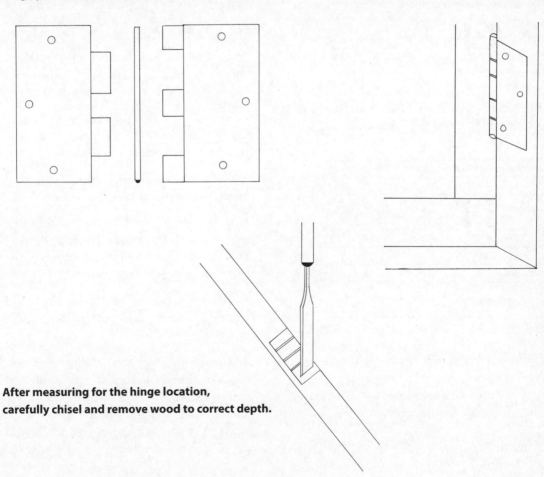

After measuring for the hinge location, carefully chisel and remove wood to correct depth.

Installing Friction Hinges

An alternative to butt hinges is to install friction hinges. I can't say which hinge type is easier to install or more useful. They both work and friction hinges mostly eliminate the need for openers. I say mostly because in a high wind a sash can still slam closed if it has an older hinge without the tighter holding power of a new hinge. I also can't say how long a new hinge will retain this holding power (longer on narrow windows, less so with wide windows).

Friction hinges are a specialty item not commonly stocked whereas every hardware and home improvement store has butt hinges. However, these stores don't all have openers/control arms so purchasing them is another consideration.

To install a pair of friction hinges in a formerly fixed sash:

· Buy a pair whose size is appropriate for your sash as noted in the following table:

Approximate sash width (inches)	Hinge size (inches)
12–16	8
16–20	10
20–24	12
24–28	14
28–30	16
30–32	18
32–36	20
36–38	24

NOTE: These measurements are not the same as those for awning or hopper vent windows. For a complete list of measurements for all window types, go to www.jcwhitney.com.

· Prime and paint all four edges of the sash and let dry.

· Decide how you want the sash to open (left to right or right to left); this will determine which side your hinges get installed.

· The hinges will install in the upper and lower rails. Measure off and mark a rectangle 1⅛" wide by the length of the closed hinge using a carpenter's square or straight edge. On the side of the rail, measure and mark a line ⅜" from the edge; this will be the depth of your cut. After marking with a pencil, take a knife blade and your square or straight edge and cut into the pencil line.

· Cut a rabbet ⅜" deep and 1⅛" wide by the length of your hinge into both sides of the sash so that the closed hinge will fit into it. The outside face of the sash is uncut. Make your cuts with a sharp wood chisel (see instructions above for cutting butt hinge mortises).

· Cut a little notch ¹⁄₁₆" deep and 1" long so the hinge track will clear when open.

· Mark the screw holes with a pencil, drill pilot holes, and screw the hinges to the sash.

· With the hinges open, fit the sash into the opening so hinge tracks are against stool and header (upper horizontal section of the jamb) and snug into the corners.

· Mark the screw holes, drill pilot holes, and screw the hinge tracks into place in the opening.

· Test the sash for smooth opening and closing. If it doesn't quite clear the jamb and close completely, and you're sure the hinges are set all the way into the corners, observe where the sash is hitting and gradually trim the corners down with a file or sandpaper.

· Continually test the sash as you trim so you don't take off an excessive amount of wood.

· Install sash locks.

You can install these same hinges for awning and hopper vent windows as well. Or, for simplicity, you can install butt hinges on either type of window and control its opening with a transom chain attached to both the sash and one of the casings. For awning windows that are high up and difficult to reach, install a transom catch, a lock that can be opened and closed with a window pole. Examples of this hardware can be found at www .kilianhardware.com/tranwinhar.html.

WEATHER STRIPPING

Weather stripping is available in the following general categories:

· Spring bronze
· Interlocking metal
· Vinyl
· Foam, both open- and closed-cell

Metal weather stripping is the longest lasting and most time consuming to install. Vinyl is quick and easy, does a decent job, and is simple to replace once it eventually comes loose or gets torn (which it will). Foam is used to fill gaps that are too wide for vinyl. Sometimes a combination of materials works best depending on the window.

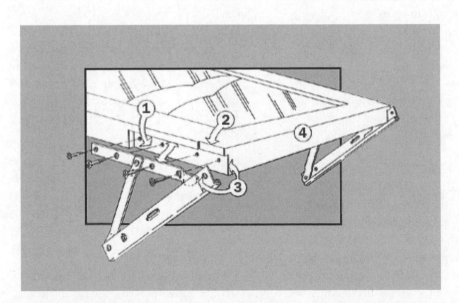

Basic friction hinge installation (illustration courtesy of the Vincent Whitney Company)
1. $^3/_8$" x $1^1/_8$" rabbet
2. $^1/_{16}$" x 1" notch
3. Testing hinge for free movement
4. Hinge edge

Spring Bronze

Spring bronze is a thin brass weather stripping available in different widths. It's available in both a V-shaped and flat material; I prefer the latter because it offers more adjustment possibilities in my view. The nailing edge of the flat material has a crease running the length of the weather stripping. After running a putty knife against the crease, it prevents the metal from lying flat as a sash either slides or closes against it (therein the "spring") forming a seal against drafts. This is a versatile, long lasting, and forgiving material that adapts to a range of gaps and misaligned windows. Pemko Manufacturing (www.pemko. com, 800-283-9988 West Coast, 800-824-3018 East Coast) makes spring bronze weather stripping in 17′ rolls of 1⅛″ wide material (enough for one door, but suitable for windows), normally sold in hardware stores. They also manufacture 100′ rolls, which are a much better idea if you're doing several windows.

I almost always install Pemko 1½″ wide spring bronze in double-hung residential lower sashes, even though it's made for thicker commercial sashes. This size is not available at hardware stores and would have to be ordered, usually from a wholesale hardware supplier (contact Pemko at one of their 800 numbers listed above or in Resources as they seem constitutionally incapable of responding to e-mail). Installed against a standard 1⅜″ thick residential lower sash, the wider weather stripping provides a much cleaner look. Depending on the size of the upper sash meeting rail, you can install either the 1⅛″ or 1½″ size spring bronze.

NOTE: Kilian Hardware (see Resources) offers spring bronze weather stripping in 1¹/₈″, 1¹/₄″, 1³/₈″, and 1³/₄″ sizes.

Installing Spring Bronze

Spring bronze is pretty easy to install, but you'd never know it at the prices some contractors charge. One key is keeping it straight and taut during the initial fastening. It's installed at the jamb and the meeting rail. You can install spring bronze between the upper sash and the jamb, but I don't recommend it. Why not? Because the metal has to be trimmed to fit around the pulley wheel and then nailed in several places so it doesn't catch on the sash when it slides up and down at the pulley. The nails flatten out the spring bronze eliminating its effectiveness as weather stripping. I suggest using V-vinyl (see below) at the upper sash jamb.

The lower sash stays out while the weather stripping gets installed at the jamb.

Here are the steps for installing spring bronze:

- Spring bronze material can be installed with nails, staples, or even screws (which no one except Mr. Window seems to consider using). A good electric stapler is a big help if you're working on a lot of windows.

- You can buy a commercial stapler (over $200) or rent one (better idea). When renting, take a piece of the weather stripping and an old board with you and test that the stapler is strong enough to punch the staples through the metal. Use galvanized or stainless steel staples as the brass-colored ones can rust.

- The nails that come with Pemko weather stripping are brass coated and the heads can corrode when they get any water on them, including overspray from latex paint.

NOTE: Nails are not included with the Pemko 100′ rolls and must be ordered or supplied separately. I recommend copper weather-stripping nails that can be found in many hardware stores. They're sold in prepackaged plastic containers in the same section as brads, tacks, and other small fasteners. They seem to be more corrosion resistant than the brass-coated nails.

· With the lower sash out, measure its height and add one inch. Using metal snips, cut two pieces of spring bronze this length.

· The nailing edge with the crease faces inward to the room. Take one piece for the left side and cut the bottom end at a slight angle to accommodate the slope of the sill.

· Take your snips and round off the top end, eliminating the sharp corners. You do this because there's a chance the corners can catch a splinter or rough edge of the sash when it closes and eliminating the corners helps prevent this.

· Line up the weather stripping so the edge facing out is about ¹⁄₁₆″ away from the parting bead. Hold the metal straight to be sure it clears for the entire length. Press the weather stripping flat to be sure it doesn't butt up against the parting bead.

NOTE: Sometimes (my favorite term, it seems) the weather stripping will not run straight up an equal distance from the parting bead. It looks like it's bowing inward at one end or the other and won't lie flat. If this happens, just move the whole piece slightly away from the parting bead until it lies flat, even if it looks like it's kind of at an arch.

· With the spring bronze in position, put one nail in as close to the bottom end as you can, hammering it in at a downward angle (toe-nailing).

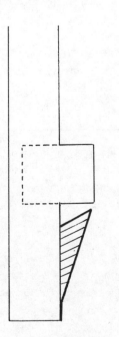

Spring bronze weather stripping installed at lower sash top view. Weather stripping flares out against the sash. Next to the weather stripping is the parting bead.

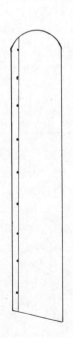

Spring bronze weather stripping at lower sash. Round off the top with sheet metal snips. Left side is nailing edge. Bottom cut to match sill angle.

- Push the top of the weather stripping hard upward, watching that it lines up with the parting bead but doesn't touch it, and toe-nail another weather stripping nail (aiming upward) in the nailing edge. By hammering in the end nails tightly and toenailing, you're stretching the spring bronze until it's taut. Now, when you finish nailing, it shouldn't bind or bend.

- Install the remaining nails (or staples) every inch and a half. The 1⅜″ material has small indentations indicating nail locations.

- Take a slotted screwdriver or stiff putty knife and run either tool along the bend in the nailing edge, pressing down on the metal. This will cause the weather stripping to flair out as though it were bent. The weather stripping will now form a tighter seal when the sash is installed and slides against it.

NOTE: On some jambs, the weather stripping staples will not shoot all the way in and will have to be hammered the rest of the way. Don't slam them too hard as this will flatten them instead of driving them in.

WARNING! The spring bronze will be nailed to any inside pocket covers. Depending on how firm your pocket covers are, the hammering might not go well as the pocket covers can be too springy. It's even worse with stapling, which really depends on a firm stapling surface. If you've got spongy pocket covers, place a stiff putty knife between the cover and the jamb (there will be a space where it's cut out, enough space for the blade), bend it towards the room to brace the pocket cover, and continue nailing or stapling.

Although you can measure and cut the spring bronze so it's flush with the top of the lower sash and the bottom of the upper, I prefer to run it about one inch longer. This way, if the edge of the sash is a bit rough, despite sanding, and catches the end of the weather stripping, you can add a nail or staple at this corner (this is opposite the nailing edge and is the edge which normally flares out) and not lose much, if any, of the seal because this end runs out beyond the sash. Is that clear? Probably not, but trust me, it's a good idea.

Q **Hey, Mr. Window, I put that spring bronze stuff in and every time the wind kicks it up it starts humming. I like**

Instead of using nails to secure spring bronze weather stripping to the pocket cover section of the jamb, or even the entire jamb, use some small, flathead brass screws. They go right through the metal without needing pilot holes, they sit flat enough for the sash to pass, and they give you a means to remove the weather stripping in the future should you ever need to get back into the weight pocket. Using a drill with a Phillips head attachment and half-inch screws (or so), you don't have to be concerned about a spongy pocket cover, and the screws will go right in once they tap into the metal. Be careful not to drill the screws so hard they go through the weather stripping.

my humming in the shower, thank you very much, and preferably Broadway show tunes ("OOOOOOKLAHOMA, where the wind comes sweepin' down the plain . . .") and not this strange buzzing from my windows. You got me into this, now you get me out of it before I go nuts.

A *Before you go nuts? Well, the insane are often the last to recognize their condition. If the weather stripping "hums" during windy weather, it indicates a lot of wind is hitting its underside and it's doing its job. That's all well and good, but it's annoying. You can eliminate the noise by running a length of foam weather stripping under the flared edge of the spring bronze. This acts as a cushion and keeps it from humming.*

Installing weather stripping at the meeting rail can be a little problematic. How come? Because it gets nailed to the meeting rail of the upper

sash and can sometimes rub against the lower sash when either sash is moved. I've never figured out why it happens with a few windows and not with most others, but you can still go ahead and install the weather stripping.

When installing the spring bronze at the meeting rail:

· For residential size windows, use 1⅜" wide weather stripping unless you have an especially thick meeting rail that can accommodate 1½" wide material.

· The sash should be installed so you can get an exact measurement for the length of weather stripping.

· The nailing edge should face up. Allow a little room at the far ends—that is, measure the length of the meeting rail on the upper sash and then take off ⅛" so it won't scrape the parting bead as the sash slides.

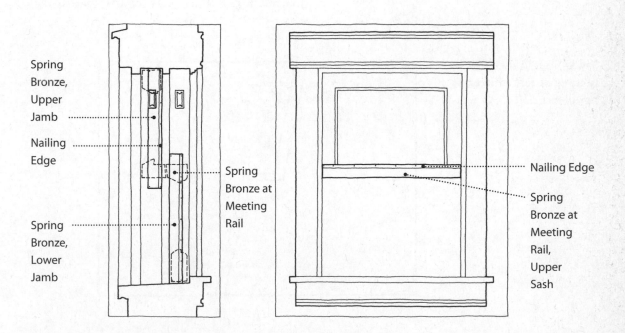

Spring Bronze, Upper Jamb

Nailing Edge

Spring Bronze at Meeting Rail

Spring Bronze, Lower Jamb

Nailing Edge

Spring Bronze at Meeting Rail, Upper Sash

- Nail one end, toenailing it, and then pull the weather stripping tight and toenail the other end as well.

- Nail the remaining weather stripping every 1½". Put your hand or a board against the outside of the lower rail to brace the sash as you pound away.

- Run a slotted screwdriver or stiff putty knife blade against the seam on the nailing edge to flair the weather stripping out.

- Move the upper sash down, raise it, and check the exterior of the lower sash to see if the weather stripping rubbed against the paint. If so, you can either compress the weather stripping back at the far edges and try to flatten it; or, if that's unsuccessful, nail the ends of the weather stripping at the edge of the meeting rail so they won't rub against the lower sash. This diminishes the effectiveness of the weather stripping in the corners, but you really don't have much choice.

After you have installed the weather stripping and before you install the stops, slowly run the lower sash up and down to check for rough spots or catching at the end of the spring bronze. Sand down any splinters or coarse edges that catch. If necessary, nail the end of the weather stripping where it's catching. See below for installing V-vinyl weather stripping at the upper sash.

NOTE: Most meeting rails are flat and can accommodate spring bronze or interlocking weather stripping. Some meeting rails, however, resemble a type of lap joint and need a narrower, flexible type of weather stripping. The best material I've found is smoke seal, whose normal function is to seal fire-rated doors, especially steel doors, to keep smoke from seeping through. Smoke seal is a self-adhesive, tear-shaped, silicone or rubber material that fits this type of meeting rail perfectly. There are other weather stripping tapes, both closed and open cell foams, that might work, but in my experience the smoke

Lap joint–style meeting rail. Smoke seal adheres to upper sash (left).

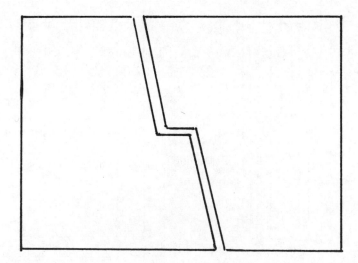

seal (which is lamentably more expensive given that its manufactured purpose isn't as a weather stripping, but as a safety material) is more reliable. Smoke seal is available in several widths from various manufacturers including Pemko and K. N. Crowder (www.kncrowder.com). It is not a common hardware store item, but is available from wholesale hardware stores catering to building contractors.

There is some debate around installing spring bronze on the sill because it may prevent water, which can blow in during a storm, from completely draining. Also, it tends to get covered with a lot of paint over the years and looks kind of wretched.

Spring Bronze and Casement Windows

Spring bronze works quite well with casement windows. The nailing edge should face outside, however, so the sash closes against the flared edge. If you have butt hinges, you can run the material right over the hinges, although some believe that spring bronze on this edge of the sash will throw it out of alignment because it's constantly forcing it away. Sometimes it does, sometimes it doesn't. I know, that's not an especially helpful observation, but you don't know until after it's installed, although you can get an indication if, after installing spring bronze on the jamb section opposite the hinges, the sash closes very snugly. With friction hinges, you can only partially weather-strip the upper jamb and at the sill.

When I find a noticeable gap between the bottom rail and the stool, I often install a strip of closed-cell weather stripping directly to the edge of the stool, taking care that it isn't so thick as to prevent the sash from easily closing. For large, uneven gaps, I have attached the closed-cell material to a section of molding, such as a bullnose stop, butted it up against the sash, and nailed the molding to the stool. You can easily do this with friction hinges, less so with butt hinges that require a casement opener or control arm that can get in the way.

Interlocking Weather Stripping

There's a heavily used park in Seattle called Green Lake. The lake has a jogging path around it and it's often full of runners, skaters, and cyclists. One of my goals in life is to never, ever run around Green Lake or any other lake and so far, I have met this goal. I can safely say I will persevere and continue to meet it in the future as well. I have the same attitude towards installing interlocking weather stripping: Let someone else do it. Installing this stuff from scratch is very much an art form, especially at the meeting rail of a double-hung window, and few contractors install it in windows any more, although some do install it for doors. Mr. Window strongly suggests you use an alternative material, particularly if you're dealing with old sashes. Mr. Window both knows his limits and further knows that spring bronze is a more intelligent choice for him. Interlocking weather stripping is still manufactured if you need replacement pieces for existing material.

Really, really, really want interlocking weather stripping? You can buy new material from Accurate Metal Weatherstrip Company (see Resources).

Vinyl

3M V-Seal Door Weather Strip, or an equivalent material from Pemko, is also used for windows. This is adhesive-backed polypropylene (plastic)

149

which folds into a V shape and is available in brown and white. In a double-hung window, this material can be pressed between the sash and the parting bead (it adheres to the parting bead) and at the meeting rail. However, I have found it works well between the upper sash and the parting bead, OK between the lower sash and the parting bead, and not well at all at the meeting rail.

3M also works with casement windows, but I still prefer spring bronze. V-Seal requires a very clean surface, preferably unpainted, for the adhesive to stick. It sticks well to new parting beads, but not as well to old casement jambs.

With double-hung windows, I usually combine the 3M and the Pemko, using the spring bronze at the meeting rail and between the jamb and the lower sash and the 3M at the upper sash stile and header.

To install V-Seal weather stripping at upper sash:

· Be sure the side of the parting bead facing the upper sash is clean and preferably free of paint. If the paint is sanded off, brush away all dust.

· Do all painting first so you don't have to cut in around the vinyl. Try to leave the back side of the parting bead, where the vinyl will attach and the upper sash slides, paint free.

· Measure from the top of the jamb to a half an inch or so below the meeting rail of the upper sash when the sash is closed. Cut a piece of V-Seal this length.

· Lower the sash and remove the first twelve inches or so of paper backing from the weather stripping.

· Starting at the top of the parting bead and with the crease facing toward the jamb, press the V-Seal against the parting bead, removing the paper backing as you go.

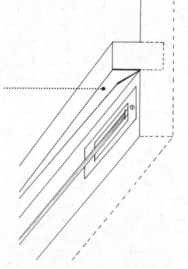

Upper sash in lowered position, with parting bead and 3M V-seal illustrated.

· When you get to the bottom few inches, you'll need to place a flexible putty knife inside the crease and push the V-Seal in and against the parting bead.

· Raise both sashes. The last half-inch of so of the V-Seal will be sticking out under the upper sash. Press a thumbtack, staple, or weather-stripping nail into it to prevent it from coming loose.

· Do both parting beads and test the sash for up and down travel.

· Measure the header section of the jamb (at the top).

· Run some sandpaper across the header and wipe away the dust. Cut a length of V-Seal and attach it to the header with the crease facing outside and the open section close to, but not rubbing up against, the horizontal parting bead.

This is a good combination of materials, vinyl and metal, and allows for an easy installation at the upper sash. Both materials will be a nuisance to paint around, the vinyl more so than the metal, which is why I recommend painting before installing the V-Seal. You can do the same for the spring bronze, but will have touch up to do after installing the lower sash and stops. Touch-up is often easier than painting around the weather stripping.

If you want to paint first:

· Paint both sashes, parting beads, and jamb before installing the sashes.

· Install the upper sash and parting beads.

· Install the spring bronze and then install the lower sash and stops.

· After caulking and filling the nail holes in the stops, touch up as needed to cover.

I'm a big believer in painting while the window is disassembled. Why make the job harder than it needs to be?

Foam

Foam weather stripping is available in different thickness and widths. Two types are manufactured: closed-cell, which is a thick, dense material, and open-cell, which is less dense, lighter, and softer. Neither type works well in double-hung windows and their performance varies with casements and doors. The closed-cell is less flexible, so if it is thicker than the gap you are trying to seal, the window (or door) will not close properly.

Closed-cell weather stripping is a good solution if you have a sizable gap between a sash and a stool. You can:

· Clean the edge of the stool and apply the foam directly.

· Nail a stop or narrow section of trim across the stool with a length of closed-cell running along the edge facing the sash, butting it up just enough to keep out drafts and not interfere with the movement of the sash.

NOTE: The stop or trim must clear any control arms or openers in the case of casement windows, either by using a very narrow stop, trimming around the opener, or installing the opener on top of the stop.

Other Materials

There are other types of rigid weather stripping available for doors which, in some instances, can be used for windows. You may have gaps or problems that defy the usual choice of materials. One type made for doors consists of lengths of aluminum with a vinyl bead on one edge. The installer cuts them to length and screws or nails them to the door jamb. They can also be nailed to double-hung window stops or to casement jambs. I have even nailed them at meeting rails when the situation called for it. That doesn't sound especially pretty, but it's not quite as ugly as you might think, either.

Occasionally you run into what appear to be homemade windows which do not fit well or tightly. You might applaud the past home-owner, who built them from self-reliance or frugality, but will think them more crude examples of folk art when you're filling the gaps around them with rags when winter rolls around. If you're not ready to replace them and you want to cut down the drafts and some of the more industrial-looking weather stripping will do the job, then by all means install it. Study the gaps and their severity and take a trip down to your hardware or home improvement store and look at their weather stripping selection. Something will fit even if it won't win you any *House Beautiful* awards. For the vast majority of windows, however, spring bronze will do quite nicely.

REPAINTING AND REFINISHING

Painting and finishing of sashes and windows is a million times easier if the window is disassembled. Some touch-up and caulking will be needed after assembly. You can even paint the outside casings and sill with the sash out—a real plus if you don't like working from extension ladders.

The following is Mr. Window's crash course on painting and finishing to complete your window repair work.

You want the simplest, cheapest weather stripping that requires no tools? Try Mordite Rope Caulk, a self-adhering clay-like material available in gray or dark brown and available at many hardware stores. Rope Caulk comes as a roll of separate flexible, narrow lengths of material that you unroll and press into the window between the sashes and the parting beads and anywhere else you feel a draft. It isn't especially pretty, but does the job for around $4 a box (90 linear feet). Given that it's so thin, it doesn't stand out all that much. If you're really frugal, you can remove it in the spring, store, and reuse the following winter. Once the Rope Caulk has been installed, you can't open the window without pulling the material loose.
For a look, go to: *www.energyfederation.org/consumer/default .php/cPath/21_392_71*

Paint

Paint is a collection of small solid particles in a liquid medium. When applied, the medium dries leaving behind a colored protective film. Paint pigment adds both color and longevity to paint by slowing down its deterioration from sunlight and weather.

Once upon a time, almost all paint was oil-based. That is, it contained oil, usually linseed, paint thinner, color pigment, and drying agents. Some old-time painters swear by it, waxing especially nostalgic about lead-based paint (lead was a terrific pigment and drying agent). "Best damn paint you could get, you know. Never should have stopped making it." Progress goes on despite personal opinions, gentlemen.

An oil-based paint stays liquefied until its oil dries to the touch while its solvent (paint thinner, turpentine) evaporates. This is a lengthy process and it can take hours and hours for a coat of oil-based paint to dry depending on the temperature and humidity.

Q **Just hold on, Mr. Window, what about something called milk paint? That's been around longer than commercial paints, hasn't it? By the way, can I pour it on my corn flakes if I'm out of regular "Boy, Oh Boy, It's Soy" milk?**

A *Sure, put it on your corn flakes. Then you can paint the kitchen with it when you're through with breakfast. Milk paint, also called casein paint, is an old finish, often homemade, whose ingredients included old curdled milk, lime, and coloring. It's really more of a furniture and cabinet finish and it would be unusual to find it on your windows or other woodwork, but not impossible. It's very difficult to remove. Go to www.milkpaint .com or www.realmilkpaint.com for more information.*

Water-based paints have actually been around since the 1800s (whitewash is one example). After World War II, water-based latex paints with their tricked-out resins were commercially available for consumer use. No more smelly paint thinners and long drying times. Latex paint stays liquid until the water in it evaporates, leaving a protective film.

Which is better? It depends on the application and with whom you consult. There is no shortage of opinions and the only common ground you'll find is both paints require proper preparation of the surface to be painted. Here's the rundown on the hits and misses of oil and latex paints:

Oil-Based Paint
- Less shrinkage than latex paint
- Durable in high-traffic areas
- Adheres to all kinds of surfaces, even if poorly prepared
- Turns brittle and yellow with age
- Long drying time, requires paint thinner for cleanup
- Colors fade faster than latex
- Chalks faster than latex
- Does not breathe, forms tight film, blistering can result
- Seals stains better than latex
- Requires good brushing technique, not as easy for beginner painters

Latex Paint
- Fast drying
- Resists fading and chalking
- Breathes, thus less blistering
- Flexible
- Does not yellow
- Water cleanup
- Mildew resistant

- Softer film, should not be used in high-traffic areas
- Adhesion problems over existing oil-based paint without extensive preparation work first

At some point in the near future the question will be a moot one because oil-based paint and finishes are gradually being phased out. In California, for instance, air quality regulations have essentially killed the market for oil-based residential paint. Although the first generation of latex paint left something to be desired, particularly for use on woodwork, the current generation with acrylic resins and advanced emulsion technology is vastly improved and is used for myriad applications. Many painters used to prefer latex for walls and oil for woodwork, although in new construction latex is used on everything.

I have no problem recommending latex paint for both the interior and exterior of your windows. The main point of failure on the inside will be on the ogee detail on the bottom rail and the first couple of inches of vertical ogee up from the bottom rail on all sashes and to a lesser extent on the bottom rail of the upper sash and any horizontal muntins. These areas near the glass are where water can condense and settle in the winter months and where exposure to sunlight is greatest. They're tough to maintain if you've got single-pane glass, no storm windows, and winter condensation on the glass.

Paint is available in various sheens or glosses the same as the clear coats—varnish, polyurethane, and lacquer. The sheen determines how much light the paint coating reflects. The higher the gloss or sheen, the more binder or resin in the paint and the tougher the dried finish coat. These are the available paint sheens in ascending order of dullest to brightest:

- Flat
- Eggshell
- Satin
- Semigloss
- High-gloss or just gloss

Every manufacturer's idea of sheen within these categories differs so don't assume Glidden's semigloss will be an exact match of Pratt & Lambert's semigloss, although they'll be close enough. Satin is pretty much the minimum sheen for woodwork because it offers a low-level sheen that's both washable and does not highlight dents, dings, and other imperfections. High-gloss will show everything, which isn't the best idea for old woodwork. Flat finish is reserved for most walls because it hides a lot of problems and is easy to touch up, although difficult to clean.

To apply latex paint:

- You'll need paintbrushes, rags, and a drop cloth. Get a top quality brush, something a good painting contractor would use. Cheap brushes don't hold much paint and the really cheap ones lose their bristles while you're painting. Foam brushes are useless for cut-in work (painting details and corners), although they work well enough for priming, and even painting, flat areas.

- All surfaces to be painted should be clean, deglossed, and dust free with any loose or flaking paint removed. Wash all dirty, greasy existing painted surfaces with a good household detergent and allow to completely dry. It is especially important that oil-based paint be cleaned and dulled by sanding or chemical agent before coating with latex paint. Otherwise, the latex can peel right off after it's dried.

- Prime any bare wood. If you're painting over oil-based paint, consider priming all painted areas as well.

NOTE: Primer and paint are two different materials. It's best to use primer as an initial sealer and "toothy" surface for paint instead of trying to substitute an extra coat of paint in lieu of primer.

- Use good quality enamel paint, applying one to two coats for coverage.

- Mix the paint well and pour a portion of it into a clean container or a clean paint pan. Dip your brush no more than halfway up the bristles, knocking any excess paint off by tapping the bristles against the inside of the container.

- Apply in even, long strokes with an angular cut-in brush.

- If you're painting with the sashes intact, move them every half an hour or so, up and down an inch, so they don't get painted shut. At the end of the day, keep the sashes open an inch or two as there is often enough paint left between the sashes and the jamb and stops to prevent them from moving after drying overnight. Allowing an inch gives you enough room to pop them and move them again the following day. An easy way to do this is to place a block of wood on each sash and tap the block with a hammer.

- Clean your brushes in warm, soapy water at the end of the job (see below). Work a brush comb through the bristles, rinse in clean water, and spin the excess out by spinning the brush between your hands while holding it inside a bucket or garbage can. Wrap the bristles in paper or put the brush in its keeper, the cardboard or plastic wrapper it came in.

Painting with oil follows the same steps as painting with latex except the drying time is much longer, the brushing is slower, and once oil-based paint starts to set up, it doesn't like anyone trying to brush over it again to touch it up. Dust is also more of a problem. Keep a wet edge, watch for drips, and paint in long strokes with plenty of paint on the brush.

What is a "wet edge"? A wet edge simply means after you dip the brush back in the can, you return to the last area painted while it's still wet and overlap it for a uniform finish. It's more critical with oil-based paint than latex.

This is worth mentioning again (and again and again): Do your painting or refinishing when the window is disassembled! It's faster, easier, and you don't have to mess with it drying shut. With the sashes out, you can paint both sides of them as well as the exterior casings and sill without climbing a ladder.

NOTE: Only prime the edges of the stiles, the section that rubs against the jamb. If you paint them, they can squeal when opening and closing against the painted jamb. Tuck the parting beads into the jamb just enough so they don't fall out and paint those, too. When you reassemble the window, you'll only have to do some touch-up and paint the edge of the stops where they meet the casings. Be sure to prefit the sashes first so you don't have to mess with shims or trimming after your painting is finished.

Cleaning Paintbrushes

In an ideal world, paintbrushes would never have any paint in the top half of their bristles, especially at their heel, the ends opposite the tips, which is secured inside a metal band called a ferrule. This ideal world only exists in magazine advertising where every paintbrush is perfectly loaded halfway up the bristles. You, along with every other painter in the world, will get paint all over the length of the bristles, inside the ferrule, and on the handle. When this paint dries, the bristles stiffen up and the brush becomes useless except as a heavy-duty fly swatter. Cleaning brushes is another nuisance of restoration work, but you have to do it.

Whether latex or oil-based paint, a paintbrush needs to be rinsed, the bristles worked either with your fingers or a brush comb (a tool available at paint stores), the paint and cleaner spun out, and the bristles reformed and wrapped so the brush can be used again. Every writer and columnist on home repair will tell you never to soak a latex brush in water because the ferrule can rust out and don't stand the brush on end when you're soaking it because the tips of the bristles can get damaged and that's all very nice, but it isn't realistic. How else are you going to get

the heel and ferrule clean if you don't soak the entire brush? This doesn't mean you soak it for days and days, by the way, just long enough to clean it.

Here are some brush care tips:

- Always keep the bristles of a stored brush wrapped in their keeper, the cardboard holder it comes in, or in plain paper secured with a rubber band or tape.

- Store your brushes hanging up or flat, but not resting on the tips of the bristles.

- When you stop working for a half-hour lunch break or so, it's OK to leave the brush standing in paint halfway up the bristles. If you have to go away for a few hours, do a rough rinse and spin out the water or solvent and paint. Dip the brush back into clean water or solvent, lightly shake off the excess, and wrap the brush tightly in plastic wrap. Spin the brush out completely inside a garbage can, five-gallon bucket, or several paper grocery bags tucked inside each other before you begin painting again.

- Don't wrap the brush and put it in the freezer! You read this all the time and it's just a dumb idea, especially if the brush is really gunked up with paint. I did this once with an oil brush and the next day everything in the freezer smelled like paint and had to be tossed out (OK, my fault, this advice is often intended for latex brushes, but not exclusively latex, so who knew? You may laugh and shake your head now at Mr. Window.). Do it with latex and you still have to clean it out before you can paint again as well as wait for it to thaw. Better to do a rough clean and wrap in plastic slightly wet with water or solvent as this will last overnight as well.

· When cleaning, wear latex gloves if you're cleaning an oil brush to keep the solvent off your skin. Use warm, soapy water for latex and wear gloves if the paint bothers your skin.

· Clean brushes until either the rinse water or solvent are clean and show no signs of any additional paint coming off the brush.

· After spinning a brush, comb the bristles back (they will have flared out from the spinning) and wrap the brush.

· Older, stiff brushes or brushes that didn't get cleaned in time can often be revived by soaking in paint remover or, for latex brushes, hot water and granulated dishwasher detergent. They will recover, but won't necessarily be the lively, accurate brushes they once were depending on how they've been neglected. Still, brushes can get a second life for exterior painting or staining decks and fences or as dust brushes.

Oil paint gets cleaned with paint thinner and the thinner can get reused regardless of how gunky it looks. How? Like this:

· Pour some thinner in a can or plastic container and rinse your brush.

· Pour the dirty thinner into a storage container that has its own top (a plastic jar, empty plastic laundry detergent bottle, etc.). Mark this container as having paint thinner inside it.

· Repeatedly clean your brush in new thinner until all the paint is out. Spin after each dunking.

· Let the dirty thinner sit undisturbed in its container. Eventually, the paint will settle to the bottom as sediment and the clear thinner on top can be poured into a clean container and used again to clean brushes. By maintaining a storage system of new, dirty, and recycled thinner, you can make your

Although some professional painters will make fun of you, consider using a Warner 380 Roller-Brush Cleaner, a tool that spins paint and water out of both paintbrushes and paint roller covers. It's a very cool tool and works like a toy plunger-style top, the type of spinning metal top that moves when the spiral plunger is pumped up and down. This tool spins the brush out far more thoroughly than you can by hand. Painters laugh because they think hand spinning is sufficient (it works, but why not use a tool?) and they toss out paint roller covers at the end of the job rather than cleaning them. This is understandable; cleaning a roller cover out by hand is time consuming, but spin it and the job goes quickly. It's worth it if you buy expensive covers, not so if you buy cheap ones unless you have concerns over garbage and waste and landfills. Insert the brush or roller into the Roller-Brush Cleaner and then spin them out inside a garbage can to catch the spatter. Then proceed with cleaning and more spinning. Afterwards, be sure to comb the brush bristles down and place the brush in its holder or wrap it in paper so the bristles stay packed together.

original gallon or so of thinner last much longer. Mark each container so you know which is which. Large professional painting companies recycle their thinner as well, but they use expensive filtration systems.

Stains, Varnishes, Oils, Shellac, and Lacquer

Unpainted woodwork is normally clear coated with or without being stained first. Think of a stain as a very diluted paint that doesn't form a durable film. Most stains bring a "wood" color (oak, walnut, etc.) to woodwork, but no real protection. The stain has to be coated with some kind of clear coat. Clear coats include:

· Varnish
· Polyurethane
· Oil
· Shellac
· Lacquer

Each clear coat (hey, stop me if you've heard this before) comes with its own properties, advantages, and quirks. With the exception of a rubbing oil, they're more demanding than paint when applying so consider practicing on a clean board or inside of a closet door before you put your work out for public view.

Stains

Interior wood stain—the stuff that's used on furniture, cabinets, floors, and woodwork—is composed of pigment suspended in a vehicle of oil and solvent or in water. Interior wood stain adds color and depth to the appearance of wood. A little stain goes a long way and it spreads much faster and easier than paint or any clear topcoats.

Both oil-based and water-based wood stains are available. Like latex and oil-based paint, there is no end to the discussion on the merits and drawbacks of each. The coatings industry has greatly improved all water-based products over the years, although they haven't done it out of charity. The industry is compelled to cut down on VOCs—volatile organic compounds, also known as those nasty smells you inhale every time you open a can of oil-based coating—and water-based is the way to go to meet those reductions.

Water-based stains are fine and they work, but there are plenty of wood workers who prefer oil-based for a sharper-looking finish. You can't go wrong with oil-based if you only want to buy one product instead of messing around with samples (although this is a good idea when you're not sure what you want). If you have any environmental qualms about adding to ozone depletion and global warming and just smelling up your house, skip the oil-based and stick with water-based. I would suggest you buy small sample cans of each once you find a color you want and test them on your woodwork before you commit to either. I would also suggest you think twice about using varnish-stains, which are mixtures of polyurethane and stain. They will not give you the same result as using stain separately from the clear coat.

To apply either stain:

· You'll need latex gloves, clean rags, a piece of scrap wood or stir stick for mixing, a narrow brush, and a drop cloth. Use a high-quality natural bristle brush for oil-based stain and a synthetic brush for water-based. Wear a respirator with organic vapor cartridges if using oil-based or if the water-based fumes bother you.

- The woodwork must be completely stripped of the old finish and be dust free.

- Stir your stain with a clean stir stick and mix periodically while working.

- Dip your brush into the stain no more than halfway up the bristles (the stain will wick up the bristles very quickly). Brush across your scrap wood to get familiar with the flow and penetration rate. If the color is too dark, apply less stain and brush lightly across the wood until the color is satisfactory. Wipe off any excess stain (less likely with water-based).

You can't control the shading much simply by applying less stain, but you can affect it some. If the color is too dark once you start staining, stop, clean it off the woodwork with a rag and lacquer thinner, and purchase a lighter shade.

- Starting at the top of your woodwork or sash, spread the stain lightly and work it in with the brush. Do the entire section and lightly wipe any excess off with a rag. Work your way down, cutting in the stain to reach all the corners and openings.

Let's say your window casings and stool have seen better days, but the finish is mostly intact and you're not interested in stripping it all down. You've sanded most of the finish off the sashes and you have to refinish those, but what about the rest? Mr. Window understands since stripping is a messy job. Once again, fearlessly facing the wrath of purists, he offers a shortcut. Lightly sand all the casings and woodwork with 120-grit sandpaper. Completely sand (you can do it by hand with 80- and 100-grit papers or machine) the worst stools since they often get pretty trashed over time, mostly from sunlight, and can have little if any finish left on them and turn rough to the touch. Clean all the dust off and then paint an oil-based stain on everything. You'll have to use the same color as the existing one or one close to it (you can experiment with a darker color as well). The stain will soak into the stool, which is bare wood, and will sit on the surface of any varnish on the casings. Lightly brush and spread the stain over the varnish until it's an even coat; watch for sags and brush them out if they occur. Let it sit for two or three days before applying any oil-based varnish. Do it any sooner and there's a good chance the stain sitting on the varnish will dissolve since it hasn't soaked into the wood as it's designed to do. The stain on the varnish might look a little cloudy, but I've done it and gotten great results. Once the new varnish dries, no one will tell the difference (well, beauty is in the eye of the beholder). To be sure you'll get acceptable results, test this process first on a section of baseboard. If you're happy with it, proceed with the windows. This method works much better than using a polyurethane/stain mix, which just leaves a muddy-looking mess.

You can also apply the stain using only a rag, but brushing is a lot easier. If applied just right, there will be very little excess to wipe off. Stain spreads very quickly so don't dawdle in one area. A light touch with a modest amount of stain is best. Be sure to stain the entire window at one time. You can't stop for lunch and come back to a half-stained board because, unlike paint, trying to cover up the area where you stopped isn't always successful and there's a terrific chance you'll see two different colors on the wood if you don't stain all at once, keeping a wet edge as you go.

After your staining is finished, you'll have to coat the stain with a protective finish. There is some debate as to whether you can cover a water-based stain with an oil-based varnish or an oil-based stain with a water-based clear coat. From a manufacturer's standpoint, the recommendation is often, if not always, to cover with a like product, that is, oil over oil and water-based over water-based. This recommendation keeps the manufacturer from getting any grief over their products failing because of incompatibility issues so you can't blame them for being conservative. It probably isn't a problem mixing your coatings, especially using an oil-based top coat; oil can cover and sticks to almost anything. I've even used oil-based paint on rubber baseboards. Unfortunately, there will always be some combination of products that don't follow Mr. Window's unwillingness to ardently follow corporate guidelines and instead recommend seemingly laissez faire approaches. With that caveat, he does recommend doing a test sample of your refinishing process to be sure all finishes and products are compatible. Let everything dry for a day or two, check that the clear top coat is still tight and intact, and then continue.

Another debate is how long you should wait before applying a clear top coat. Well . . . the directions will state how many hours, even overnight for oil-based stain. Mr. Window has waited twenty whole minutes before applying a coat of varnish without any ill effects. Floor finishers do this as well; they can't afford to lose a day between coats. Let me correct that: They don't want to lose a day between coats. I've never had a problem with this, figuring it takes hours for most varnishes to dry before forming a film and this is plenty of time for any remaining solvents in the stain to escape as well.

Varnish

Varnish has been around for centuries. It's a durable finish made from oils (mostly linseed, soybean, or tung), resins, and a solvent such as turpentine or paint thinner. The type and amount of oil used determine the varnish's properties (degree of hardness, resistance to weather, etc.). Varnish is categorized by:

· Interior or exterior usage
· Oil content
· The sheen of its film (flat, satin, semigloss, high-gloss)

Exterior varnish, usually called marine or spar varnish, has plenty of tung oil in it, to resist moisture, and UV (ultraviolet) light inhibitors. Its oil content makes it softer and somewhat flexible, which is great for dealing with the weather, but it won't provide the harder finish you want for interior work. Interior varnishes have less oil and dry harder, but like all varnish finishes, they'll show scratches. Varnish offers pretty decent resistance to water, solvents, and heat. This doesn't mean it's a good idea to sit a potted plant leaking water out the bottom on a varnished window stool. Do that and eventually you'll get a nice black ring.

Varnish formulations vary by manufacturer and product. Don't know a phenolic resin from an alkyd? You don't need to. Just buy a can of McCloskey varnish, available at many paint and hardware stores, and you'll do fine. McCloskey offers a full line of interior and exterior varnishes.

Q Ahem, excuse me, Mr. Window, but my hardware store doesn't sell McCloskey varnish. They sell their own brand called "I Can't Believe It's Varnish." They even set up a hotplate next to the cash register to cook up the resins and stuff so you'll know it's fresh. I mean, who wants to be using stale varnish? How do I know you're not some highly paid lobbyist for McCloskey and the various other products you recommend in this book?

A *It appears my road to great wealth and financial independence is being thwarted by your keen insight. I recommend products that are readily available and have been proven to work. This doesn't mean other products won't do the job and this being America, land of infinite consumer choice, you'll never lack for another brand of varnish or filler or hardware to buy for your window restoration. Do you really want to try out seven different varnishes only to find out they all look pretty much alike? Or do you want to buy a quality product and get on with the job and finish it? Say, just how many windows have you worked on since you started reading this book anyway?*

Once in a while, a homeowner (I was one of them) gets the bright idea to strip all the paint from the exterior of their windows and then stain and varnish them. It looks really, really cool . . . for maybe a year. Then, as all wooden boat owners know, the varnish deteriorates and needs to be sanded and recoated, year after year after year. Think twice before you take this route; it really isn't worth it. That said, I have seen the exterior side of windows varnished in England and Ireland, two sunlight-challenged countries where they can pull this off, and they were generally in pretty good condition (presumably, they were maintained). Unless you're living under overcast skies most of the year, stick with exterior paint.

Varnish comes in flat, satin, semigloss, and high-gloss finishes. Satin, also called matte, works well for interiors, offering just enough shine without highlighting every imperfection in your woodwork. Satin and flat varnishes have a flattening agent in them that settles on the bottom of the can and must be regularly mixed during application to keep it suspended in the varnish.

Applying Varnish

Oil-based varnish is less forgiving than latex paint. It likes clean, dust-free surfaces, dry, warm weather, and the right brush (sorry, no discount brushes should be used with varnish). Here's what you do:

· You'll need a tack cloth (available at paint stores), a clean rag, a small container of paint thinner (in a squeeze bottle is good), a drop cloth, and a good natural bristle brush (badger or ox hair or china hog bristle are all good). A recently introduced alternative, the Purdy Syntox brushes (www.purdycorp .com) claim the longevity of synthetic bristles but can be used with both water and oil-based finishes. Use a 2″ or 2½″ angular cut-in brush of your choice for best results. Wipe the area to be varnished with a tack cloth, which is a piece of cheesecloth with rosin worked into it. The cloth is sticky and picks up dust without leaving any residue.

- The room has to be warm and dry and the windows mostly closed. In the summer, closing them prevents dust and pollen and bugs from blowing in on your work; in the winter, this keeps cold breezes from causing the resin to harden up prematurely and mess up the finish (it will look like big chunks of dust have blown into it).

- Wear a respirator with organic vapor cartridges.

- Stir, don't shake, your can of varnish. This isn't a James Bond cocktail. Shaking can cause the finish coat to have bubbles in it.

- Tape a pencil or Popsicle stick across the top of the open varnish can. This is where you'll wipe the brush to get rid of any excess varnish before applying it to the woodwork. If you wipe the brush against the rim of the can, the varnish hardens and little bits of it can fall into the can and contaminate the varnish.

- Dip the bristles no more than halfway into the varnish. Apply with long, steady strokes following the grain of the wood.

- After doing a length of wood, "tip off" the finish by lightly running the brush across the varnish without dipping it into the can (the tips of the bristles will be relatively dry). This action smoothes out the varnish.

- If any varnish drips onto the glass or floor, squirt a bit of paint thinner on one of your rags and wipe it up.

The brush won't move as easily as it does when painting with latex paint. If you find the varnish is just too thick, dilute it with paint thinner, one or two capfuls per quart until you find a mix that's more comfortable to use. Be careful, if you overdilute the varnish, it will run while you're applying it. Some writers even call for the first coat of varnish to be greatly diluted for better penetration, but this is unnecessary.

The first coat of varnish isn't going to look all that great. In fact, it will look pretty incomplete. It normally takes three coats for a full, rich finish. Between coats, lightly sand any dust or imperfections with 220-sandpaper and run a tack cloth over the sanded areas. Some refinishers will sand all the varnish, but the necessity of this is questionable. It certainly can't harm anything to lightly sand each coat, however.

It usually takes up to twelve hours before you can recoat so figure this as a three-day job plus the staining.

Your staining is finished, you don't have time to apply the varnish, but you don't want to leave the woodwork unprotected until you can get back to it. Go ahead and apply a coat of clear wiping oil (Danish oil, Watco, etc.) with a rag as an initial sealer. You can varnish right over it and it will offer some protection until you can commit the time to varnish. Don't wait too long; a single coat of wiping oil doesn't offer as much protection as varnish.

Polyurethane

Polyurethane is a varnish with a synthetic resin and is commonly used today on interior woodwork when a brushable clear finish is called for. It dries faster than varnish and produces a tough film. Some liken its appearance to plastic (no kidding, that usually happens when you have a plastic resin) and don't care for it. Modern polyurethane looks less plastic-y than earlier versions and offers adequate UV protection. Polyurethane is available in several finishes as well as oil-based and water-based products. You apply it as you would varnish.

Oils

Those cans of oil finish you see in hardware and paint stores (Watco is probably the best known) are basically diluted varnishes. They're a snap to apply, dry quickly, and you can put on multiple coats easily. They're not especially durable unless you reapply regularly, which can mean once a year or more depending on the number of initial coats. Although they're really meant to be brushed or ragged on and the excess wiped off minutes later, I've been able to brush them on very heavily without wiping them down and got a thicker finish as a result, almost a varnish finish. I also got a finish that took a long time to dry. This is Mr. Window improvising again and although I can't expressly say it will work for you, you can always experiment. I will add that the manufacturers don't recommend it even if it worked for me.

To apply a rubbing oil-type finish:

· Apply to clean, dust-free wood. Dust isn't as much of an issue with rubbing oils, but the wood should be as clean as possible.

· All finishes emit fumes so wear a respirator if needed.

· Brush on liberally, and use any brush you want. Since you'll be wiping off the excess with a rag, you don't need to be as concerned with brush marks.

· Allow to dry as per the directions on the can before wiping. Follow the directions! If you let it go too long, the oil can get tacky and a lot more difficult to wipe down and you'll have a mess on your hands.

Tung and linseed oil are true drying oils. They don't contain any solvent or resin and are a lot more work to apply than Watco or similar products. They dry by polymerization (small molecules combine to form larger molecules) rather than the evaporation of a solvent. If you want to go this route, use tung oil which leaves a tougher finish and doesn't darken as linseed oil can. Pure tung oil (also called China wood oil):

· Is expensive.
· Isn't readily available.
· Requires a lot of rubbing.
· Takes days and days to cure.
· Is a labor of love, but looks really cool.

Pure oil finishes are great for some furniture pieces, but can be a lifestyle choice when applied to your windows and woodwork.

To apply tung oil:

· Brush a moderate amount of oil onto clean, dust-free woodwork.

· Do one section—say, a single window—at a time! If you get too far ahead, the oil might start tacking up (getting sticky) and becoming harder to rub down.

· Allow the oil to soak in for twenty to thirty minutes, but monitor it, as it could set up faster depending on the weather and dryness. Put on a pair of latex gloves and wipe with a clean rag (T-shirts and old cotton diapers work well), rubbing the oil in, and removing any excess. Tung oil is thick and the rubbing is time consuming.

· Allow to dry overnight and recoat. Figure on doing at least two coats and possibly three.

· After the final coat has dried, you can apply a coat of wax using a clean rag or ultrafine steel wool.

Before you commit to a tung oil finish, do a sample on a board. After your final coat, let it dry a couple of days, wax and buff if desired, and see if this is what you want. It will look fabulous and tung oil is easy to touch up, but it won't be as low maintenance as varnish or polyurethane.

Shellac

Shellac is in a category all by itself. Shellac:

· Is made by and from bugs.
· Dries in minutes and is nontoxic.
· Dissolves in alcohol.
· Is a traditional finish on antiques.

Laccifera lacca is an insect that feeds off of lac host trees in India and southern Asia. It sucks sap from the tree branches and then secretes an amber-colored resin that surrounds the bugs and provides for incubation, feeding, and protection of themselves as well as the next generation of these critters. This hardened resin, called lac, is scraped off, crushed, dried, and cleaned (it's full of dead insects, insect parts, and bits and pieces of trees). Shellac is sold in both flake and liquid form in different colors and has a limited shelf life (old shellac can take forever to dry).

Aside from being an ancient finish, shellac is also used as a coating for:

· Time-release medications.
· Certain candies.
· Apples and other hard fruits.

Yes, that's right, a bug excretion can not only coat your woodwork, but some of your snacks as well. It almost sounds like skit material from "Saturday Night Live," but this is why shellac is in a category all by itself.

Shellac isn't used much on woodwork except for those wanting to reproduce a historic finish. One use in the 1920s was to coat glazed woodwork which had had a very diluted coat of light-colored paint rubbed into it and then wiped off, leaving the grain visible. Mr. Window's unsolicited opinion of this particular finish is that it's ugly-ugly-ugly and should be painted over.

Shellac sticks to anything and can be used as an undercoat for varnish, although varnish manufacturers won't recommend this. I've even used it as an undercoat for polyurethane without any problems.

If you decide to use shellac:

· It dries fast so brush on a full coat as quickly and neatly as you can. The wet edge won't last. With fast drying, dust isn't as much of a problem as it is with varnish or polyurethane.

· Although the alcohol vapors aren't as nasty as those from other clear coats, wear a respirator when applying shellac.

- Apply at least three coats.

- Use a fresh can, not one left in your garage by the last homeowner.

- Remember shellac dissolves in denatured alcohol. You can rub some into any problem areas should you need to fix drips or excess buildup.

NOTE: Orange shellac will leave a visible amber finish.

Shellac is a very old, traditional finish. It is not as tough a finish as varnish or polyurethane, but is more easily repaired and touched up. I might use it as an experiment in one room, but not throughout a house. The world's largest manufacturer of shellac is the Zinsser Company (www .zinsser.com) for more information.

Lacquer

Lacquer is a fast-drying clear coat that is most often used as a furniture finish and always sprayed in a production setting. It's highly flammable, smells awful, and forms a durable film. If you have a ton of woodwork to do—like your entire house—and are prepared to really stink the place up, a sprayed lacquer finish isn't a bad way to go. You can do multiple coats in a day and be done with it. This is what a professional painter would do on a new home. For those looking for something a little lower key, there are brushing lacquers available from Deft, Minwax, and McCloskey. They contain solvents that extend the drying time, allowing the lacquer to be brushed. They'll still stink and all your brushes and tools will need to be cleaned with lacquer thinner. I can't see that they offer any clear advantage over a longer-drying varnish other than a shorter drying time.

If you use lacquer on your woodwork:

- Wear a respirator with organic vapor cartridges and change them at the first whiff of lacquer.

- Clean your brushes immediately after finishing the job. Should you take a break, leave the brush in a container of lacquer thinner.

You can apply a first coat of sanding sealer, a lacquer-based product that dries even faster than brushing lacquer, prior to applying the brushing lacquer.

CHAPTER 5

— · —

Moldings

WOODWORK: MOLDINGS AND CASINGS

Moldings are simply decorative pieces of wood used for transitions from one surface to another (a floor to a wall, for instance). They also provide a degree of protection. Baseboards, which run at the bottom of a wall and rest on the floor, prevent plaster and paint from being nicked by vacuum cleaners, furniture legs, and toy trucks. Door casings, which run around a door frame or jamb, prevent the corners or edges of walls from being chipped. Picture molding was once installed so pictures could be hung from it rather than being secured by nails or hangers pounded into the walls (although later on, in the 1920s and '30s, it was installed for mostly decorative purposes).

In a sense, you can document social and economic changes by the types and size of woodwork in American homes. In grander eighteenth- and nineteenth-century American homes, baseboards could be 16–18″ wide with additional trim on top and a wide base shoe. Ceilings in these homes were quite tall, up to ten feet or so, which almost required a wide baseboard, and wider door and window trim, to offer a sense of proportion. Trees were everywhere and since the locals weren't using them to build casinos yet, they were free for the taking. As the years progressed, and demand increased and a supply of readily available trees diminished, woodwork gradually shrunk until you have the whopping one-and-a-half inch finger-jointed baseboards of today's homes. Economics probably dictated shrinking dimensions more than fashion tastes. As baseboards narrowed, ceiling heights were lowered while Americans were gradually getting taller. Maybe the early colonists and settlers just had a massive Napoleonic complex.

Going into the 1800s, moldings were rendered by hand planing. Special molding planes produced a variety of patterns and styles. The results were very labor intensive and consequently were not found in common homes. Life would have been a lot simpler if Black & Decker had been around (electricity would have been helpful, too). Sawmills, where available, basically did rough cutting. Smoothing and shaping required skilled hand labor and a lot of it. Even flat boards were planed and smoothed by hand.

Toward the end of the nineteenth century and certainly into the twentieth, even the most basic homes featured some kind of trim around doors, windows, and floors. This was evidence of cheaper production costs (boards could now be machined for smoothing and shaping) and a rising gentrification, no matter how humble its manifestations. A simpler or less expensive home might have had only plain baseboards and casings, but they were present nevertheless.

Since woodwork and molding don't perform any mechanical functions (opening and closing), the main issue you'll deal with as a homeowner is refinishing or repainting. As with window sashes, you will have to remove the old finish or prepare it for painting. Also like sashes, woodwork can be removed, which is sometimes a good idea. First, a short history lesson on carpentry and finishes.

Once upon a time, carpentry, like many trades, paid modestly. Now, with more and more people spending their days in front of computer monitors, carpenters and contractors can rightfully demand higher fees for their labor for doing work that everyone's grandfather used to be able to do as a matter of course. Up until the 1940s (by my observations), carpenters followed the LOTS-O'-NAILS philosophy of finish carpentry. If they needed eight nails to secure a piece of trim, they used fifteen. This will affect how you remove your woodwork should you decide to do

so. Fortunately, these guys didn't have automatic nailing guns.

In the 1920s, clever carpenters introduced the neat trick of nailing up through the stool of a window into the vertical painted casings. Mitered horizontal casings would be nailed both to the wall and down and into the vertical casings they butted up against. This was very thorough, very unnecessary, and very annoying to anyone trying to remove the trim.

Other styles of window casings were also assembled in their own unique fashion. Victorian structures built at the end of the nineteenth century frequently had bull's-eye pieces where vertical and head (horizontal) casings met over doors and windows. The bulls' eyes were often overnailed and can split during removal, although they are easily reglued.

Nails from stool into casings.

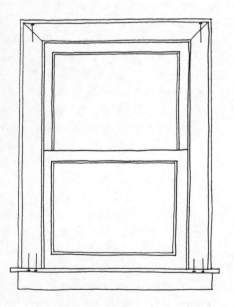

Victorian style woodwork.

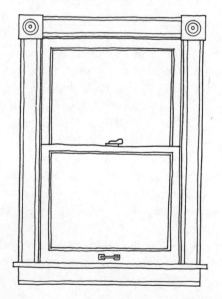

Common casing style with placement of nails.

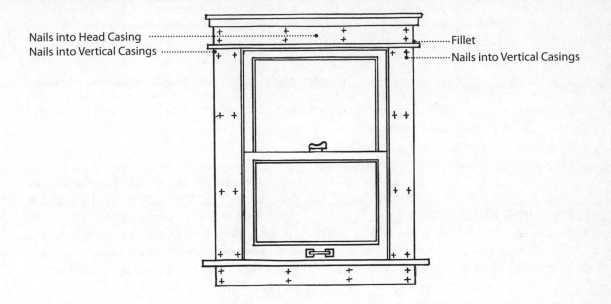

Nails into Head Casing ········
Nails into Vertical Casings ········
Fillet
Nails into Vertical Casings

A common casing style around the turn of the century consisted of a cap molding, a 1″ x 6″ head casing, a fillet or bullnose trim, and two vertical casings. The fillet was nailed down and into the vertical casings and sometimes up and into the head casing in the center with one or two nails.

Some styles were plainer, without the fillet but simply a head casing with ends cut at a 45-degree angle as shown on this page.

Finishes varied depending on the era and, to a lesser extent, geography. Shellac was often used in the late 1800s and early 1900s, with and without a wood stain for color. The same was true for varnish, although the color of choice seems to have been either a dark walnut or dark oak oil stain. Kitchens and bathrooms were typically painted starting in the early 1900s. In the 1920s, almost all woodwork was painted with the general exception of some Craftsman homes and masonry

45-degree-angle casings

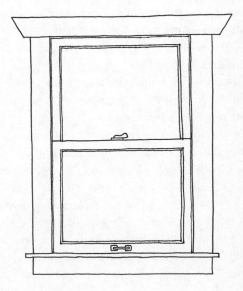

Tudors. Craftsman style featured dark-stained woodwork and Tudors usually had varnished mahogany woodwork in the entry, dining and living rooms, and a varnished staircase, railing, newel posts, and spindles while the second floor, kitchen, and bathrooms were painted. Milk paint, an inexpensive alternative to oil-based paint, was sometimes used on the East Coast prior to the twentieth century. Ever vigilant to the problems of paint-induced corpulence, milk paint was made from nonfat milk. I suppose to remove it you need to mix crushed cookies with solvent.

REFINISHING AND REMOVAL

If you have your heart set on refinishing your woodwork, do a small sample piece first to test the results. Different finishes strip off with varying degrees of effort and you may or may not find the results to your liking. As woodwork gets nicked and dented and then painted over the years, these holes and depressions are difficult to strip paint-free and require a lot of picking at with small hand tools, including dental-style tools. An original finish of either shellac or varnish offers a decent chance of stripping it clean and refinishing, regardless of whether it's been painted over or not.

However, if your woodwork has always been painted, stripping it will be a long, Zen journey: a lot of work, a lot of patience, and an ultimate encounter with the theory of solipsism (which states that one cannot know anything other than one's own thoughts, feelings, or perceptions, which is all you'll be left with after your spouse, children, and dog move out because you insist on stripping everything). Try as you may, it's a safe bet you won't get this woodwork clean enough to stain and coat with a clear finish. Find out for yourself by stripping a small section. Scrub it with

solvent and sand it smooth. Then go over it with a wet rag and watch small bits of primer show up, buried away in the grain of the wood. This will always happen in shaped molding. One approach even calls for coating the woodwork with shellac after you've stripped the paint off and then stripping the shellac a few days after. The idea is the paint left in the wood will attach to the shellac and come off with it when it's stripped. Doesn't this sound like a good time?

Q Hey, Mr. Window, what's with all the negativity? Who says I can't strip woodwork that's always been painted? Where's your can-do spirit? Don't you ever watch self-improvement infomercials? I bet if I really put my mind to it, I could strip this and it would be beautiful.

A *And I bet you've built up quite a real estate empire from all those zero-down seminars, too. Yes, if you really, really, really wanted to strip always-painted woodwork clean—it's your grandest dream—you could, with dental tools and little bits of sandpaper and plenty of solvent and stripper and time, strip this woodwork to the point that you might get away with staining and/or clear coating it. Why go to all the trouble for dubious results when you can take some sample pieces to a millwork company and get the same pattern reproduced so you can just replace it all? (There is a set-up fee for every order or run so order everything you'll need the first time.) Or grain your painted wood (see below)? Better yet, change your dream because this one can quickly turn into a nightmare.*

Replacing woodwork brings up its own problems. Where do you stop? Do you do the box-beam ceilings or leave them? What about all those doors and door jambs and window jambs? You can't just replace the easy stuff and leave the rest painted; it will look awful.

Refinishing woodwork is a messy procedure, although varnished or shellacked woodwork without any paint on it is simpler. Paint over varnish or shellac can be very messy depending on the number of coats of paint and the intricacies of the woodwork. I generally advocate removing painted woodwork with the exception of wide baseboards (anything over four inches). Removing casings and moldings is not an intimidating process and can give you cleaner results than stripping in place.

To test your woodwork for ease of removal and refinishing, remove the trim from inside a closet as a test sample first. If it seems worth the trouble, follow up with one room at a time.

How do you remove it?

· Follow the procedures for removing window casings on page 44. Just be certain you insert a wide, flat, chisel-type putty knife between the wood and the wall or the jamb and pry it out slightly each time. Continue to do this, gradually pulling out a little further. Cut the nails with a hacksaw blade or cut them with wire clippers if necessary. Then insert a flat pry bar for the final removal.

· If you have to remove a fillet (page 169), loosen the head casing first and pry it out from the wall, starting at the top. Move it back and forth a few times and the nail from the middle of the fillet into the bottom of the casing will loosen, allowing you to pull the casing off. Next, remove the fillet from the vertical casings and proceed to remove them as well.

· A window stool is nailed into the sill and the nails are at an angle. Pry the stool off by inserting a stiff putty knife between it and the sill and slowly forcing the stool upward; complete the job with a flat pry bar.

· Depending on the width, baseboards often have two nails at each wall stud, usually every sixteen inches. Removing narrow baseboards is much easier than removing wide baseboards so think twice before removing the latter. In either case, consider a practice run by removing a section inside a closet.

· Don't even think about removing door or window jambs!! Can you remove them? Sure, what went in can come out, but you'll regret it. Each jamb was fitted to its individual location and then shimmed in place so it was square and level. Strip them in place and be sure to install the door and sash that go with them.

· Mark or otherwise tag the woodwork that you do remove!! Make a map so you know where it goes. Mark the jambs and locations as well. It may look the same size from one window to the next, but casings can be off an eighth of an inch or so. All the pieces around any window make up a happy family and if you separate them they can become very dysfunctional. Then you'll have obnoxious TV talk show hosts and their camera crews knocking on your door demanding to know why you are contributing to the growing trend of delinquency and petty crimes among the hitherto productive woodwork society.

· Varnished window stools often deteriorate prior to painting, allowing the paint to soak

One way to remove picture molding is to simply hang on it by your fingers. It will pull away making it easier to get a pry bar behind it and finish the job. Some people will have to hang longer than others, I imagine.

into the wood, but the paint usually sands out. Bear in mind if the paint is old enough, it could be lead-based and you'll have to contain any sanding dust.

· You can trace the changes in window coverings by the number of screw holes in the casings from curtain holders, shutters, shades, and blinds. As the hardware changes, the old screw holes get filled with Spackle or some kind of patching compound. The easiest way to clean out the fillers is with a nail set or punch. Tap with a hammer and then refill the hole with wood putty or color putty, which is a wax type material available in different colors to match wood stains. It does not need finishing and can be applied after your finish coats of stain and clear topcoat have been applied. Putty sticks can also be used, but the color putty works better for larger holes. Wood putty works OK, but requires finishing and does not take the stain and clear coats with the same results as the surrounding wood.

STRIPPING AND FINISHING

Whether you remove the woodwork or leave it intact, the stripping methods are the same except you can be a little sloppier working off workbenches in the garage than you can over a finished floor in your living room. You'll need the same

protective gear and materials needed for stripping sashes alone (see pages 73–90) which include:

· Respirator, long gloves, and eye protection
· Long sleeves and pant legs
· Drop cloths and rags
· Cabinet scrapers
· Paint remover of your choice
· Can or plastic container and old or cheap paintbrush
· Solvent, preferably lacquer thinner
· Medium-grade steel wool
· Flexible putty knife
· Plastic to cover the remover
· Refuse container (an old box)

The easiest finish to remove is old varnish. Oftentimes the varnish is disintegrated and brittle and much of it can be scraped off with a cabinet scraper, requiring less chemical stripping. Scrape with just enough pressure to remove the brittle varnish without gouging the wood.

Cabinet scrapers come in all shapes and sizes. One of the most useful for scraping varnish off the wide, flat sections of woodwork is a card scraper, which is a flat piece of steel, commonly 6" x 3", with four burnished edges. A card scraper is simple and cheap ($5–6 or so), and does a great job cutting through deteriorated varnish and reducing the amount of paint remover you'll need to complete your stripping work.

To remove varnish with paint remover:

· Lay down plenty of drop cloths.

· Paint on a thick coat of remover, brushing once in one direction.

· After the varnish has softened, test a small area by scraping with a putty knife. If the varnish comes off easily, continue scraping gently to avoid gouging the wood.

· Clean any details with steel wool.

· Apply a second, lighter coat of stripper if necessary and clean everything off with steel wool dipped in lacquer thinner.

· Wipe clean with a rag dipped in lacquer thinner as a final rinse.

· Watch out for stripper that drips onto the back of the boards; be sure to wipe this off, too. Otherwise, you'll inadvertently put your ungloved fingers in it later.

If the varnish is very thick and the first coat of stripper starts to dry out too soon, immediately apply more over it. You want to keep the remover wet so it will keep working. Use a medium grade of steel wool (the very coarse grade tends to catch on every possible splinter). For intricate work, paint stores sell brass brushes for cleaning out detailed grooves and such. Synthetic brushes for cleaning auto parts, available at auto parts stores, can also be used. You can cover the remover with plastic wrap if you want to get a lot of it working at once; the plastic will keep the stripper from drying out.

To avoid repainting your walls when stripping woodwork in place, put several layers of wide masking tape on the plaster, right up next to the woodwork. Use the longer-lasting blue masking tape which is manufactured with an adhesive that does not dry out as quickly as regular masking tape. Painters use this for masking work because it can be pulled away 24 hours or more after use and not leave a sticky residue or pull paint off the surface it's adhering too.

Painted woodwork that has been removed can be stripped faster if the majority of the paint is scraped (see lead-based paint below and on pages 72–73) off first down to the varnish with a Red Devil carbide scraper (see page 86) or similar scraper. Scrape the worst of the paint off and then apply a thick coat of paint remover. Don't grind down too hard with the scraper as you could leave digs in the woodwork. Cover the remover with plastic wrap and let it sit for a few hours before removing with a flexible putty knife and steel wool. Your woodwork can also be tank-

Line the floor area with plastic and put a drop cloth on top of it. Wear old shoes that you can slip off easily if you have to walk off the drop cloth and onto a finished floor or carpet. It can now be told that Mr. Window himself didn't always follow this caveat and tracked bits of gummy, gooey paint stripper gunk across a floor or two, albeit quickly rectifying and disguising the fact before any witnesses showed up.

dipped (see pages 85–86), but be prepared for discoloration and raised grain that will have to be sanded. As always, try a sample piece first to observe the results.

NOTE: Once again, the ugly specter of lead-based paint stares you in the face with the same leering eye as King Kong looking at Fay Wray, except you won't be carried up to the top of the Empire State Building only to watch your interspecies boyfriend be shot down and take a really big tumble. Removing lead-based paint (see pages 72–73 and 90) exposes you and yours to potential hazards and demands proper procedures for handling and disposing of it. I've hopped out of an airplane (well, more correctly dropped from an airplane) and bungee-jumped off of a bridge, but there's no way Mr. Window is going to stick his neck out and try to provide definitive legal information involving lead-based paint. My own experience has been that the rules and their enforcement are somewhat fluid, which is fine if the fluid isn't being dumped on you. Call your local air quality control office or the EPA for guidelines.

PAINTING, FINISHING, AND GRAINING

Paint and painting have already been covered with regards to window sashes alone and the same advice pertains to the rest of your woodwork. The main things to remember are:

- Do plenty of preparation work in the form of cleaning, sanding, and deglossing before applying a new coat of paint.

- Prime all bare wood.

- When applying latex over oil-based paint, deglossing is critical and it's a good practice to prime all the woodwork before painting. The primer acts as a good base for the latex.

- Deglossing can be done with commercial liquid deglossing agents, which soften up the old paint, or by sanding sufficiently with 100- or 120-grit paper to dull the paint. Machine sanding will remove all the old brush marks and produce a smooth, wonderful surface for repainting, but also produce a lot of dust (which often means lead-based paint dust).

- Repainting with oil-based paint requires a very clean work area and hours of drying time. During the winter months, close off or restrict any heat ducts to the room you're painting in order to keep the dust controlled. And wear a respirator!

- Although most people will brush on new paint, it's worth considering spraying out your woodwork if you have a lot of it to do. The trade-off is, depending on what kind of paint you're using, you might have to tape all the woodwork off at the walls and certainly at the floors and taping is time consuming. The result is an awesome finish if it's done right (a big qualifier) and the painting part goes much faster than if you were brushing. Sprayers and compressors can be rented from tool rental and paint stores.

NOTE: A sprayer can pump out a lot of paint in a short amount of time. If you go this route, consider practicing with the sprayer by painting a basement room or your garage first. Every paint store and home improvement center has incorrectly tinted paint and paint that was mixed and never picked up by customers for sale at steep discounts. This paint is perfect for garage painting and practice painting.

· For refinished woodwork, you will probably want to stain the woodwork before applying a clear-finish top coat. Stain will even out the irregularities resulting from the stripping and sanding. Do a sample piece first! Take that piece of stained trim around to different rooms at different times of the day. The oak stain that looks so warm and cozy at high noon may be too dark and foreboding in the evening when it shows up in room after room. A good rule of thumb is to go one shade lighter than your first choice.

Graining

Graining is a technique that duplicates the grain and appearance of different varieties of wood. An associated technique, marbling, reproduces the appearance of marble or other types of stone. A number of books and articles have been written on these techniques and when done properly, they look incredible. Here are the general steps for graining:

· An eggshell or satin base color is applied to the wood or metal surface being grained.

· A second paint or glaze is applied and sometimes a third. Each is manipulated with rags, special brushes, combs, even feathers, to produce a wood grain look.

· A coat of varnish can be applied to protect the painted surface.

Good graining looks very much like the real thing. It's a great disguise and offers an option to stripping and refinishing woodwork that's always been painted without any varnish or shellac undercoat. There are books and classes available on both graining and marbling or you have the option of hiring a local practitioner. Regardless of who does the job, try a sample piece first so you know what you're getting.

CHAPTER 6

— · —

Stupid Windows, Leaded Glass

STUPID WINDOWS

Once in awhile, I run across some strange old hardware or track system and have to improvise the repairs. Some of these systems are retrofits, that is, the original pulleys and weights may have been discarded in favor of a plastic track system that would allow the sashes to tilt in for easier cleaning. The current equivalents are products such as Marvin Windows Tilt Pac, although these include new replacement sashes along with the track hardware.

The old systems are just about impossible to repair once the hardware starts breaking unless the original installer was clever enough to leave some extra parts with the building owner. Since no one in the history of home building or repair has ever done this, there isn't much you can do once these systems start failing except patch them up with parts you adapt from whatever you have out in the garage. I know, this isn't especially helpful, but does reinforce one redeeming feature about pulleys and weights, which is they can always be repaired.

PIVOTING WINDOWS

I have worked on two types of pivoting windows; one with pivoting pins on the vertical stiles and one with them on the horizontal rails. The vertical ones are simple enough to deal with. The sash has a steel pin in the center of each stile. The pins fit into corresponding hardware installed in the jamb. The sash simply rotates on these pins. They are removed by lifting them out of the jamb hardware.

The horizontal ones, however, are nightmares demanding an extensive Freudian analysis of their designer. Some have a crank located in the center of the bottom rail. You rotate the crank and the entire sash lifts up about two inches or so. It is now free to swing out on its center pivots, one attached to its top rail and one at the bottom. These are about the stupidest window design imaginable. Depending on their size, you almost need a crane to remove them.

These are primarily commercial windows that showed up around the early twentieth century. They can be repaired using the same techniques as casement windows, but if you can avoid removing them, all the better. Well, the chances are you won't be able to remove big ones at all, at least not safely. I once did an eight-story building full of these windows without removing any of them. I trimmed and adjusted them in place and secured the loose bottom rails. The exterior stripping and painting was done by a painting contractor. Of course, I tied all of the tools off and was totally paranoid about dropping so much as

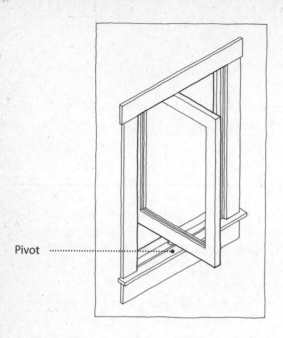

Pivot

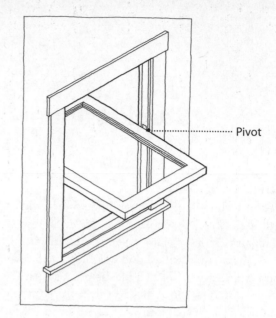

Pivot

a loose screw to the sidewalk below. As it ends up, both the owner and I were having our own distinct nightmares over removing these windows and he was very relieved when I came up with an alternative plan.

Some of these pivoting windows do not have the crank system, but simply push out. They never seal well at the stool and are generally haphazard. I suppose the original appeal was the ease in cleaning because the exterior side swings around to the interior. They're still stupid.

LEADED GLASS WINDOWS

Leaded glass windows are constructed from either plain or colored glass inserted in and held together by a series of cames or channels that are joined by lead solder. The cames are most commonly made of zinc or lead and less often from copper. Additional saddle bars or braces were added to some windows when further support was needed. Zinc was more common with geometric designs while more malleable lead was used for curved and circular glass installations.

Colored glass, used to make stained glass windows, can be painted, enameled, or tinted with true glass stains. Leaded glass windows became plainer and simpler after the early 1900s and essentially disappeared from new house construction after the 1930s.

The glass in these windows usually survives just fine other than the occasional errant baseball or tree branch falling during a storm. The problems arise when wood sashes decay and cames and joints deteriorate. Poor design, age, and questionable workmanship can result in glass that bows, bulges, or sags. The most common problem, though, is the deterioration of the cement or grout that seals the glass to the weather and strengthens the window. This stuff

Diamond Pattern

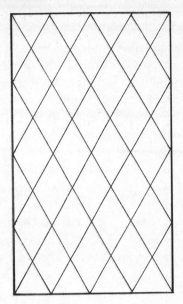

Rectangular Pattern

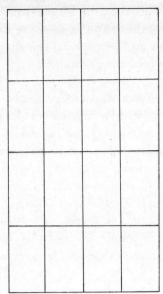

isn't made to withstand the weather forever without an occasional makeover, but almost no one ever attends to it.

As the cement deteriorates, water and air can leak in and the glass loosens and rattles. What to do? Well, you can haul everything down to Mr. or Ms. Stained Glass Artisan who, for a rate similar to a Mr. Glazier, will solder the joints and tighten the glass. If a lot of work is involved, inquire about replacement costs. There are some Mr. Window alternatives, however.

Nontraditional Repairs for Leaded Glass

Low budget? No budget? No problem. You can tighten the glass up easily enough. Here's what you do:

· Take a putty knife and carefully dig out any loose cement near the glass.

· Follow up with a soft brass brush to clean the came.

· Force a small amount of DAP '1012' Glazing Compound into the came and smooth it out. Be sure to use 1012, not DAP '33,' which is made for wood windows. DAP '1012' does not require painting or sealing to preserve it and is designed for steel windows. If you use DAP '33' and leave it unsealed in the came, it will eventually fall out. DAP '1012' usually isn't available at hardware and paint stores, so call around or try a supplier to the glass and glazing trade.

· Knife the excess glazing compound off, leaving a very slight beveled edge.

179

Q I have to protest, Mr. Window. This isn't a proper repair at all and you know I'm all for propriety. You're suppose to remove the window and mix special cement and then cover it with whiting and then . . .

A *That's right and it's a lovely idea if you have the time and materials and you want to remove the sash. If you were restoring a Tiffany window, of course, take the complete restoration route. Does an upper sash with six plain rectangles of leaded glass justify that same degree of work? I can't make that decision for every reader, obviously, but I can offer a reasonable compromise that will extend the life and function of the window and still fall within the working talents of a range of homeowners . . . even those who are big on propriety.*

As an alternative to glazing, you can use a dark gray latex caulk and carefully shoot it into the came using as small an opening in the tube as possible. Smooth the bead with a putty or glazing knife and wipe off the excess. You may also prefer to use clear caulk.

Latex caulk is difficult to smooth out with a tool without smearing it on the glass, although this excess can be cleaned off with a moist rag or a razor blade. Try caulk on one section of a window first and see if this process agrees with you. The caulk does a good job of sealing the glass and reinforcing all of the cames. If you ever have to replace a piece of glass, the caulking is a pain to remove and you will probably think malevolent thoughts about Mr. Window. Such is the price of offering an affordable fix to his readers.

Cracked joints can be patched up with clear exterior polyurethane or other exotic caulk to secure the joint. No, this isn't as good as professionally soldering, but it does help. If the joint is really bad, even soldering can only improve it to a point and if you cannot afford to replace the glass, you might as well caulk it and leave it. I am nothing if not practical. Caulking the cames on both sides of the glass will help strengthen weak cames even further.

For a good summary of leaded glass repairs and structural issues, take a look at Historic Preservation Brief 33, The Preservation and Repair of Historic Stained and Leaded Glass, from the National Park Service (www2.cr.nps.gov/tps/briefs/brief33.htm). They won't endorse a single one of my simpler repairs even for what were originally plain, inexpensive windows, but their projects aren't exactly subject to the time and budget restraints of the average homeowner. For minor repairs and maintenance, you can do fine with glazing compound and caulk. If your glass is sagging or bowing out more than 1½" from its original plane, consider removing the sash for a more thorough repair if the glass is weak or loose; if it isn't, leave it alone. Occasionally a glass shop can do these repairs, but more often you'll need to go to a stained glass artisan for the work.

Replacing single panes of glass, called a drop-in or slip, can be done by experienced glaziers (this usually means older glaziers), but call your local shop first before carting the sash down to them. Sometimes replacement can be done by bending back the flange of the came and slipping in a slightly smaller pane of glass.

CHAPTER 7

— · —

Screens and Storm Windows

SCREENS

Window-framed screens come in a lot of flavors, but the main distinction is between fixed screens and both retractable and adjustable screens. Fixed screens are single-framed screens that are installed either on the interior or exterior of a window. Traditional wood screens were installed in the spring and removed in the fall to make way for traditional wood storm windows. These fun chores were usually performed by Dad. Mom and the kids no doubt cheered him on, being at least momentarily thankful for sex and age-determined cultural values as Dad huffed and puffed up ladders carrying screens down and second-story storm windows up.

Fixed screens were normally associated with double-hung windows because casements could not open with exterior screens. To get around this, some clever people installed fixed screens on the inside, but hinged them to the window casing or jamb so they could swing out of the way while the window was opened and closed. I've only seen this arrangement a couple of times, but suspect it's more common in other parts of the country (screens are not a common item in low-bug Seattle except in newer homes). The alternative to a hinged fixed screen for a casement is a retractable screen.

Retractable Screens

Retractable screens have been around since the 1920s, probably to answer the casement window/screen problem. They roll up like a window shade except they're concealed inside decorative housing. The edges of the screens move up and down on tracks, clips, or magnets attached to the casings or jamb and, when open, lock at the stool. The original retractable screens were all steel and the survivors are pretty stiff today and likely torn in a few places. New models use fiberglass screen that is both flexible and strong. Retractable screens can be installed for double-hung windows as well as other styles.

The advantages to a retractable screen are it only gets installed once and it's up and out of the way on days when you want the windows closed and don't want the screen obscuring the view.

Adjustable Screens

There is an alternative to fixed screens and retractable screens for double-hung windows: the adjustable window screen. These are very slick, inexpensive (their largest one sells for less than the price of a movie ticket), and long lasting with almost no maintenance. Made by the W. B. Marvin Company (www.wbmarvin.com) and sold in hardware stores everywhere, these adjustable screens range from 7″ to 24″ high and extend to from 19″ to 37″. These metal screens are the bargain of the universe and require no tools to install. The only maintenance is an occasional washing, lubricating the sliding metal parts, and a bit of varnish every so many years on the wood ends that slide against the window jamb.

The adjustable screens come with a couple of caveats, however. They fit between the open lower sash and the sill or the open upper sash and the header. When you want to close the window, the screen must be removed and stored. This is probably less of a concern on second and third floors, but could be considered a nuisance on a first floor, especially if you're in and out all day and lock up as you leave. When a rain storm comes, you have to run around and remove all of them to close the windows. In an apartment building, an owner runs the chance of a tenant dropping the screen onto someone below. An owner could get around this by attaching a small eye (a piece of hardware that looks like a threaded hook, but the hook end is closed to form a circle) to the screen and tying it off to another eye inside the room, but this would look more than a little tacky.

Fixed Wood Screens

Unless your wood screens have been maintained (as in washed yearly, painted, etc.), yours might be in need of repairs. Wood screens are not as thick as sashes. Their thickness matches the casings or blind stop they butt up to and are installed against, which is typically ¾″ thick. You would repair a damaged wood screen the same way you would a damaged wood sash:

· Reinforce loose corners with dowels, 16d finish nails, screws, or corner irons.

Adjustable Screen

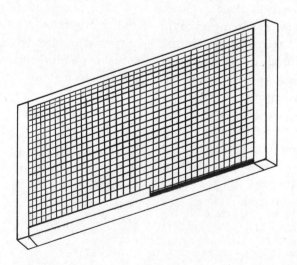

- Dig out any rot or badly damaged wood and replace with epoxy.

- Remove loose, flaking, or blistering paint as needed.

- Prime and paint all bare wood or wood in need of another coat of paint.

Repairing the screen itself is another matter. Screen damage ranges from small holes to major tears, the latter requiring complete screen replacement. Here is a rundown on repairing metal screens in wood-framed screens:

- For small holes, dab in some clear caulk or model airplane glue. You might not see the point in such a small repair, but it can grow larger if not attended to and it will be the one place a fly will use to come inside and pester you.

- If the hole is less than 2" x 2", buy an aluminum screen patch kit at your hardware store. The patches are self-adhering, no tools needed, just put the patch over the hole and press.

- Complete screen replacement (see below) is a bit of a nuisance. This is a common repair service offered at many neighborhood hardware stores so you might compare costs before doing this yourself or invest in an adjustable screen.

FULL-SCREEN REPLACEMENT

I want to thank Michigan State University* Extension for the following instructions on screen repair and this wonderful disclaimer on their Web site: "This information becomes public property upon publication and may be printed verbatim with credit to MSU Extension." If only writing the rest of this book was so easy.

Replacing Screen on a Wooden Frame

Michigan State University Extension
Home Maintenance and Repair
12/04/98
www.msue.msu.edu/msue/imp/mod02/01500163.html#visuals

*Unsolicited endorsement for Michigan State University: America's first land-grant university founded in 1855. Located in East Lansing, Michigan. Ranked 20th in Playboy magazine's 2004 list of top 25 party schools. Go Spartans.

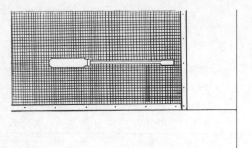

Step 1.
Remove wooden strips covering the edge of the screen. Be careful not to break them. Pry up with the screwdriver close to the nails to prevent cracking the strip.

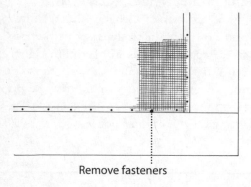

Remove fasteners

Step 2.
Remove the old screen material by taking out the tacks or staples.

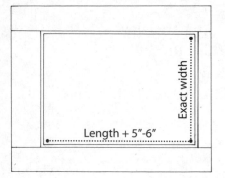

Exact width

Length + 5"-6"

Step 3.
Cut the new screen to the width between the shoulders on the frame and 5" or 6" longer than the frame.

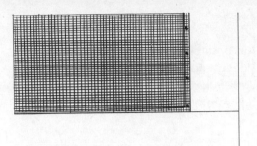

Step 4.
Attach the new screen fabric at one end with regular $1/2$" carpet tacks. A stapler works well also.

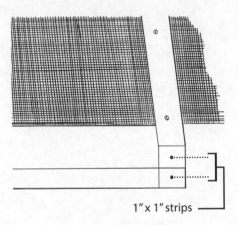

1" x 1" strips

Step 5.
Stretch the screen over the frame so it extends beyond the frame at the opposite end. Stretch it tight. One way is to nail two 1" x 1"" strips to each side of the screen and to the workbench or large piece of plywood. Be sure the frame is snug up to the 1" x 1" with the loose end of the screen extending over the end of the frame. Another procedure is to clamp the frame to a board or table.

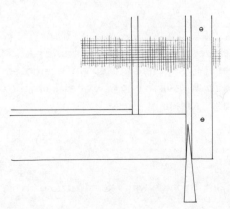

Step 6.
Drive a wedge between the frame and the 1" x 1" on both sides of the frame so it tightens the fabric over the frame.

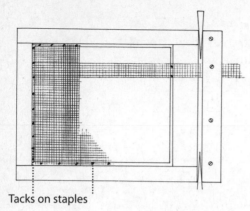

Tacks on staples

Step 7.
Nail or staple the screen fabric on all four sides of each panel about every 4" to 6". Work from center to each end to prevent a bulge from developing.

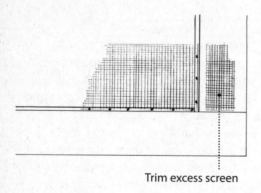

Trim excess screen

Step 8.
Cut off the excess screen with a knife, household shears, or tin snips. A razor blade will also work for plastic. Nail the loose end.

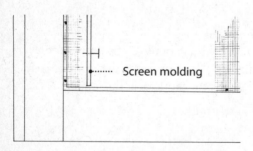

Screen molding

Step 9.
Replace the wooden strips around each panel. If they were broken when removed you may have to buy new ones. Paint the entire screen.

This article was written by Anne Field, Extension Specialist, Emeritus, with references from Michigan Extension bulletin "Repairing and Replacing Screens."

Doesn't that look like fun? I didn't think so. Consider taking your broken screens to the hardware store or replace them with adjustable screens.

BUILDING WOOD-FRAMED SCREENS

If you like the look and appeal of traditional fixed screens and want to make your own:

- Use straight grain redwood, cedar, or fir. These choices display my West Coast bias against pine, but I can live with that. For all you Southerners who really object, I was born and raised as a Yankee as well, so neener-neener.

- The stiles and top rail call for 1" x 2" stock lumber and the bottom rail requires a 1" x 4". You can go wider on the stiles and top rail, but they will then be wider than the corresponding pieces in the window sashes. 1" x 2" is a little narrower.

- Decide on a molding—there is an actual screen molding available—to cover the edges of the screen.

- Choose hardware to attach the screen (see below).

- Measure the outside opening between the vertical casings and from the header casing to the sill. Measure in three locations—top, middle, and bottom—in each direction and use the narrowest measurement for the wood screen.

- The bottom edge of the bottom rail should be beveled to match the slope of the sill. You can bevel it with a table saw or a belt sander (the saw is faster, but how many homeowners have table saws?).

- You can connect your four pieces with corner irons or by screwing, nailing, or doweling them together through the corners.

Joining corner using wood dowels.

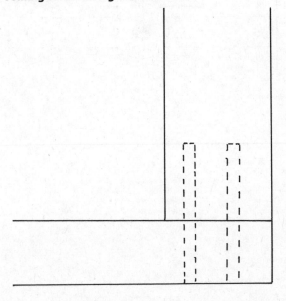

Corner joined with screws.

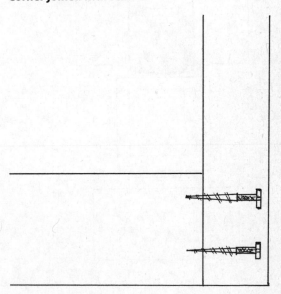

- On the interior side at the center of the opening for the screen, attach four sections of 1½" lattice, leaving ½" overhanging the open space (see illustration, page 190).

- Prime and paint or otherwise finish the wood frame and screen molding before installing the screen.

- Measure, cut, stretch, and secure a new piece of screen to your frame following the directions provided above for replacing a screen. The screen will staple against the lattice.

- Fasten the screen molding to cover the edges of the screen. If you use small brass or galvanized screws, you can more easily remove the molding in the future should repairs be needed.

- Attach and fasten all screen hardware and install your screen.

- Stand inside your house and taunt flies, mosquitoes, and other insect nuisances who haven't figured out how to use cutting tools yet.

SCREEN AND STORM WINDOW HARDWARE

Wood-framed screens and wood storm windows use the same types of hardware to attach to your windows. You have several choices:

- Hangers
- Snap fasteners
- Turn buttons

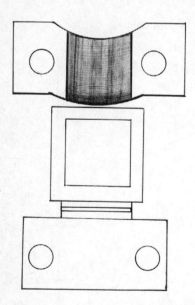

Exterior storm window and screen hanger.

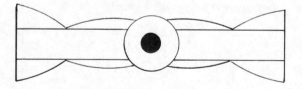

The turn button.

Hangers, which attach to the upper rail of a wood-framed screen or wood storm window as well as to the upper/header casing or brick molding, are the most traditional hardware for hanging storms and screens. They allow you to hang from inside a room, although it's easier to line them up on the outside. To secure the storm window or screen at its bottom rail, a screen door hook (found on wood screen doors) is fastened, allowing you to pull inward and secure to an eye fastened to the sill.

Snap fasteners are fancier arrangements and attach to the stiles as do turn buttons, which hold the storm or screen tight to the casings as the buttons are turned and tightened. All three types of hardware are still manufactured and available at hardware stores and businesses such as Rejuvenation (www.rejuvenation.com) that specialize in antique and reproduction hardware.

WOOD STORM WINDOWS

A single-glazed window, that is, a window with a single pane of glass, has an R-value of approximately R-1. The R-value is the window's resistance to heat flowing from your warm, cozy home to the cold outdoors. R-1 is a pretty lame R-value, considering that a wood-framed wall without insulation has an R-value of 4 or greater. Doubling the number of glass panes approximately doubles the R-value. Modern insulated windows do this by separating two panes of glass, filling the space between them with a gas like argon, and then sealing the space between the edges of the panes with a tough, exotic caulk. Adding a wood storm window approximates this design by trapping air between the storm window and the primary window.

It's not perfect, but it works. The questions are, at what price and are the savings worth it? Old windows are a major source of heat loss, much of it through the gaps around the sashes, but before you install storm windows, you should:

· Caulk any gaps around your windows.
· Replace any loose, broken, or missing glazing compound.
· Be sure your windows close and lock tightly.
· Install weather stripping.

From a comfort standpoint, storm windows do make a difference in a cold climate. Storm windows will make you feel more comfortable as well as cut down on any outside noise levels. You can do better by installing insulated window coverings, but then you can't see out the window. The payback period can take years if you pay a contractor to fabricate and install wood storm windows, but less so if you make them yourself.

Styles

Storm windows come in all kinds of styles:

· Interior mounted
· Exterior mounted
· Glass, rigid plastic, and flexible plastic
· Wood, metal, and vinyl

If you really want to do it on the cheap and relive the early 1970s impoverished college student chic, staple some clear (or black if you're still into Goth fashion or feeling particularly vampirish) construction plastic over your window and cover the stapled edges with tacked down wood strips. Be prepared to listen to flapping plastic every time the wind comes up. Hardware stores also sell storm window kits with plastic that you tape to the interior of the window.

Interior vs. exterior storm windows comes down to a few simple factors:

· Convenience
· Appearance
· Protection of the primary sashes

It's a lot more convenient to mount an interior storm window and if they're done right, they won't look unattractive. However, an exterior mounted storm window protects your main window sashes from the weather and this is a real plus. Several companies specialize in interior storms. Their windows consist of vinyl or aluminum components attached via tracks, magnets, or other attachments. Some are easily removable and others less so. For a review of a variety of interior and exterior storm windows, go to www .alliedwindow.com, the Web site for the Allied Window Company or call (800) 445-5411 for more information.

Making Your Own

You would fabricate a wood storm window the same way you would a wood-framed screen. The storm window has to accommodate a piece of glass or plastic and provide room for glazing compound or wood strips to secure it to the sash. Normally this is done by routing out the sections of wood that form the sash, but since Mr. Window has never owned a router, he would take the easy way out:

· Cut and assemble the four sections of the sash.

· On the interior side, right at the center opening for the glass, attach four sections of 1½″ lattice or similar size molding, evenly spacing them so half an inch of the lattice overhangs the open space. Essentially, you're framing the opening.

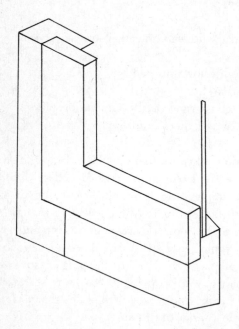

Interior/exterior storm window: illustrating location of glass, 1^1/$_2$″ lattice, and 1″ x 4″ rail.

· Flip the sash over. You can now install the glass against the lattice and glaze it.

Exterior wood storm windows are installed the same way wood-framed screens are installed with the same choice of hardware.

Interior wood storm windows are a little trickier. Factory-made windows come with attachment systems; the ones you make in your shop do not. And a homemade wood storm window is heavier than a factory-made vinyl window with a Plexiglas insert.

Installing an interior storm window over a fixed sash installed from the outside or a casement gives you plenty of room in the jamb for different types of hardware, including sash pins, various latches, or even casement sash locks if you don't mind their appearance. A double-hung window offers little room because you're installing between the stops and the stool and you have to allow for the sash lifts, which means routing out part of the storm window's lower rail so it will clear the lifts. The easiest solution is to use drywall screws, two or three per stile, inserted at a 45-degree angle into the window stop (after drilling pilot holes). When the storm windows are removed, fill the holes in the stops with small brass screws, which will simply look like normal fasteners holding in the stops.

NOTE: Although moisture buildup shouldn't be a problem between the main sashes and the storm, check for it and any accompanying mildew as the weather turns cold. If moisture does collect, drill some small weep holes in the bottom of the interior storm window. Be sure to mark and number all your storm windows so they get reinstalled in their original locations later.

Once these storm windows are in, they're there to stay for the season.

An inventive carpenter or cabinet maker will no doubt come up with a different system of attachment to which I say, "Bravo!" There are an awful lot of fasteners in the world that can offer more elegant solutions than mine, but this will work for anyone and uses readily available materials. Mr. Window is willing to admit his experience with storm windows is limited due to working in Seattle's temperate climate where storm windows are few and far between on older homes.

Mark all your storm windows and screens so you know where to install them as the seasons change. Traditionally, brass tacks with numbers on their heads were used; one tack would go into the side of the storm or screen and the other into the jamb of the respective window. These are still available from some renovation suppliers. You can also chisel a Roman numeral (remember those?) into the stiles, use indelible laundry markers, or come up with your own marking system. Keep a paper or electronic copy as well.

WARNING! You need to provide egress out of bedrooms in the event of a fire or other emergency. Regardless of the type of storm window you install, keep at least one window per bedroom accessible for emergency exits (you can even attach these storm windows with hinges and casement window locks for a simple solution).

Plastic vs. Glass

Glass is clearer than plastic, it doesn't scratch, and it lasts longer unless someone tosses a baseball through it. Plastic is lighter and more flexible, but some plastics will yellow over time and clarity degrades. It's easy enough to compare the costs. Take your glass sizes to a plastic supplier and to a glazing shop—who might also sell plastic—and get prices for the cut pieces. Look to the future, though, and decide how important a window will be to you on a sunny winter day when looking through plastic won't be quite the same as looking through glass.

WARNING! Exterior storm windows need weep holes or small gaps between their bottom rails and the sill to allow any water that washes in to drain out as well as any condensation that develops between the storm and main window. If you install wood storm windows, you can leave a $1/16$" gap between the bottom rail and the sill to allow for this. Otherwise, you can drill small holes every six inches or so at the very bottom edge of the bottom rail. Interior storm windows can eliminate the need for weep holes because any condensation should escape through the primary window. The wood can rot if the moisture doesn't escape so be sure to monitor your windows regardless of which type of storm window you install and adjust them accordingly.

ALUMINUM SCREENS AND STORM WINDOWS

If you can get past their looks—they really don't go with traditional homes all that well—aluminum triple-track storm/screen combination windows are a convenient way to go. The triple-track refers to two movable sections of glass and one movable screen; they all slide on separate tracks. These storm/screen combos are made to order and installed either by the manufacturer or an approved subcontractor. They are a secured installation, meaning they're screwed in to stay, and are a nuisance to work around when it comes to painting the windows.

CHAPTER 8

— · —

Security

Single-pane wood windows aren't exactly the Fort Knox of home security. A burglar could put some tape across a piece of glass to keep it from breaking into small, noisy pieces, tap on it with a rubber mallet until it cracks, and in he goes. All it takes to force open a double-hung window is a good pry bar. The ne'er-do-well only has to force up two screws, the ones holding the strike on the upper sash. Casement windows are tougher to pry open, but it's easy enough to break the glass and flip open the lock.

The most sophisticated alarm and security systems in the world can be overcome, but that doesn't mean you can't secure your windows a bit more than the standard single lock allows. Here are some steps you can take:

· For the locks, installing the longest screws you can into solid wood beats keeping the old, corroded short screws that aren't tightly attached to the sash.

· On large double-hung windows, install two locks, equidistant from the stiles; on casements, two locks equidistant from the top and bottom rails or equidistant from the ogee detail.

· Install pin locks and/or ventilation locks on all first-floor and basement double-hung windows.

· Block shut any non-egress required windows you aren't using and won't be using in the near future.

· Consider installing security film or window grates.

· Clear all shrubs and hedges away from your windows so they can't conceal anyone snooping around or breaking in.

So many factors go into determining your risk for a home break-in: Is your house occupied during the day? Do you have a dog? Is there a neighborhood watch program? Is your home highly visible or isolated? The windows are just one factor, but where else to address them than a book about windows?

NOTE: One oddball lock available from National Manufacturing Company (www.natman.com to find a local dealer) is a keyed sash lock. It replaces your standard double-hung lock with a more contemporary version that can be locked with its own key. This prevents someone from opening the lock, and thus the window, after breaking the glass near the lock.

PIN LOCKS

You can easily and inexpensively improve the security of any double-hung window by "pinning" the two sashes together. Here's what you do:

- Buy either a simple sliding door pin lock or a deadbolt-type, key-operated lock for sliding doors for every window you want to secure.

- For a standard pin lock, close the window you're working on and drill a hole in the upper right- and left-hand corners of the lower sash into the lower left- and right-hand corners of the upper sash as per the lock's instructions (each will require its own size hole). The hole will be drilled at a slight angle.

- Install the lock(s).

- If you install key-operated locks, do not leave the keys in the locks, but be sure everyone in your home knows where they're located.

If you want to do this on a budget, you don't even need to purchase a lock (although the basic pin locks are pretty inexpensive, usually under $3). Just drill a large enough hole to accommodate either a 16d nail or a large eye or bolt, whatever fastener you're comfortable installing and removing when you need to either lock up or open the window. The advantage of the sliding door pin lock is it has a large head—either plastic or metal—that's easy to grab as well as a small chain and holder that screws to the window stop so you can store it when the window is open. The illustrated example is made by M.A.G. Manufacturing and Engineering Company, Inc.

Sliding patio door pin.

Insert pin in angled hole drilled through meeting rail.

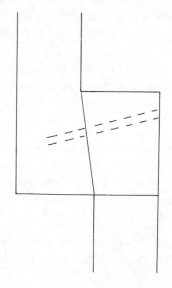

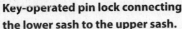

Key-operated pin lock connecting the lower sash to the upper sash.

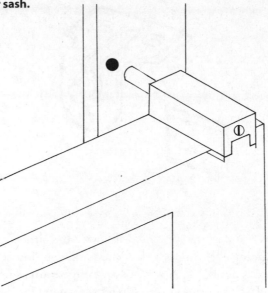

(www.magsecurity.com, 800-624-9942) who also manufactures a full line of window and door hardware available at major hardware and home improvement stores.

Whichever locking method you choose, these locks cannot be forced out by prying the lower sash up; the sashes will break first.

VENTILATION LOCKS

There are two styles of ventilation locks that I've used. Each is installed on the upper sash and, when opened, prevents the two sashes from moving past the lock. This way you can have the window open enough for ventilation, but not enough for someone to climb in.

One style, the less expensive of the two, features a small brass wedge that flips open and closed like a hinge. It's a simple, contemporary design, and it provides enough clearance that I've never found a double-hung window that couldn't accommodate it. M.A.G. Security makes one version of this lock (Double-Hung Wood Window Locks #8760) and it retails for around $2 at hardware stores.

Another version, a heavier duty, screw-on affair, has a thick, sliding pin that is housed in a curved metal track that bends around the upper sash ogee near the glass. It's a very nice lock (with either type, you normally install two to a window), but it's too large for some sashes and won't allow them to pass each other even when the pin is out of the way. I've found some windows with these locks and the installers carved out sections of the upper sash so the lock would recess enough for clearance. Well, OK, this kind of follows Mr. Window's if-it-works, try-it philosophy, but it looks pretty tacky.

Ives ventilation lock.

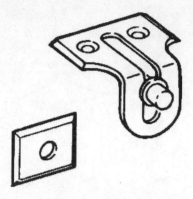

SECURITY FILM

Various manufacturers, including 3M, produce synthetic, mostly clear (tinted is available), protective films that attach to glass to improve its resistance to shattering (as though it has much to begin with). I have only seen one of these products installed and it is straightforward enough. A technician thoroughly cleaned the interior side of the window glass and carefully applied the self-adhesive film. It won't stop someone who's really intent on entry if, say, a hammer is repeatedly pounded against the glass, but it vastly increases the difficulty and the noise factor since it takes a lot more pounding to break in. A Web search on "security film glass" will bring up a host of businesses that provide this product.

WINDOW GRATES

There are very few attractive window grates and probably none that will win any fashion awards for your home. However, if you have basement windows you either never open or they open inward and you don't need them to be available as an escape route, some tasteful security grates aren't the worst idea in the world if you live in an area with regular break-ins. You can make your own out of pipes (your windows can resemble a jail and your kids can stage breakouts with their friends) installed between the jamb header and the sill or put them on the interior side if the window does not open.

WARNING! If a window has to be available for egress, don't install key locks or hard-to-remove (for kids or the elderly) pins. Unless your basement has an outside entrance door, do not put grates on all these windows, either. The code normally calls for operable grates on bedroom windows.

CHAPTER 9

— · —

Glass Cleaning

We've all grown up with a certain blue spray window cleaner which does an adequate job of cleaning windows and other surfaces, but you won't see a professional window cleaner using it. Why? Because it's a consumer grade product too slow for certain types of cleaning. Old window glass that hasn't been really cleaned for years can have all kinds of pollutants and gunk on it, including paint spatters. It could need nothing more than a good scrubbing, some scraping with a razor blade, or some cleaning with polishing compound depending on the desired results. This doesn't mean you can clean it with anything (one of those green scrubbing pads will leave some very nice scratches, a reminder that you should have listened to Mr. Window). Glass seems to be pretty tough stuff that can resist all kinds of cleaning abuse, but that's not quite the case.

Just what is glass? Well, according to my handy *American Heritage Dictionary of Science*, a reference book that has on more than one occasion allowed me to appear much smarter about the ways of the world and how it's put together than by any stretch of the imagination is justified, glass is "...a hard, brittle, amorphous material, especially a transparent ceramic consisting mostly of silica. Glasses behave like solids, but their atomic structure is disorganized like that of a liquid." Amorphous simply means glass does not consist of crystals (thank you again, *American Heritage Dictionary of Science*). It is this liquid nature that has led to the question of whether the distortion in old glass is due to the glass moving (also known as super viscous flow), like some strange, mostly dormant liquid reacting to gravity, leading to a wavy appearance. Physicists say no, you dumb non-physicists who should have studied science stuff in college like they did. The wavy and irregular appearance is due to the way the glass was manufactured.

For centuries, glassmaking was a handcrafted process and the glass itself expensive. Mass production began during the Industrial Revolution. Flat glass production in the early twentieth century economized sheet glass, making it more affordable. Float glass manufacturing was introduced in the 1950s and is the predominant method used today to produce flat glass. Unlike flat glass methods which required glass to be pulled through rollers for flattening and then ground and polished, float glass is made by a process that just sounds weird, but works. The raw materials are placed in a very hot furnace where they melt together to form liquid glass. The glass flows in a continuous ribbon onto a bath of molten tin. The glass flattens out perfectly because it doesn't mix with the tin and requires no polishing or grinding to make it flat. It is then cooled and cut to size.

There's a definite difference in viewing through old "wavy" glass and clear new glass. Some find it charming and will go to great expense to replace broken, older glass with art glass that reproduces this distorted effect. Others, like Mr. Window, have no problem installing new glass when replacing broken glass because he likes viewing a seemingly muddled world with as much clarity as he can find.

How you clean your glass depends on what you're trying to clean off.

GENERAL DIRT AND GRIME

I suppose every window cleaner has a specific cleaner they use or mix as they wish, but more than once I've heard the simplest cleaner is a couple *small* squirts of Dawn liquid dish soap and a bucket of warm water. Why Dawn as opposed to another brand? I don't know, its name comes up and not Dove or Ivory or Palmolive. *It doesn't take much soap, just a little!* Too much and you'll be cleaning soap film off all afternoon. Professional window cleaners also use professional products formulated to not only remove dirt and grime, but keep the glass wet longer than water alone. This assures the squeegee won't stick on a dry spot when wiping off the cleaning solution.

Window cleaners use special window washer tools, which resemble squeegees but have scrubbing covers on them to efficiently remove dirt. A natural sponge also works for mere mortal non-professional cleaners, although professional products such as those made by Ettore, whose founder invented the modern day squeegee, are available at chain hardware stores.

The main thing to remember is to apply sufficient cleaning solution without soaking the

Ettore ProGrip Squeegee

Ettore ProGrip Washer

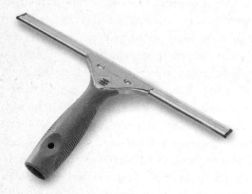

window. If you're washing the inside, place an old towel down at the bottom of each sash as you clean them to catch any drips. Depending on the cleaning solution you use, you don't want to let it remain on painted or varnished woodwork as it can affect the finish.

Q **Once again, Mr. Window, you seem to think your readers need fancy tools and such to do the job. Just what's wrong with cleaning my windows with water and vinegar and wiping them off with newspaper like my grandmother did? Are you saying my Nana didn't know what she was doing? I liked my Nana, she always tucked me into bed and told me a bedtime story when she visited, although I have to say my college roommate found this a little strange.**

A *Your Nana, like Mr. Rogers, must have liked you just the way you are. If you want to follow the vinegar and newspaper routine, be my guest. The Vinegar Institute will thank you wholeheartedly. However, it's not especially efficient and you'll end up with a pile of wet newspaper and missed spots. A squeegee isn't exactly the cutting edge of modern technology, but it's a fine tool and superior to yesterday's sports section. Also, vinegar isn't recommended for leaded glass because of its acidic nature (see below) which can weaken the lead joints. Stick with the dishwashing soap and leave the vinegar to your salad.*

Other Tips

Window cleaning is taken very seriously by, well, professional window cleaners. There is even a yearly international speed contest sponsored by the International Window Cleaning Association (who else?).

For cleaning your own windows:

· Clean your windows at least twice a year, inside and out, working from the top of each window downward.

· Buy a professional quality squeegee; cheap ones have hard rubber edges that just don't do the job and leave streaks. Keep the rubber blade clean and replace it if the edge becomes rough or deteriorates.

· For smaller panes of glass, cut a squeegee down to size using a hacksaw. First, remove the rubber blade and then cut the metal channel an inch or so narrower than the window pane. Cut the rubber blade half an inch or so longer than the channel and reinstall.

· If some windows are hard to reach, attach the squeegee to an extension pole.

· After pulling the squeegee across the glass, wipe the excess water off the blade with a clean rag.

· Clean stubborn water spots with fine steel wool (000 or 0000) and your window cleaner or with Zud cleaner on its own. Sprinkle a small amount of Zud on a damp, clean rag and rub out the water spots, always testing a corner of the glass first to be sure the Zud doesn't scratch (it shouldn't, but shouldn't is a big and dangerous word).

· Try not to wash your windows in bright, direct sunlight. The heat can sometimes dry out the cleaning solution faster than you can work it.

PAINT DRIPS AND OVERSPRAY

Painters' razor blades, which are single blades that can be used with or without a blade holder, are great for removing paint from window glass. They're sold in small packs of five or ten and in boxes of 100, the latter normally purchased by window cleaners and painters. *Wet the glass first* with a generous amount of soapy water solution and then hold the blade as flat as you can against the glass and push it against any paint on the glass. Do a small test section first to be sure you're not scratching the glass (unlikely with a new razor blade, possible with an old one if the edge has rusted).

A razor blade is also good for cutting away any over-painting on the window glazing. Keep in mind if you cut into the paint line on the putty too deeply or aggressively—which you might want to do if it's a really sloppy line—you'll need to seal it again with fresh paint. Otherwise, you've created an entry for water to undermine the glazing. This is why good painters will run a razor blade first around the glazing's errant paint line so they're not extending it even further onto the glass.

Listen to the razor blade as you're pushing it across the glass. If it makes a coarse noise, either the blade is old or the surface isn't wet enough. Correct this before scratching the glass.

Another way to remove fine overspray or small drips of paint is to use fine (000 or 0000) steel or bronze wool, again on wet glass. Use a fresh piece, not one with any hint of rust on it.

REMOVING DECALS AND STICKERS

Stickers and decals just seem to migrate to window glass. Do we or our children bother to attach them with a bit of clear tape while leaving the backing intact so we could easily remove them later when we've discovered we really have no idea why we put a sticker proclaiming "Our House is Trans-Fat Free" up in the first place? Or do we peel off the backing only to expose an adhesive so strong that had it been mixed with the foundation of the Leaning Tower of Pisa, there would *be* no Leaning Tower of Pisa? Yes, it's another trick question from Mr. Window.

To remove stickers:

· Spray the sticker, especially the edges, with your window cleaning solution.

· Take a new razor blade and lift one corner of the sticker.

· Grab the corner and pull as much of the label off as you can.

· Keep the sticker wet, remove as much of it and the backing as you can with the razor blade.

· To remove any remaining glue and residue, spray with WD-40 or Goo Gone ("...a combination of Citrus Power and scientific technology designed to eliminate the very toughest problems," according to its manufacturer and if true, has implications *way* beyond its ability to merely clean off stickers) and scrape with a razor blade; finish up with a clean rag or paper towel.

· Wash the glass after all glue residue has been removed.

STAINED AND LEADED GLASS

Both ammonia and acid-based cleaners such as vinegar can negatively affect leaded and zinc cames and joints, the metal sections of leaded windows. Painted glass can be damaged by using the wrong cleaner.

A leaded window containing multiple small pieces of glass won't lend itself to a squeegee, but can be cleaned with a benign window cleaner and wiped dry with clean, soft cotton cloths. Go easy on the amount of water you use as it can fill any cames which have lost some of their cement.

Are you uncertain if your colored glass is painted or not and how you should clean it? You *should* be able to stick with clear water or water with just a bit of liquid dish soap. Test a corner first and pat it dry. If the coloring isn't affected, you *should* be safe doing the entire window, but "should," like "shouldn't," is also a big and dangerous word.

POLISHING YOUR WINDOWS

Glass can be polished *if* it doesn't have any kind of film on it (sun blocking, tinting, or security film, for instance). Some glass stains resulting from hard water or residue running off chimney mortar or even oxidized window screens need a little stronger treatment than steel wool or Zud. Polishing can also remove minor scratches in most glass.

Standard white automotive polishing compound and a moist rag are all you need to try and deep clean hazy windows that don't respond to standard window cleaning. Don't use the cleaner/polish/wax combinations on glass because they'll leave a waxy residue. Always test the cleaner in a less-than-noticeable section of an out of the way window first. For large glass areas, use a buffer—I like the Bosch six-inch dual random orbit polishers myself, which are also used as sanders—on a moderate speed. Again, experiment on a closet or basement window to test the process.

GLASS CLEANER

An excellent aerosol glass cleaner is made by Sprayway, Inc. (www.spraywayinc.com) and is used by glass installers to clean off residue and fingerprints from their work. It's available at glass supply companies and some automotive detail shops, but call first or do an Internet search. Some sellers only deal in case quantities.

Want to make your own glass cleaner? There are all kinds of formulas available, many of them including either ammonia or vinegar, which tend to streak and aren't recommended for leaded glass or stained glass windows. Some are kind of bizarre and include corn starch, vinegar, *and* ammonia, a strange triumvirate. Better ones are one half isopropyl alcohol, one half water, and a tablespoon or so of vinegar (a *little* vinegar probably won't hurt anything . . .). Fine, you can make these, or you can just buy a can of Sprayway which will last for months and always work. Modern chemistry in a can is a fine thing.

CHAPTER 10

— · —

Shutters and Awnings

I live near Seattle. No one (all right, *almost* no one) here has shutters and few have awnings. Shutters protect against hurricanes and keep the summer sun out while allowing ventilation inside a house. Given that we have no hurricanes and the summer sun is mostly a rumor, shutters serve little purpose in the Northwest except for expat Southerners who need reminders of the muggy and buggy world they left behind. The same holds true for awnings.

AWNINGS

According to Preservation Brief 44, "The Use of Awnings on Historic Buildings Repair, Replacement & New Design" by Chad Randl of the National Park Services Technical Preservation Services toward whom I am immensely grateful for this non-copyrighted material which is freely available to other writers who know nothing about awnings—the ancient Egyptians and Syrians used awnings to shade market stalls and homes. The Roman poet Lucretius, in 50 BC, likened thunder to the sound that "linen-awning, stretched, o'er mighty theatres, gives forth at times, a cracking roar, when much 'tis beaten about, betwixt the poles and cross-beams." Well, of course he did, what else would one possibly compare thunder to? Awnings block out the sun and are especially protective of shop window displays which would otherwise fade in direct sunlight. Storefront awnings were common in nineteenth century America with the canvas duck sections stretched over a fixed wood or cast iron framework. The latter half of the century brought about hinged extension arms, allowing awnings to be conveniently opened or retracted as the weather changed. Roller awnings followed, offering even greater convenience and better storage when an awning was retracted.

Awning manufacturers expanded into the home market, offering a broad choice of frame and canvas options, awning shapes, colors, patterns, and hardware to fit a variety of window, door, and porch styles. twentieth century innovations included folding-arm and lateral arm awnings. I'm sure these terms mean something *very significant* to awning aficionados.

As pragmatic as awnings were and remain, fashion often trumps practicality. Modern building design, tinted glass, air-conditioning, and the arrival of aluminum awnings marked a major change in the canvas awning business. In addition, canvas duck's "tendency to stretch and fade, and its susceptibility to mildew, and flammable materials like cigarettes and matches motivated the awning industry to search for alternatives."

No kidding.

These alternatives included synthetic materials that resist UV radiation and an even greater variety of shapes more befitting to modern architecture.

Repairs and Maintenance

Existing awnings in decent condition—no tears in the fabric and all moving parts operating—need little maintenance other than cleaning the fabric as needed and lubricating the gearboxes, arms, and rollers. "As needed" varies depending on the fabric's exposure to tree sap, bird droppings, and pollution. A monthly hosing and a twice-a-year cleaning with mild soap and water will extend an awning's life. Be sure to clean on a sunny day, leaving the awning fully extended so it can completely dry. Some awning companies offer professional cleaning and re-stitching which are appropriate services for ignored, but still usable, awnings.

Older awning frames and hardware that have corroded can be cleaned off using a drill with a wire brush attachment. Once any superficial rust is removed, spray the metal with a rust inhibiting coating and monitor it from time to time to ensure the corrosion doesn't return. Missing or damaged hardware can be replaced by some awning suppliers. In some cases, new marine and boating hardware can substitute for missing historic awning hardware. Damaged pieces of galvanized pipe frames can be bent back into shape or replaced with virtually identical new material.

In addition:

· If a covering begins to sag between cleanings, the cause (an object on top stretching the material, loose laces, or a damaged seam) must be addressed as soon as possible.

· When other maintenance or repair work is undertaken on the building, remove fixed awnings temporarily, as they are easily damaged or stained by materials dropped from above.

· Small holes or tears in acrylic coverings can be immediately treated with a hot needle or awl that will melt the frayed edges and prevent the damage from spreading. Patch kits are available that keep torn edges together. These patches, glued or sewn to the fabric, let the awning color show through but do have a semi-gloss sheen to them.

What if you don't have an awning but want one anyway? You'll need to snoop around period books and magazines showing a home similar to yours and hope you run across a photo or drawing of it with awnings. This helps in selecting both the style and fabric color for a new awning. When original photographs indicate a building had distinctive awnings, install new awnings that replicate their appearance. Storefront remodeling projects often uncover concealed and disused awning hardware that can either be repaired or at least suggest what type of awning was formerly in place.

Where no awning currently exists, and there is no evidence of a past one, it may still be possible to add an awning to a historic building without altering distinctive features, damaging historic fabric or changing the building's historic character. A new awning should be compatible with the features and characteristics of a historic building, as well as with neighboring buildings, or the historic district, if applicable.

On both commercial and residential buildings, awnings were only wide enough to cover the window openings that they sheltered; a single awning rarely covered two or more bays. New awning hardware should not be installed in a way that damages historic materials. Clamps and fasteners used to attach awning frames should penetrate mortar joints rather than brick or other masonry surfaces. If new backboards and rollers are installed, care needs to be taken not to damage cornices or transoms.

SHUTTERS

Traditional shutters were installed for their practical benefits in the days before air-conditioning. Operable louvers allowed air circulation while blocking out direct sunlight and some of the heat that came with it. It's been written that ancient Greek shutters were made from marble—they must have weighed a ton. Shutters also provided protection and solid shutters, as opposed to louvered style, were used to cover window openings before glass was obtainable and affordable.

As glass became more available, exterior shutters gave way to interior versions which were used for both decoration and privacy. The really fun interior versions are installed in their own cabinets and fold away inside them when not in use.

Exterior shutters are still used when weather is a consideration. In the Southern United States, the plantation shutter developed with wider louvers, presumably for more air circulation during hot, muggy summers. Current day metal hurricane shutters protect windows from extreme wind damage. New non-functional, for-looks-only exterior shutters are made from vinyl or other synthetic materials.

Repairs and Maintenance

An exterior shutter is exposed to just as much weather-related wear and tear as a window. The outer section of a shutter is composed of horizontal rails and vertical stiles, the same as a window sash. Movable or fixed louvers are wood slats with doweled ends installed between the stiles; the dowels insert into holes drilled into the stiles. A tilt rod attaches to each movable louver with a shutter staple or equivalent so they can be adjusted up and down allowing light and air to pass through. Various types of hinges mount the shutters to the window and a locking mechanism or shutter latch secures them when closed.

The same coating and epoxy repairs done to window sashes hold for shutters:

· Remove any deteriorated paint from the shutters and the hardware

· Patch missing wood or deteriorated areas with epoxy and dowels as needed

· When all repairs have been sanded smooth, coat the shutter with an appropriate sealer, which will most likely be paint

· Lubricate all moving parts

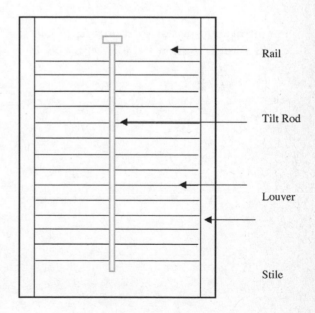

Rail

Tilt Rod

Louver

Stile

Q My shutter has a broken louver. Just how do you replace that, Mr. Smarty-pants Window, without knocking the whole shutter apart? I made a new louver with those wood thingies at the end that fit inside those holes in the sides and there's no way it will fit without defying all the laws of physics, geometry, and cosmetology.

A *You say cosmetology, I say cosmology, but that's beside the point. You're right, the dowled ends of the new louver make it too long to fit back into the stiles. When a new shutter is assembled, the rails and stiles are not fitted together until all the louvers have been installed in one of the stiles. Then, the other stile and the rails can be fitted and secured. You can do one of two things: slightly trim down (and I do mean slightly, just a bit at a time) the doweled ends until you can fit the louver first into one stile and then slip it into the other; or, install a louver pin available from SHUTTERMEDIC at www.shuttermedic.com.*

For further information on shutter repair, please see "Resources" section at the end of the book.

Window repair doesn't require a lot of fancy or even expensive tools. Most of your work will be done with a hammer, a small saw, some kind of cutting tools, putty knives, sandpaper, and paintbrushes. You won't need everything in this list and you probably have most of it if you own an old house and do your own work on it.

These tools will get you through your window repairs.

TOOLS

- Claw hammer
- Flexible putty knife
- Stiff blade or chisel-type putty knife
- Small pry bar
- Large pry bar
- Screwdrivers
- Diagonal cutting pliers
- Needle-nose pliers
- Hacksaw
- Glazing knife
- Paint scrapers and file
- Dust brush
- Paintbrush(es)
- Plastic containers for mixing epoxy
- Metal snips
- Small wire brushes
- Nail set
- Small canister-style vacuum cleaner
- ⅜″ or ½″ electric drill
- Belt sander
- Orbital sander and finish sander
- Heat gun
- Bench grinder with buffing wheels and wire wheel

TOOL USES

- You'll use a hammer for everything from removing sash stops to chopping out old glazing by hitting a chisel or hackout tool. Get one with a weight and handle size that's comfortable for you and your grip. It doesn't need to be especially heavy given that you're only going to do finish work and minor prying.

- Flexible putty knives work well with Spackle, wood dough, and epoxy fillers for even spreading. In a pinch, you can use them for glazing compound as well. The metal knives are better than the plastic ones.

- Stiff blade or chisel-type putty knives are thicker, and more expensive, versions of flexible blade putty knives. They're useful for prying open stuck sashes.

- Pry bars are also needed for opening painted-shut sashes and removing stops and parting beads.

- Screwdrivers are needed for removing hardware and sometimes latching onto the tops of sash weights inside the pockets. Screwdrivers are also the most abused tool you'll ever own given that they often serve as chisels and even scrapers and easily get lost. Cheap ones deform quickly so buy decent middle-range screwdrivers such as those made by Stanley, in addition to some cheap ones. Also, keep a screwdriver around that comes with interchangeable multiple heads in case your other screwdrivers won't fit a particular screw. These multiple heads can also be used in electric drills.

· Diagonal cutting pliers are perfect for cutting sash ropes. These are generically referred to as wire cutters. Invest in a good pair because cheap ones dull quickly and require more effort to cut (or more accurately chew through) the rope.

· Occasionally a sash weight is stuck inside a pocket and you'll need needle-nose pliers to fish a rope through the hole at the top of the weight before tying it off. Just about any pair will do given that they will serve more as pinchers than pliers.

· A hacksaw is a handy and portable tool for cutting parting beads or sash stops to size. I usually cut using only the blade because it takes up even less room in a toolbox than the saw.

· Although you can apply and clean off glazing compound with a putty knife, a glazing knife is a better tool for the job, especially when glazing the corners of a sash. Inexpensive knives, available at most paint and hardware stores are all right, but they're not as good as the English-made knives sold at businesses that supply the glass and glazing trade. It's worth the trip and few extra dollars to buy these superior knives if you have a lot of glazing to do.

· For removing thick, obstructing paint from jambs, it's quickest to use a paint scraper. A scraper can also be used in place of a carpenter's plane to trim down the edges of sashes, particularly casements, by shaving off excess wood. A scraper is also a lot easier to use than a plane, as no training is required. The quality, styles, and prices of paint scrapers are quite extensive, covering everything from almost throwaway tools to high-end Swedish scrapers such as the Skarsen and Sandvik brands. Even the types of metal blades vary, from regular carbon steel (at different quality levels) to longer-lasting and more expensive tungsten carbide blades. Scraper preferences are very individual: The handle shapes are different with each manufacturer; blades also come in different shapes; and carbide blades cannot effectively be sharpened unless you have a diamond file.

· Since steel scraper blades can dull after hard use, keep a file on hand to sharpen the blade. Hyde Tools makes an excellent sharpening file.

· A dust brush is either an old paintbrush no longer usable for painting or a cheap new paintbrush. Either works well to brush dirt and debris off a windowsill or dust off a sash.

· You can use disposable foam or inexpensive bristle paintbrushes for your priming and painting if you're only coating flat areas without any cut-in work, meaning inside corners or painting close to glass or a surrounding wall. For more extensive painting or more exacting painting, you'll need higher quality brushes such as the Wooster or Purdy lines. Paint brushes come with either synthetic bristles (polyester or nylon) for latex coatings or natural bristles (ox hair or China bristle from hogs or boars) for oil in sizes starting at 1″ or 1½″ upward. For your purposes, a 2″ or 2½″ cut-in brush will fulfill most of your painting chores. Inexpensive bristle brushes will leave more brush marks than better brushes.

· Plastic containers, such as used yogurt or other food containers are useful for mixing epoxies, body fillers, or for small amounts of paint. They're also good for storing hardware and screws as you remove them.

· If you install weather stripping, you'll need a good pair of metal snips. Also referred to as tinner's snips, this tool comes in (you guessed it) more than one style. My own preference is for the straight pattern snips that handle like heavy-duty scissors as opposed to the compound-action aviation snips. If you don't have any other cutting tools available, snips can also be used to cut sash rope.

· In the event you run into a rusty pulley or other piece of hardware, small wire brushes come in handy for removing rust and corrosion. You can also buy wire brush attachments for power drills.

· When reinstalling trim and sash stops, you'll need a nail set to set the finish nails prior to filling their holes with putty or Spackle. Nail sets are sold individually by size—$1/32''$, $2/32''$ or $3/32''$ common sizes—or in sets of three with all three sizes represented. Nail sets are easily lost and in a pinch you can use a 16d nail (flatten the sharp end first by striking it with a hammer while the head of the nail rests against a solid surface such as a bench vise or a concrete floor).

· It isn't necessary or desirable to haul around a shop vac to job sites, particularly in occupied homes. A small canister-style vacuum cleaner is the ideal tool. If needed, some come in HEPA (High Efficiency Particulate Air) models to collect lead dust. I had fabulous luck with a Eureka Mighty-Mite which lasted through years and years of vacuuming plaster dust, small nails and screws, bits of splintered wood, you name it. Eureka also makes a very affordable HEPA version of this vacuum cleaner.

· A $3/8''$ or $1/2''$ electric drill will fulfill all your drilling requirements, including drilling prior to installing dowels or screws or for cutting openings into jambs to access ropes in the absence of pocket covers. Every power tool company makes a decent line of drills so find one whose fit is comfortable to you. For installing hardware, consider a cordless (battery-driven) drill in addition to an electric drill. When buying a cordless drill, be sure to purchase an extra battery so a fresh battery is available while the other is being charged.

· Belt sander size is a matter of preference. A 3" x 21" model is plenty suitable for trimming down sashes, removing small amounts of paint in a controlled environment, or sanding down epoxy fillers. A 4" x 24" is quite a bit heavier and more power than you really need for this work. There are many brands available and they all do a decent job.

· Orbital sanders and finish sanders come in a variety of styles and sizes. They're really the only convenient and efficient way to smooth out wood that's been deeply sanded or otherwise stripped of paint. I prefer the Makita palm sander because it's lightweight and user-friendly when doing basic maintenance such as replacing its clips, brushes, and pad.

· A heat gun serves multiple purposes, including paint removal, drying out wet wood, speeding the drying time of some fillers in cold weather, even heating up your lunch! Choose a heat gun that offers variable temperatures, which allow you to choose the ideal heat setting for the job at hand. By my informal survey, many modern heat guns' maximum temperature is just under 1100 degrees, the temperature at which lead can vaporize. By staying under 1100 degrees, the guns can be used for removal of lead-based paint, provided certain safety procedures are followed. There are a number of tool manufacturers who have heat gun product lines, including Makita, Milwaukee Electric Tool, and Master Appliance. If you don't want to purchase a heat gun, you should be able to rent one from a tool rental business.

· The best way to clean and polish hardware is to use a bench grinder with a buffing wheel and a wire wheel. Old hardware can quickly be given a new life with this tool. A very serviceable bench grinder can be purchased for under $100 (some are under $50). Since your intent is to polish hardware, you will need to buy optional wire brushes to replace the grinding wheels that come with a bench grinder. Should you want to take your polishing endeavors further, you'll need buffing wheels and polishing compound, which comes in stick form wherever bench grinders are sold.

Your materials list will vary depending on the job, but here are the essentials:

· Glazing compound
· Glazing points
· Sandpaper
· Spackle
· Primer
· Epoxy or similar filler
· Finish nails, including galvanized
· Weather-stripping nails
· Various sizes of screws
· Weather stripping
· Sash rope
· Parting beads
· Caulk
· Tape
· Baling wire

MATERIAL USES

· Glazing compound seals the edge of the glass to the sash. It is soft and pliable and available in cans, plastic tubs, and tubes. Both oil and latex versions are sold by national manufacturers, the best known being DAP.

You don't have to be on a budget to shop at the various dollar and just under-a-dollar value stores that have popped up all over the country the past ten years or so. I have been surprised at the hand tool selections at some of these stores: paintbrushes, chisel-type putty knives (which normally cost at least $6–7 at hardware stores), wire cutters, and pliers, all for a buck. Are they great tools? Not at all, but many are more than serviceable, especially the putty knives and cheap paintbrushes. They even carry bags of disposable foam paintbrushes for a dollar.

Oil-based glazing compound always works unless it's dried out in the can and cannot be revived. Latex-based is considered too sloppy and sticky by some users. Some versions of glazing are barely glazing at all, but more like Spackle and are very hard to use; I do not recommend them. Unfortunately, you won't know a product's consistency or nature until you've opened the can and for that reason I recommend you always have a can of DAP '33' with you in case another brand turns out to be difficult to tool and smooth out. When purchasing DAP '33,' be sure to have the store clerk shake the can on the paint shaker. This thoroughly mixes the ingredients and yields a very smooth, easy-to-work material and saves you the effort of doing the mixing by hand. If you forget, empty the entire can out and knead it like bread dough until it's soft and completely mixed.

· Glazing points are small fasteners with sharp ends that are installed against the edge of a pane of glass and then pushed into the wood to secure the glass. The best ones, those that sit flushest against the glass and install easily, are the diamond or triangle points installed with a point driver, which is like a staple gun, but shoots glazing points. Push-in type points are sold at hardware stores and will do the job, but some are a bit clunky and do not sit as flat as diamond or triangle points, thus making them harder to cover with glazing compound.

· Sandpaper is made by gluing abrasive grit to some kind of backing in the form of a belt, disc, sheet, or self-adhesive custom shapes for specialized sanders. The most popular and fastest cutting grit is aluminum oxide. Sandpaper is categorized by the amount of grit per square inch, for example, 100-grit paper should have 100 particles PSI. This grit size, normally marked on the back of the paper, determines the grade of sandpaper. Sandpaper is sold as closed coat (the entire paper is covered with grit) or open coat (50–70 percent is covered with grit). Closed coat is best for preparing bare hardwoods to receive a finish. Window restoration calls for open coat because you'll be cutting through paint, fillers, and weathered wood and closed-coat paper will clog too quickly during these applications. You will also be using coarse grades for part of your work.

· Spackle is a soft, premixed plasterlike material used for filling holes and small cracks in woodwork, plaster, and drywall. It is not a structural material. Although a trademarked product, the term Spackle has lost much of its affiliation with a specific manufacturer. Note that Spackle comes in both interior and exterior types. Spackle is appropriate for filling nail holes and very small chips in a sash, but it should never be used on a sill or to fill multiple cracks or splits across a sash.

· The first coat of finish in a painting system is the primer, either oil-based or latex, which is applied as a sealer or base coat. Primer should always be applied to bare wood prior to painting and serves as an intercoat between oil and latex paint. There is no overall agreement on whether to use oil primer only on weathered old wood and then coat with latex paint or always use latex primer with latex paint and there never will be an agreement. This argument will keep up until the sun turns cold and humans are living on other planets. I've always used oil primer and never had compatibility problems.

- Epoxy mix consists of a tough, durable, synthetic resin and a catalyst. When mixed together, the two harden into a material tougher than the wood you're repairing. The mixture has a limited "pot" life before it becomes too stiff and hard to apply or work. Pot life varies depending on the individual product, the temperature, and the catalyst. Every marine supplier and many paint stores sell epoxies. Every brand has its champions and detractors. National brands include West System and System Three. Other fillers appropriate for window restoration include automotive body fillers, fiberglass-reinforced polyester resin, and various "plastic wood" and wood hardener products. Each has its place in your repair work, but they are not interchangeable. Epoxy is especially appropriate for structural repairs.

- Finish nails, including galvanized, are needed for reinstalling window stops and occasionally for securing parting beads. A galvanized nail comes with a zinc coating to prevent rust and should be used for exterior applications (it also works for interiors, but is more expensive than plain steel nails). Nails are identified by their length which is expressed as a "penny" size, thus 2d means 2-penny, 3d means 3-penny, and so on. Initially, in the early days of nail manufacturing, this designation stated the weight of the nails per hundred. Most of your finish work will require 4d and 6d finish nails. However, you will need 16d (3½″ long) finish nails, when appropriate, for firming up loose sash corners.

- There are several finishes available for weather-stripping nails: copper, brass, and stainless steel. In my experience, the brass-coated nails tarnish and corrode when exposed to water, including overspray of latex paint. Staples, including galvanized, can also be used, but you'll need a power stapler to install them through metal weather stripping. Copper-plated nails aren't always easy to find and the only readily available suppliers are hardware stores.

- You will need screws of various sizes and types for installing hardware, tightening loose sash corners, installing sash stops that are secured with screws and washers instead of nails, and, in cases where the jamb is insufficiently rigid, installing metal weather stripping. Wood screws come in an assortment of sizes, finishes, and designs. You'll also use drywall screws, which come in black, silver, and gold finishes. Drywall screws have become increasingly used for all kinds of fastening purposes for which they were never designed. Why? Because they're a lot cheaper than wood screws and quickly bore into soft wood. They are acceptable for installing window hardware. They are not weatherproof and will rust if exposed to the weather.

- Weather stripping is a good idea even in moderate climates because its installation, aside from minimizing drafts, also tightens up loose sashes and keeps them from rattling around in the wind or every time a heavy truck drives by and shakes a building. Older weather stripping was primarily metal, often rigid, sometimes coupled with a felt strip. Modern versions include metal, but also vinyl, rubber, and felt. Metal is the longest lasting and the most labor-intensive to install. The simplest metal weather stripping to install is spring bronze, which is a somewhat flexible material sold in rolls and either nailed or stapled for attachment. Vinyl often comes with a self-adhesive strip and is sometimes attached to metal strips which are secured with screws. Whenever possible, it's worth saving and reinstalling older rigid weather stripping and replacing felt and any deteriorated or mangled weather stripping with new material.

- Modern sash rope is normally a mix of cotton and synthetic material such as polypropylene. One hundred percent cotton sash rope is still available, but should be avoided for the stronger mixed rope. Sash rope is sold in convenient fifty- and one hundred-foot hanks or bundles. Hanks are sold individually and by the box (twelve hanks). Common sizes include #6 ($\frac{3}{16}$" diameter), #7 ($\frac{7}{32}$" diameter), #8 ($\frac{1}{4}$" diameter), #10 ($\frac{5}{16}$" diameter), and #12 ($\frac{3}{8}$" diameter). For almost all residential purposes you should use #8. Anything larger can be difficult to get through the opening in a smaller pulley. You can use pure polyester rope as well, but it will lack the traditional feel and appearance of a poly/cotton mix. One good brand of rope is made by Sampson Rope Technologies and sold nationally. Sash chain, available in steel, brass-plated, copper-plated, and bronze, is sometimes used in place of sash rope, particularly in commercial and public buildings with larger, heavier sashes. Sash chain costs several times as much per foot as sash rope and theoretically should last forever, but I've occasionally run across broken chains.

- Parting beads separate upper and lower sashes as they slide past each other. The most common standard size is $\frac{1}{2}$" x $\frac{3}{4}$" and is available in a good number of lumberyards, but not all parting beads are created equal.

For ease of installation, they sometimes come with rounded corners and are sanded or planed down to smaller dimensions. They are indeed easier to install, but can be undersized and produce a sloppy sash fit. Better to buy parting beads cut to full size that allow you to trim them if needed. Note that other sizes exist, including $\frac{3}{4}$" x $\frac{3}{8}$" and $\frac{7}{8}$" x $\frac{3}{8}$". Occasionally you'll run into an odd profile or a style that's particular to a geographical locale. In San Francisco, for instance, parting beads in older Victorians almost always have a rounded edge on the outside as opposed to a more common square edge on most parting beads.

- Caulk is a pliable sealant packaged in a tube that fills gaps and joints between sections of wood as well as masonry. During your repair work, you'll periodically use latex caulk to fill and finish the seam between window stops and jambs and any exterior gaps between different sections of the window. Basic latex caulking is made from synthetic latex mixed with fillers, glycols, and colorants. Acrylic latex caulking, which is a step up from basic latex, contains acrylic resins and is a good choice for interior work while siliconized latex holds up better outside.

- Tape has multiple uses: holding together glued wood pieces while the glue sets, temporarily securing a cracked piece of glass, securing baling wire around broken sash weights (the wire then holds the sash rope), securing plastic to epoxy repairs to keep them in place, and securing plastic wrap to paintbrushes to prevent them from drying out. I try to keep rolls of electrical tape and masking tape in my toolbox at all times and often have use for both. Whenever taping off an area to be painted, use painter's blue masking tape, whose adhesive is designed to be longer lasting than standard masking tape. This makes all the difference in the world when it's time to remove the masking tape as less expensive tape can dry out and leave a messy residue to clean off.

· Baling wire is available in small rolls at hardware stores. It's an all-purpose, flexible wire good for fishing reluctant ropes out of crowded wall pockets and for giving ropes something to anchor to if you have to repair or fabricate a sash weight. One roll will last you for years.

RESOURCES

An Internet search on "repairing wood windows" currently brings up 125,000 hits. I am grateful to say this book is included among them. A search on "wood window hardware" brings up close to half a million. You will never lack for information or sources for hardware and replacement parts or even entire windows. I've listed a few pertinent ones here that have been referenced in the text and others I thought would be helpful. It is by no means exhaustive.

TOOLS AND MATERIALS

Glazing Compound and Caulk

· DAP (www.dap.com) makes an extensive line of caulk, glazing compound, and fillers. They are available at every hardware, paint, and home improvement store in the universe.

· Liquid Nails Concrete Repair (www.liquidnails.com) is one of many caulk products available from Liquid Nails.

Epoxy

· West System (www.westsystem.com) is one of many epoxy manufacturers whose products are normally available at marine supply stores and some paint stores. Their site offers a list of local dealers.

· Abatron, Inc. (800-445-1754, 5501 95th Ave., Kenosha, WI 53144 or www.abatron.com) is a regularly recommended epoxy repair product, available in paste and liquid form.

· J-B Weld Marine Weld or Waterweld fillers (www.jbweld.net).

Paint Removers

· Peel-Away (Dumond Chemicals Inc, New York, NY; 800-245-1191; www.dumond.com) is a lye-based caustic paint remover regularly used for paint removal on large, high-profile restoration projects.

· Jasco (www.jasco.com) is available at paint and hardware stores everywhere.

Tools for Paint Removal

· Speedheater 1100 or Silent Paint Remover (www.silentpaintremover.com) removes paint by infrared technology. A competing infrared tool, the Paint Peeler, is available from the Scott Machine Tool Company (www.paintpeeler.com or 800-613-1557).

· Heat guns for paint removal are available from several manufacturers including Master Appliance (www.masterappliance.com), Milwaukee (www.milwaukeetool.com), and

Makita (www.makita.com). Heat guns are sold at tool and home improvement stores and available at tool rental outlets.

Finishes

· The world's largest manufacturer of shellac is the Zinsser Company (www.zinsser.com) for more information.

· McCloskey Varnish (www.valspar.com/val/resident/mccloskey.jsp) is sold at paint and hardware stores nationally.

Window Hardware and Suppliers

· Duplex pulleys are manufactured by Duplex, Inc., 909-397-9003, in Pomona, California and available at wholesale hardware stores. Call Duplex, Inc., if you can't find a local supplier.

· Sash controls are manufactured by Wright Products Corp., Rice Lake, WI 54868 (www.wright-products.com/products/misc_hardware/MWdwHardware) and are available at many hardware stores.

· Jamb liners, which can be installed in lieu of pulleys and ropes, are available from Intek Plastics, Inc. (www.intekplastics.com).

· One supplier of replacement sash weights is Kilian Hardware (www.kilianhardware.com, 215-247-0945). Kilian also sells weather stripping and window hardware among other restoration items.

· Rejuvenation of Portland, Oregon (800-787-3355, www.rejuvenation.com) makes a fine line of window hardware, including sash pins and pulleys, in addition to reproduction lighting and other household hardware. Offers online ordering.

· Ives Hardware (www.iveshardware.com) makes an extensive line of hardware at all price levels. Ives is a major supplier of window hardware to both retail and wholesale hardware stores.

· M.A.G. Engineering and Manufacturing Company, Inc. (www.magsecurity.com, 800-624-9942) for pin locks and other window and door hardware.

· The Vincent Whitney Company (www.vincentwhitney.com or 800-332-3286) manufactures friction hinges and other window hardware. Offers online ordering.

· Builders Hardware & Supply Company, Inc. (www.builders-hardware.com) carries a large selection of window hardware and Pemko weather stripping.

Weather Stripping

· Accurate Metal Weatherstrip Company (800-536-6043 or www.accurateweatherstrip.com) for interlocking weather stripping.

· Pemko Manufacturing, Inc. (www.pemko.com, 800-283-9988 West Coast, 800-824-3018 East Coast) carries several sizes of spring bronze weather stripping and self-adhesive vinyl.

Sash Rope

- Sampson Rope Technology (www.sampson
.com, 800-227-7673) makes an excellent sash
cord along with a complete line of commercial and recreational rope.

Handtools

- Red Devil (www.reddevil.com) manufactures
an excellent carbide paint scraper.

- Prazi Putty Chaser (www.praziusa.com/
puttychaser.html) attaches to an electric
drill and removes hardened window putty.
This is an accessory that takes some getting
used to.

- Purdy paintbrushes (www.purdycorp.com)
are sold at paint stores everywhere.

- Hyde Tools (www.hydetools.com) manufactures a complete line of paint and finishing
tools, including putty knives and scrapers.

Sanders with Dust Collection Systems

- American-International Tool Industries Inc.
(1116-B Park Ave., Cranston, Rhode Island,
02910, 401-942-7855) offers a S344 Sander
Vac 5″, a modified Makita disc sander with a
good dust collection system.

- Fein Power Tools, Inc. (800-441-9878 or
www.feinus.com for local dealers) produces
a line of dust-free (up to 98 percent recovery)
sanders and vacuum systems.

- Festool (888-337-8600 or www.festool-usa
.com) is a competitor of Fein and produces
similar tools.

Window Screens

- W. B. Marvin Company (www.wbmarvin
.com), manufacturer of adjustable screens.

Storm Windows

- Allied Window Company (www.alliedwindow.
com or 800-445-5411) for interior and exterior storm window ideas.

Shutters and Awnings

SHUTTERMEDIC offers every part you never
knew you needed for your shutters www.shutter
medic.com

The following articles, current as of this
printing, display various shutter repairs and
installation:

- www.oldhousejournal.com/magazine/
2002/july/shutter-dos-donts.shtml

- www.diynetwork.com/diy/hi_house_exterior/
article/0,2037,DIY_13923_3672668,00.html

- http://woodblindsrepair.com/woodblind
repair/woodblindrepair.htm

- http://lifestyle.msn.com/homeandgarden/
bejane/article.aspx?cp-documentid=838903

- www.onthehouse.com/wp/19970210

- www.nps.gov/history/HPS/tps/briefs/
brief44.htm is a history of shutters published
by the National Parks Service

Window Washing

- Sprayway, Inc. (www.spraywayinc.com) An excellent foaming window cleaner.

- The Ettore squeegee is the professional's choice. Their Web site displays their products and lists local sales outlets (www.ettore.com or 800-438-8673).

Window Screens

Retractable or hidden screens are made by various manufacturers and *each one makes the best screens in the entire world!* Here are four manufactures and their Web sites:

- www.rollaway.com/index.htm

- www.screen-time.com/screens/window_screens.html

- www.phantomscreens.com/index.com

- www.eclipsetechnologies.com/

MISCELLANEOUS

- The Window and Door Manufacturers Association offers an interesting glossary of window terms at www.nwwda.org/i4a/pages/index.cfm?pageid=3687.

- To read an article on constructing a sash in your workshop, please see www.sommerfeldtools.com/tutorial-windowsash.asp.

- For more information on lead-based paint and abatement practices, please contact the

National Lead Information Center (www.epa.gov/lead/nlic.htm, 800-424-LEAD [5323]), an organization under contract to the EPA, whose site www.epa.gov/lead/leadinfo.htm also offers lead information.

- *The Old House Journal,* a restoration publication, also publishes the *Old House Journal Restoration Directory* (www.oldhousejournal.com/restoration_directory/rd_home.shtml), which lists a number of wood window related merchants.

WHAT THE WORLD HAS TO SAY ABOUT *WORKING WINDOWS*...

- As an architect with the seventh largest firm in the world, I am obviously qualified to endorse *Working Windows*. This is the best text on the subject I have ever read. So maybe it's the only book on window repair I've ever read. You got a problem with that? I wouldn't consider repairing an old window without consulting this book first. Of course, I only work on new construction so I never have to repair old windows, but that's besides the point.

  —Jim Smotherman, AIA,
  Callison Partnership

- If I had had this book a few years ago, when Meany was supposed to have finished it, we would have repaired our windows ourselves instead of hiring him. We could have bought a ton of the books for the big bucks we paid to Mr. Window.

  —Dale Kisker, Cornell & Associates

· You mean he was writing this book when he was supposed to be working on our windows? As the biggest and most self-important general contractor in the Renton Highlands, I find this very disturbing. I would be even more disturbed if we had ever actually paid Mr. Window for his work.

—Bill Briere, Vice President,
Briere & Associates

· You said this book was a birthday present. You're charging me for this? I'm your mother!

—Peg Meany, complaining despite her
10 percent family discount

· *Working Windows* is the most profound treatise on window repair I have ever read. I fully expect it to be on the best-seller lists for years to come. It is a privilege and honor to offer my endorsement.

—T. F. Meany
(No relation to the author, really.)

· I repaired my windows a few years ago and it took forever. It would have been a lot easier if Meany had finished the book on time like he was supposed to.

—John Warner, Research Historian

· Well, I don't do windows, but if I did I would certainly use this book.

—Misty,
Misty's Personalized Cleaning Service

· Using the techniques outlined in *Working Windows,* I repaired all the windows in our house. It was better than having Mr. Window mucking around the place. For that matter, it was better than having my husband/spouse/partner/significant other–type person trying to do them either since I had to fix the one he broke when he tried doing it without the instructions from the book.

—Gail Petersen

· Whoa, I thought this book was about Windows® for my computer. I want my money back.

—some whiner on the Internet

An Offer from Mr. Window...

Terry Meany is available for fee-based on-site, online, and telephone consultations for your window projects, especially large restorations. This service is particularly helpful to nonprofit and community groups doing their own restoration work on limited budgets. Terry has even been known to answer questions from readers as his time permits. Please contact him at tfmeany@msn.com or (425) 481-4059.

INDEX